THE REVELꞏ

Former general editors
Clifford Leech
F. David Hoeniger
E. A. J. Honigmann
J. R. Mulryne
Eugene M. Waith

General editors
David Bevington, Richard Dutton, Alison Findlay,
and Helen Ostovich

# MOTHER BOMBIE

Manchester University Press

# THE REVELS PLAYS

THE REVELS PLAYS

# MOTHER BOMBIE

## JOHN LYLY

## edited by Leah Scragg

MANCHESTER
UNIVERSITY PRESS

Manchester and New York

*distributed in the United States exclusively by*
*Palgrave Macmillan*

Introduction, critical apparatus, etc
© Leah Scragg 2010

The right of Leah Scragg to be identified as the editor of this work has
been asserted by her in accordance with the Copyright, Designs and
Patents Act 1988.

Published by Manchester University Press
Oxford Road, Manchester M13 9NR, UK
and Room 400, 175 Fifth Avenue, New York, NY 10010, USA
www.manchesteruniversitypress.co.uk

Distributed in the United States exclusively by
Palgrave Macmillan, 175 Fifth Avenue,
New York, NY 10010, USA

Distributed in Canada exclusively by
UBC Press, University of British Columbia, 2029 West Mall,
Vancouver, BC, Canada V6T 1Z2

*British Library Cataloguing-in-Publication Data is available*

*Library of Congress Cataloging-in-Publication Data is available*

ISBN 978 0 7190 9688 4 paperback

First published by Manchester University Press in hardback 2010

This paperback edition first published 2014

The publisher has no responsibility for the persistence or accuracy of URLs for any
external or third-party internet websites referred to in this book, and does not guarantee
that any content on such websites is, or will remain, accurate or appropriate.

Printed by Lightning Source

# Contents

# General Editors' Preface

Clifford Leech conceived of the Revels Plays as a series in the mid-1950s, modelling the project on the New Arden Shakespeare. The aim, as he wrote in 1958, was 'to apply to Shakespeare's predecessors, contemporaries, and successors the methods that are now used in Shakespeare's editing'. The plays chosen were to include well-known works from the early Tudor period to about 1700, as well as others less familiar but of literary and theatrical merit. 'The plays included', Leech wrote, 'should be such as to deserve and indeed demand performance'. We owe it to Clifford Leech that the idea became reality. He set the high standards of the series, ensuring that editors of individual volumes produced work of lasting merit, equally useful for teachers and students, theatre directors and actors. Clifford Leech remained General Editor until 1971, and was succeeded by F. David Hoeniger, who retired in 1985.

Ever since then, the Revels Plays have been under the direction of four or five general editors: initially David Bevington, E. A. J. Honigmann, J. R. Mulryne, and E. M. Waith. E. A. J. Honigmann retired in 2000 and was succeeded by Richard Dutton. E. M. Waith retired in 2003 and was succeeded by Alison Findlay and Helen Ostovich. J. R. Mulryne retired in 2010. Published originally by Methuen, the series is now published by the Manchester University Press, embodying essentially the same format, scholarly character, and high editorial standards of the series as first conceived. The series now concentrates on plays from the period 1558–1642. Some slight changes have been made: for example, starting in 1996 each index lists proper names and topics in the introduction and commentary, whereas earlier indexes focused only on words and phrases for which the commentary provided a gloss. Notes to the introduction are now placed together at the end, not at the foot of, the page. Collation and commentary notes continue, however, to appear on the relevant pages.

The introduction to each Revels play undertakes to offer, among other matters, a critical appraisal of the play's significant themes and images, its poetic and verbal fascinations, its historical context, its characteristics as a piece for the theatre, and its uses of the stage for which it was designed. Stage history is an important part of the story. In addition, the introduction presents as lucidly as possible the criteria for choice of copy-text and the editorial methods employed in presenting the play to a modern reader. The introduction also considers the play's date and, where relevant, its sources, together with its place in the work of the author and in the theatre of its time. If the play is by an author not previously represented in the series, a brief biography is provided.

The text of each Revels play, in accordance with established practice in the series, is edited afresh from the original text of best authority (in a few instances, texts), in modern spelling and punctuation and with speech headings that are consistent throughout. Elisions in the original are also silently regularised, except where metre would be affected by the change. Emendations, as distinguished from modernized spellings and punctuation, are introduced only in instances where error is patent or at least very probable, and where the corrected reading is persuasive. Act divisions are given only if they appear in the original, or if the structure of the play clearly points to them. Those act and scene divisions not in the original are provided in small type. Square brackets are also used for any other additions to, or changes in, the stage directions of the original.

Rather than provide a comprehensive and historical variorum collation, Revels Plays editions focus on those variants which require the critical attention of serious textual students. All departures of substance from the copy-text are listed, including any significant relineation and those changes in punctuation which involve to any degree a decision between alternative interpretations. The collation notes do not include such accidentals as turned letters or changes in the font. Additions to stage directions are not noted in the collations, since those additions are already made clear by the use of brackets. On the other hand, press corrections in the copy-text are duly collated, as based on a careful consultation of as many copies of the original edition or editions as are needed to ensure that the printing history of those originals is accurately reported. Of later emendations of the text by subsequent editors, only those are reported which still deserve attention as alternative readings.

One of the hallmarks of the Revels Plays is the thoroughness of their annotations. Besides explaining the meanings of difficult words and passages, the annotations provide commentary on customs or usage, on the text, on stage business – indeed, on anything that can be pertinent and helpful. On occasion, when long notes are required and are too lengthy to fit comfortably at the foot of the page below the text, they are printed at the end of the complete text.

Appendices are used to present any commendatory poems on the dramatist and play in question, documents about the play's reception and contemporary history, classical sources, casting analyses, music, and any other relevant material.

Each volume contains an index to the commentary, in which particular attention is drawn to meanings for words not listed in the OED, and (starting in 1996, as indicated above) an indexing of proper names and topics in the introduction and commentary.

Our hope is that plays edited in this fashion will promote further scholarly and theatrical investigation of one of the richest periods in theatrical history.

DAVID BEVINGTON
RICHARD DUTTON
ALISON FINDLAY
HELEN OSTOVICH

# Acknowledgements

I am grateful to many scholars and institutions for help afforded to me in the production of this book. The British Academy facilitated the collation of the early editions through a travel grant enabling me to examine copies held in the United States, and I am grateful both to them and to the staff of all ten libraries in which the extant copies of the first and second quartos of the play are preserved (the British Library, the Victoria and Albert Museum, the National Library of Scotland, the Bodleian Library, the Pepys Library (Magdalene College, Cambridge), Boston Public Library (Massachusetts), the Folger Shakespeare Library (Washington), the Houghton Library (Harvard), the Huntington Library (San Marino, California), and the Harry Ransom Research Center (University of Texas at Austin) for all their assistance in promoting my research. I am also grateful to The British Library for supplying the reproduction of the title-page of Thomas Heywood's *Philocothonista* (1635) which appears on p. xviii, and permitting its use in this edition. Among the many individuals who have offered their advice and support, I am particularly grateful to Roger Holdsworth, for his help with Elizabethan bawdy; Gale Owen-Crocker for unravelling a sixteenth-century embroidery term; Martin Wiggins for locating a relevant passage from William Bullein; Anthony Wilson of the Tonbridge Historical Society for information on the production of knives in the Tonbridge area; Anne Bradley of The Bristol Grammar School for supplying me with a wealth of materials relating to the Shakespeare Quatercentenary performance of *Mother Bombie* at Bristol; Sue Hall-Smith for her exhaustive (if largely fruitless) research on my behalf into the post-sixteenth-century production history of the play; and Patrick Spottiswood of the Education Department of Shakespeare's Globe for his enthusiastic support for the current project, and the insights afforded by his active promotion of staged readings of the entire corpus of Lylian drama in Globe Education's 'Read Not Dead' series.

Once again, however, it is to the wisdom and learning of that most distinguished of Lylian scholars, David Bevington, to which I am most deeply indebted. The editing of a body of material deeply rooted in a culture increasingly removed from twenty-first-century thought has been no easy task, and it has been a source of considerable reassurance to know that his advice, as General Editor, was always available when required. It has been a great privilege to work with him in bringing the Revels Plays' project to publish Lyly's complete dramatic work to fruition.

# Abbreviations

### ANCIENT TEXTS

Wherever possible, classical texts are cited by through line numbering in the case of drama, and to book (where applicable), poem, and line number for verse. The Loeb Classical Library (LCL) offers a convenient edition for many classical authors, and all citations are to the most recent volumes in the series.

| | |
|---|---|
| Horace, *Epi.* | *Epistles* |
| Ovid, *Am.* | *Amores.* In *Heroides: Amores.* |
| Ovid, *Ars am.* | *Ars Amatoria.* In *The Art of Love and other Poems.* |
| Ovid, *Fa.* | *Fasti.* |
| Ovid, *Heroides* | *Heroides.* In *Heroides: Amores.* |
| Ovid, *Met.* | *Metamorphoses.* |
| Ovid, *Rem. am.* | *Remedia Amoris.* In *The Art of Love and other Poems.* |
| Pliny, *Hist. nat.* | *Historia Naturalis.* |
| Terence, *Adelpoe* | In *Phormio: The Mother-in-Law: The Brothers.* |
| Terence, *Andria* | In *The Woman of Andros: The Self-Tormentor: The Eunuch.* |
| Terence, *Eunuchus* | In *The Woman of Andros: The Self-Tormentor: The Eunuch.* |
| Terence, *Heauton Timorumenos* | In *The Woman of Andros: The Self-Tormentor: The Eunuch.* |

## OTHER WORKS

The place of publication is London unless otherwise indicated. All references to the works of Shakespeare are to *The Arden Shakespeare Complete Works*, general eds Richard Proudfoot, Ann Thompson, and David Scott Kastan (1998, rev. 2001), except where otherwise noted. Abbreviations of the titles of Shakespeare's plays are those adopted by the Revels Plays. References to plays other than those of Shakespeare are to the Revels editions, unless otherwise stated.

| | |
|---|---|
| *Anatomy* | *Euphues: The Anatomy of Wit.* See Lyly. |
| Andreadis | A. Harriette Andreadis, ed., *Mother Bombie*, Elizabethan and Renaissance Studies (Salzburg, 1975). |
| Baldwin | T. W. Baldwin, *Shakspere's Five-Act Structure: Shakspere's Early Plays on the Background of Renaissance Theories of Five-Act Structure from 1470* (Urbana, 1947). |
| Bevington, ed., *Sappho and Phao* | See Lyly. |
| Bl / Blount | *Sixe Court Comedies...by...John Lilly* (printed by William Stansby for Edward Blount, 1632). |
| $Bl^2$ | *Sixe Court Comedies...by...John Lilly* (printed by William Stansby for Edward Blount, 1632), corrected reissue. |
| Bond | R. Warwick Bond, ed., *The Complete Works of John Lyly*, 3 vols (Oxford, 1902). |
| *Campaspe* | See Lyly. |
| Chambers | E. K. Chambers, *The Elizabethan Stage*, 4 vols (Oxford, 1923). |
| Cooper | Thomas Cooper, *Thesaurus Linguae Romanae & Britannicae* (1565). |
| Daniel | Carter A. Daniel, ed., *The Plays of John Lyly* (Lewisburg, PA, 1988). |
| Dent | R. W. Dent, *Proverbial Language in English Drama Exclusive of Shakespeare, 1495–1616* (Berkeley and Los Angeles, 1984). |
| Dilke | Charles Wentworth Dilke, ed., *Old English Plays*, vol. i (1814). |

| | |
|---|---|
| *Endymion* | See Lyly. |
| *England* | *Euphues and His England*. See Lyly. |
| Fairholt | F. W. Fairholt, ed., *The Dramatic Works of John Lilly*, 2 vols (1858). |
| Gair | Reavley Gair, *The Children of Paul's: The Story of a Theatre Company*, 1553–1608 (Cambridge, 1982). |
| *Galatea* | See Lyly |
| Greg | *A Bibliography of the English Printed Drama to the Restoration*, 4 vols (1939–59). |
| Grosart | Alexander B. Grosart, *The Life and Complete Works in Prose and Verse of Robert Greene*, 12 vols, Huth Library (1881–83). |
| Harrison | G. B. Harrison, ed., *Thomas Nashe: Pierce Penilesse, His Svpplication to the Divell*, Elizabethan and Jacobean Quartos (Edinburgh, 1966). |
| Hazlitt | William Hazlitt, *Lectures on the Literature of the Age of Elizabeth* (1820), republished in *Lectures on the Literature of the Age of Elizabeth, and Characters of Shakespeare's Plays*, ed. W. C. Hazlitt (1870). |
| Hazlitt, W. C. | William Carew Hazlitt, *Dictionary of Faiths and Folklore* (1905, reprinted 1995). |
| Hinman | Charlton Hinman, *The Printing and Proof-Reading of the First Folio of Shakespeare*, 2 vols (Oxford, 1963). |
| Houppert | Joseph W. Houppert, *John Lyly*, Twayne's English Authors Series (Boston, 1975). |
| Hunter | G. K. Hunter, *John Lyly: The Humanist as Courtier* (1962). |
| Hunter, *Lyly and Peele* | G. K. Hunter, *Lyly and Peele*, Writers and Their Work 206, British Council and National Book League (1968). |
| Hunter and Bevington, eds, *Galatea* and *Midas* | See Lyly. |
| Jeffery | Violet M. Jeffery, *John Lyly and the Italian Renaissance* (Paris, 1928). |

| | |
|---|---|
| Lancashire | Anne C. Lancashire, 'Lyly and Shakespeare on the Ropes', *Journal of English and Germanic Philology*, 68 (1969), pp. 237–44. |
| Linthicum | M. Channing Linthicum, *Costume in the Drama of Shakespeare and his Contemporaries* (Oxford, 1936). |
| *Love's Metamorphosis* | See Lyly. |
| Lyly | References are to the Revels Plays (Manchester) for *Campaspe* and *Sappho and Phao* (ed. George K. Hunter and David Bevington, 1991), *Endymion* (ed. David Bevington, 1996), *Galatea* and *Midas* (ed. George K. Hunter and David Bevington, 2000), *The Woman in the Moon* (ed. Leah Scragg, 2006), and *Love's Metamorphosis*, ed. Leah Scragg, 2008). References to *Euphues: The Anatomy of Wit* and *Euphues and His England* are to the modern-spelling edition in the Revels Plays Companion Library Series (ed. Leah Scragg, Manchester, 2003). References to *Pappe with an Hatchet* are to Bond. |
| Macfarlane | Alan Macfarlane, *Witchcraft in Tudor and Stuart England: A Regional and Comparative Study* (New York and Evanston, 1970). |
| McKerrow | R. B. McKerrow and F. S. Ferguson, *Title-page Borders Used in England and Scotland 1485–1640* (1932). |
| McKerrow, ed., *Nashe* | Ronald B. McKerrow, ed., *The Works of Thomas Nashe*, 5 vols (1904–10). |
| *Midas* | See Lyly. |
| *OED* | *The Oxford English Dictionary.* |
| *Pappe with an Hatchet* | See Lyly. |
| Pincombe | Michael Pincombe, *The Plays of John Lyly: Eros and Eliza*, Revels Plays Companion Library Series (Manchester, 1996). |

| | |
|---|---|
| *Q1* | MOTHER / BOMBIE. / *As it was sundrie times plaied by* / *the Children of Powles.* / [lace ornament] / LONDON, / Imprinted by Thomas Scarlet / for Cuthbert Burby. / 1594. |
| *Q2* | MOTHER / BOMBIE. / As it was sundrie times / *plaied by the Children of Powles* / [device] / LONDON / Printed by Thomas Creede, for *Cuthbert* / *Burby.* 1598. |
| Robinson | F. N. Robinson, ed., *The Complete Works of Geoffrey Chaucer* (2nd ed., 1957). |
| *Sappho and Phao* | See Lyly. |
| SOED | *Shorter Oxford English Dictionary.* |
| STC | A. W. Pollard and G. R. Redgrave, *A Short-Title Catalogue of Books Printed in England, Scotland, and Ireland...1475–1640*, rev. W. A. Jackson and K. F. Panzer, 3 vols (1976–91). |
| Tilley | Morris Palmer Tilley, *A Dictionary of the Proverbs in England in the Sixteenth and Seventeenth Centuries* (Ann Arbor, 1950). |
| Tydeman | William Tydeman, ed., *Four Tudor Comedies* (Harmondsworth, 1984). |
| Williams (1994) | Gordon Williams, *A Dictionary of Sexual Language and Imagery in Shakespearean and Stuart Literature*, 3 vols (1994). |
| Williams (1997) | Gordon Williams, *A Glossary of Shakespeare's Sexual Language* (1997). |
| Wilson | John Dover Wilson, *John Lyly* (Cambridge, 1905). |
| *The Woman in the Moon* | See Lyly. |

(Thomas Heywood, *Philocothonista*: title-page)

# Introduction

THE TEXT

*Mother Bombie* is first mentioned in a Stationers' Register entry for 1594:

> Xviij Iunij [1594]
>
> **Cuthbert Burby.** / Entred for his copie vnder thand of m<sup>r</sup> warden Cawood / a booke intituled Mother Bumbye beinge an enterlude / v j <sup>d</sup> C / [B 309<sup>b</sup>][1]

The play was published in the course of the same year, with the following title-page:

> [within lace border] / MOTHER / BOMBIE. / *As it was sundrie times plaied by* / *the Children of Powles.* / [lace ornament] / LONDON, / Imprinted by Thomas Scarlet / for Cuthbert Burby. / 1594.

Though still at the start of his career, Burby was to become a major publisher of dramatic texts,[2] while Scarlet had previously printed Lyly's *Midas* for Joan Broome.

The text, which survives in two copies (BL C.34.d.15 and Bodl. Malone 251 (3)),[3] collates A–I4, and has 36 unnumbered leaves. The title-page is on A1r (A1v blank), while Act 1, with factotum initial, and headed '*Actus primus. Scena prima.*' begins on A2r below an ornament and HT ('A pleasant conceited Comœdie, / called *Mother Bombie.*'). The play concludes with 'FINIS.' and a further ornament on I3v (I4 blank). The text is cleanly printed, with no substantial variation between the two extant copies[4] and relatively few significant errors. Act 1. Sce. 2 is mistakenly designated Act. 2. Sce. 2 on A4r;[5] 'my' is printed for 'your' on B1r (1.3.9 this ed.); the sense is disrupted by an error of punctuation on B3r (1.3.136–7 this ed.); a speech prefix is omitted on D2v (2.4.21 this ed.); an erroneous direction (and implied entrance) is signalled on E2v (3.3.01 this ed.); a stage direction is printed as speech on H1r (5.3.64.1 this ed.); while speeches are misassigned on D2r and G2v (2.3.88 and 4.2.204 this ed.), and a further six on F4v and G1r (4.2.90–6 this ed.), the last group of errors, together with a confusion in familial relationships on G1v (4.2.150 this ed.), possibly arising from corruption of the copy text (see below). A more major problem is presented by variation in the representation of the characters' names. Risio appears as both *Riscio* and *Risio* on his first entrance on A4r, and the two forms of the name occur in roughly equal frequency throughout. Similarly, Lucio (abbreviated to *Liu* on C3r, *Lu* on C3v, and both *Luc* and *Lu* on D2v) becomes *Luceo* on E1v, and *Linceo* from F3v (usually abbreviated to *Lin*, but to *Lu* on F4v), with a single instance of Lincio on H4v. The potential for confusion is furthered by the contracted forms of some characters' names. Livia (beloved of Candius), for example, is denoted by both *Liu* and *Li* (as on F2r), allowing for confusion with Lucio/Linceo, servant to Prisius (see above).

While the pervasive variation between Risio and Riscio implies a similar uncertainty, or lack of clarity, in the representation of the name in the copy text, the distribution of the variant forms of Lucio/Linceo has been adduced in evidence that more than one compositor was at work. In a detailed bibliographical analysis of the play, Harriette Andreadis has argued that there are 'important changes in the nature of the typesetting which coincide at sheet E',[6] including the shift from *Lucio* to *Luceo*. Pages have two more lines on average than sheets A–D, and the compositor's stick is six millimetres longer, while a further set of changes begin in the inner forme of sheet F, with *Lucio* appearing as *Linceo*, and '*mee* and *hee* [as opposed to *me* and *he*, used] with…greater frequency'.[7] Nevertheless, though three compositors may have been involved in the printing process, the recurrent use of some pieces of broken type (e.g. the initial '*D*' of *Dro.*/*Drom.* on A2v, F1v, and F2v (1.1.19 SP., 3.4.179 SP., 4.1.33 SP., this ed.) precludes the possibility, as Andreadis shows,[8] that the text was printed in more than one shop.

Like the rest of the Lylian comedies published in the course of the dramatist's lifetime, the layout of the text is largely orderly and consistent. The names of the characters are usually grouped at the head of the scene on the classical model, rather than being specified as entrances occur, though the names are not always printed in the order in which the characters speak (e.g. at the head of 3.4 on E3r, and 4.1 on F2r). As in all Lyly's plays but for *The Woman in the Moon*, there are few directions regarding stage business, though singing is signalled (incorrectly) on E2v ('*Memphio and Stellio singing*': 3.3.01 this ed.), E3v ('*Cantant*': 3.4.41.1 this ed.), and H1r, where the direction 'Sing' is printed as text (5.3.64.1 this ed.). None of the songs that punctuate the action is included in the text, an

omission common to all the Lylian comedies with the exception of
*The Woman in the Moon*, while the relatively few props required by
the action (e.g. the pack with which Rixula enters in 3.4, and the
'stool' to which Serena alludes at 3.1.55) are not specified, characteristically, in the directions. The text differs in a number of respects,
however, from other early editions of Lyly's plays. The practice of
listing characters' names at the start of a scene is not consistently
observed (cf. B1r at the head of 1.3), while mid-scene entrances and
exits are specified, and afford an indication, in one instance, of
staging ('*Sperantus lookes out*' on H1r: 5.3.27.1 this ed.).

Taken together, the evidence suggests that, though the text ultimately derives from authorial copy, it was not prepared by the
dramatist himself for publication, as may have been the case with a
number of his plays,[9] and this inference is supported by the nature
of the errors that occur in 4.2. As Bond shows, the assignment of a
sequence of speeches on F4v and G1r (4.2.90–6 this ed.) does not
accord with the tenor of the plot, a mistake hardly ascribable to the
dramatist himself, and the probability that the text has been subject
to misguided intervention is heightened by the confusion of familial
relationships that occurs in the same scene (G1v: 4.2.150 this ed.).[10]
Similarly, though the uncertainty over the spelling of Risio/Riscio is
attributable to the idiosyncrasies of a particular hand, the disjunc-
tion between the variant forms of Lucio/Linceo is more radical, and,
though ascribable to minim confusion, militates against careful,
authorial preparation of the text.

One of only three Lylian comedies to be republished in the dramatist's lifetime,[11] the play appeared in a second edition in 1598,
prompted perhaps by the revival of Paul's Boys towards the close
of the decade, following their dissolution circa 1590.[12] The title-page
reads:

> MOTHER / BOMBIE. / As it was sundrie times / *plaied by the Children of*
> *Powles* / [device, McKerrow 299][13] / LONDON / Printed by Thomas
> Creede, for *Cuthbert* / *Burby*. 1598.

Like Thomas Scarlet, Creede was an experienced printer of dramatic texts, entrusted by Burby with printing the second quarto of
*Romeo and Juliet* the following year.

The text, of which thirteen copies are currently thought to
survive,[14] collates A–H4 and has thirty-two unnumbered leaves.
The title is on A1r (A1v blank), while Act 1, with factotum initial,
and headed '*Actus primus. Scena prima.*' begins on A2r below an

ornament and HT ('A Pleasant conceited / Commœdie, called / *Mother Bombie.*'). Act 5 concludes with 'FINIS.' on H4v, and is followed by a further ornament, which occupies the remainder of the page. Described by Greg as 'a rather inaccurate reprint' of $Q_I$,[15] the text corrects a number of the errors of the previous edition ('my girle', on $Q_I$, B1r, for example, is emended to 'your girle' ($Q_2$, A4v: 1.3.9 this ed.), 'carnes durt' on $Q_I$, D1v to 'cranes durt' ($Q_2$, C4v: 2.3.65 this ed.), and 'that' on $Q_I$, F4r to 'thats' ($Q_2$, F2v: 4.2.48 this ed.)), but fails to address any of the more major difficulties noted above, and introduces a large number of additional mistakes.[16] Another two scenes are misnumbered ('Act. 3. Sce. 3:' for 'Act. 3. Sce. 2.', and 'Act. 5. Sce. 8' for 'Act 5. Sce. 1.'), while further variations are introduced in the representation of the characters' names (e.g. Riscio/Risio becomes *Risco* on A4v and *Rosio* on E2v, Dromio appears as *Romio* on A4v, Bedunens as *Bedunenus* (the form preferred in this edition) on G2v, and Vicinia as *Vicina/* Vicina on G2r and H2v. The potential for reader confusion is heightened, moreover, by a yet greater inconsistency in the abbreviated forms of a number of names. Livia, Lucio, and Silena, for example, are all denoted, at some point, by *Liu* (e.g. on B2r, C2r, and D1r), while Lucio is indicated by *Liu* and *Lu* on C2v, *Luc* on E2r, *Lin* on F2r, and *Siu* on F2v, inviting confusion with Silena, who appears in the same scene. At the same time, the problems arising for the reader from both the misrepresentation of the text and the complexities of the plot (see pp. 40–1 below) are aggravated by a number of significant omissions. Eight words have fallen out on D2r, for example, probably through eye-skip, from Memphio's expostulations regarding the intemperance of contemporary youth (2.5.21–4 this ed.), undermining the force of his allusion to King Rufus; the omission of a speech by Serena on D3v (3.1.18–20 this ed.) has led to two successive speeches by Maestius, the second an unintelligible response to the missing lines; the loss of a speech prefix on G3r (5.3.48 this ed.) invites the supposition that a line by Sperantus is spoken by Synis; while the omission of a speech by Stellio on F4r (4.2.132–3 this ed.), again probably through eye-skip, has led to two successive speeches by Memphio.

The carelessness suggested by the many inaccuracies of the text is curiously at odds with the evident attention given to the checking of some, at least, of the printed sheets. The inverted ornament on A2r, which survives in three of the extant copies,[17] is corrected in the other surviving witnesses; ink corrections of erroneous type are numerous and common to all extant copies (e.g. on B1r, D2r, and F1v); while 'cudge.' on B1v is carefully altered to 'cudgell.' in every case, but for the second Folger Library copy, where the word is accurately printed. An attention to sense is indicated, moreover, by the detailed corrections to E1v and E3v. Whereas the Boston and Huntington Library copies of Stellio's penultimate speech on E1v (3.3.32–5 this ed.) read, 'I perceiue sober men tell most likes, for in *vino veritas, If* they had drunke wine , they would haue tolde, the trueth', with the 'l' of 'tolde' inverted, 'likes' is printed as 'lies' in the other extant texts, and the inverted letter is reset.[18] It is the corrections to E3v, however, that are more surprising given the deficiencies of the text overall. Whereas the Huntington and Boston Library copies of the opening lines of Lucio's second speech (3.4.119–20 this ed.) read, 'Thou fool, how could it come in? vnlesse it had bin a leg,', the marks of punctuation are reversed in the other ten in which the relevant page survives,[19] with 'come in' followed by a comma and a question mark following 'leg'.[20]

No further edition of the play appeared in the dramatist's lifetime, and the Stationers' Register records that the rights to the work, together with those to five other Lylian comedies, were transferred to Edward Blount in 1628:

9" Ianuarij 1627 [/ 8]

M<sup>r</sup>. **Blount:** Entred for his Copies by order of a full Court Sixe playes of Peter [*sic*] Lillyes to be printed in one volume vixt: Campaste, [*sic*] Sapho, and Phao. Galathra: [*sic*] Endimion Midas and Mother Bomby. vj<sup>d</sup> [D 158][21]

Though a collected edition was clearly projected, the planned volume was not published until 1632, when it appeared in 12° with the following title-page:

SIXE / COVRT / Comedies. / Often Presented and Acted / *before Queene* ELIZABETH, / by the Children of her Ma- / iesties Chappell, and the / Children of Paules. / *Written* / By the onely Rare Poet of that / Time, The Wittie, Comicall, *Facetiously-Quicke and* / vnparalelled / IOHN LILLY, Master / *of Arts.* / Decies repetita placebunt. // LONDON / Printed by *William Stansby* for *Edward* / *Blount.* 1632.[22]

The text of *Mother Bombie*, which occupies Z4r–2D12r (2D12v blank) and concludes the volume, is clearly derived from the second quarto, in that it replicates the majority of its errors. The same eight words, for example, are missing from Memphio's speech on youthful indulgence in 2.5 (Blount, Bb2r), Act 3 scene 2 is again misnumbered, and consecutive speeches are once more assigned to the same character in 3.1 and 4.2 (Blount, Bb3v–4r and Cc7v–8r). The edition is nevertheless significant in editorial terms[23] in that it restores four of the five songs signalled in stage directions or the text,[24] missing from the earlier quartos, but integral to the action of the play.[25]

An error of imposition in the first issue necessitated the reprinting of some passages of text, and the volume was reissued in the same year. In the case of *Mother Bombie*, in which the unsigned 2C9v and 2C1or were initially transposed, there are extensive differences of lineation, spelling, capitalization, and the use of contractions between the two editions, in both the transposed pages and the conjugate leaves, while 'knowest', omitted in the first issue, has been restored to a speech by Lucio on 2C1ov (4.2.245, this ed.). In all other respects, the text of *Mother Bombie* is identical in the two issues, and the second (a copy of which is preserved in the Huntington Library) is consequently of no significance in terms of the transmission history of the play.

In view of the clear priority of the first quarto over the editions of 1598 and 1632 it is upon that text that this edition is based. The four songs recovered by Blount have been incorporated, however, into the text, though in two instances the parts allocated to the singers have been reassigned (see 3.3.1–14n. and 3.4.41.2–61n. below).

AUTHORSHIP AND DATE

Although his name does not appear on the title-page of either quarto, and there are significant differences between *Mother Bombie* and the remainder of Lyly's plays (see pp. 14ff. below), Lyly's authorship is attested by evidence of a variety of kinds. The inclusion of the play in Blount's *Sixe Court Comedies* (see pp. 5–6 above) carries considerable weight, given the publisher's standing, and the personal interest in the project evidenced by the tone of the prefatory material, and the recovery of the songs that intersperse the work.[26] The title-page announcements of the two quartos that the play belonged to the repertoire of Paul's Boys, the company with which Lyly was associated throughout his career, supports Blount's attribution, while a casual reference to *Mother Bombie* by Nashe in his *Have With You to Saffron-Walden*,[27] a work overtly aligning the

writer with Lyly in a war of words against Gabriel Harvey, strength-
ens the probability of Lyly's authorship of the play. The action is
set in Rochester not far from Canterbury, where Lyly himself grew
up, and shows considerable familiarity with aspects of Kentish life.
The production of knives in Tonbridge, for example, is the subject
of a joke at 2.1.121–2; the cost of hiring a horse to ride from
Rochester to Canterbury is the basis for a satiric allusion to the
undervaluing of learning at 4.1.24–6; and another Kentish town,
Ashford, is invoked at 2.5.54.[28] Like the rest of the Lylian corpus,
the language of the play teems with proverbial sayings (see p. 15
below), many used by Lyly elsewhere, while the dialogue resounds
with echoes of works more securely located in the Lylian canon.
Memphio's promise of reward to Dromio, for example, at 1.1.44–6,
is strongly reminiscent of a passage from Euphues' 'Cooling Card
for Philautus' (*Anatomy*, p. 92); the opposition between youth and
age is formulated by Livia in similar terms to those employed by the
Siren to the supposed ghost of Ulysses in *Love's Metamorphosis* (cf.
*Mother Bombie*, 1.3.89–91 and *Love's Metamorphosis*, 4.2.81–3); the
exit line '*I prae, sequar*', used by Dromio at 2.4.21, occurs on three
occasions (two in translation) in *Endymion* (at the close of 1.4, 3.3,
and 3.4); the phrase '*Sine Cerere & Baccho friget Venus*', reportedly
used by Halfpenny and repeated by Sperantus at 2.5.56–7, which
has its origins in Terence, is quoted by Cupid to Ceres in *Love's
Metamorphosis* (5.1.53); and the joke turning on a passage from
William Lily's Latin grammar at 3.2.13–17 echoes an exchange
between Epiton and Sir Tophas in *Endymion* (3.3.3–6).

Though the language of the play is colloquial, in keeping with the
provincial setting of the work (see p. 15 below), the style also pro-
claims the play's affinity with the prose works on which Lyly's reputation was initially built, and the comedies with which he cemented
his position. Insistent word-play, the antithetical structuring of sentences, and the pointing of opposites through the use of alliteration
(exemplified in Prisius' lengthy speech on filial ingratitude at
1.3.183ff.), all echo the trademark style of *The Anatomy of Wit* and
the ensuing sequence of plays, written for performance at court,
exploiting the dramatic potentialities of the euphuistic mode. The
large number of juvenile roles, embracing five young servants, two
under-age fools, and four young lovers, is similarly characteristic of
the dramatist's work (see pp. 38–9 below), while the nimble-witted
boys who weave their way through the plot are figures common to
all but one of Lyly's plays.

For all the mass of evidence in favour of Lyly's authorship, however, some doubts have been raised regarding the security of the accepted attribution of the work. The late publication of the play, the absence of the dramatist's name from the title-pages of the two quartos published prior to Lyly's death, and the Roman New Comedy origins of the piece (see p. 11 below), together with the marked difference between its urban character and mundane concerns and the pastoral idealism of the court comedies, have all invited speculation that the play is by a different hand. The first two objections may be readily discounted. Though not among the group of comedies published by William and Joan Broome, *Mother Bombie* was, in fact, published considerably earlier than either *The Woman in the Moon* (1597) or *Love's Metamorphosis* (which did not appear until 1601), while, of the seven comedies attributed to Lyly at some point in the Stationers' Register, only *The Woman in the Moon* carries the dramatist's name on the title-page, and *Mother Bombie* is thus by no means exceptional in this respect. The last objection, by contrast, is firmly rooted in the specificities of the text and thus appears to command a greater measure of respect. The reservation rests upon the assumption that the Lylian corpus is a uniform body of work, characterized by a delicate craftsmanship and a sophisticated handling of abstract ideas entirely at odds with the broad humour of a work turning on the day-to-day actualities of English provincial life. In the words of John Dover Wilson, 'Though it presents many points of similarity in detail to [Lyly's] other plays, its general atmosphere is so different (displaying, indeed, at times distinct errors of taste) that [one would] be inclined to assign it to a friend or pupil of Lyly, were it not bound up with Blount's *Six Court Comedies*'.[29]

There is considerable evidence to suggest, however, that Lyly's dramatic output was, in fact, far more varied than is generally supposed and that his tastes were considerably more robust. A letter from Jack Roberts to Sir Roger Williams in 1584, warning the recipient to 'take heed and beware of my lord of Oxenford's man called Lyly, for if he see this letter he will put it in print or make the boys in Paul's play it upon a stage',[30] implies that the dramatist had gained a reputation as a satirist at an early stage in his career, and the implication that he was not averse to lampooning his contemporaries is supported by Gabriel Harvey's comment in 'An Aduertisment for Papp-hatchett' (1593) that 'all you, that tender the preseruation of your good names, were best to please Pap-hatchet, and see Euphues betimes, for feare lesse he be mooued, or some One of his Apes hired, to make a Playe of you; and then is your credit quite vn-done…Such is the publique reputation of their Playes'.[31] The fact that Lyly's aid was enlisted in the pamphlet campaign designed to discredit the anti-Episcopalian movement runs counter to the supposition that he was exclusively associated by his contemporaries with elegant compositions for production at court, while the racy colloquialism and ribald humour of *Pappe with an Hatchet*, his contribution to the Martin Marprelate debate, shows that he was capable of a kind of writing wholly at odds with the subtlety and grace of the majority of his extant plays. The twentieth-century view that the cut-and-thrust of sixteenth-century religious polemic ran counter to his natural bent[32] is contradicted by contemporary responses to the work,[33] while a passage in the pamphlet regretting the prohibition of plays written in support of the anti-Martinist cause indicates that he was far from unappreciative of the impact of broad comic effects. Instead of imagining the exposure of 'Martin Marprelate's' pretensions by verbal means, as might have been expected from a writer inexorably associated with a literary style, he devises a scene entirely dependent on visual effects, culminating in the hanging of 'Martin' on-stage.[34] Rather than being the work of a different hand, or an experiment in a new dramatic mode as a number of commentators suggest,[35] *Mother Bombie* may thus be the sole extant witness of a much broader style of comedy that the dramatist was accustomed to write for public performance at Paul's, while the seven more marketable plays that survive (see p. 10 below) may possibly offer a distorted picture of the Lylian corpus overall.

Though the authorship of the play may be determined with reasonable certainty, its precise position within the chronology of the Lylian corpus is complicated by the publication history of the text. The appearance of the first quarto in 1594 provides incontrovertible evidence that it was in existence by that time, while its attribution to Paul's Boys strongly implies that it was written prior to 1590 when that troupe (with which Lyly was associated throughout his career as a playwright) was dissolved. Echoes of *Endymion*, *Love's Metamorphosis*, and *Midas*[36] indicate, moreover, that it was his later rather than his earlier comedies that were running through the dramatist's mind when the piece was composed, while Nashe's reference to the play as 'old Mother *Bomby*' in 1596 (see n. 27) confirms a late date by the implication that, though not a new work, the drama was one that his readers could be confidently expected to recall.

While the evidence points to composition at the close of the 1580s, the fact that the play was not among the five comedies acquired by William and Joan Broome subsequent to the closure of Paul's Boys and published by them in 1591 and 1592 not only supports the contention that it occupies a different niche from the other comedies that survive from the later phase of the dramatist's career but opens the door to speculation that it might post-date them.[37] Bond suggests, however, that, rather than being a later work, the play was withheld from publication, either by the playwright himself or by the company to which it belonged, with a view to prolonging its theatrical life with a different troupe, in that its 'more popular character' would have given it 'a better chance of acceptance at other theatres' than the generality of Lyly's works.[38] Andreadis similarly concludes that, for all its late appearance on the bookstalls, the play was composed before the inhibition of the boys, but does not discount the possibility that it may have continued to be performed by that company, outside London, subsequent to the closure of their playhouse in Paul's.[39] An equally tenable possibility, also turning on the distinctive character of the work, is that the delay in its publication may be ascribable to consumer demands. As Hunter notes, though 'its title-page tells us that we have the play "as it was sundry times played by the Children of Paul's"...the absence of any reference to the court...leads one to suppose that it was never presented before the Queen'.[40] Given that the five plays published by William and Joan Broome all carry title-page announcements of a performance at court, it may be that those works were seen by the publishers as more marketable commodities than a play with a less exalted provenance, announcing itself, not as a sophisticated work directed towards a discerning clientele but as a popular piece turning on a figure from small-town life.[41] Nevertheless, though its different character may explain the fact that it was not among the comedies published in 1591–92, it does not explain its subsequent appearance in 1594, and much of the history of the text consequently remains obscure.[42]

## SOURCES AND CONTEXTS

Like the majority of Lyly's plays, *Mother Bombie* is not founded on one particular work,[43] but draws on disparate historical periods, motifs, and traditions. The play is set in Rochester, in England, and turns on numerous aspects of contemporary sixteenth-century life (e.g. the situation of an heir intellectually incapable of managing his own affairs, the making of marriages, and putting out of children to nurse), and evokes the day-to-day affairs of a small-town community, subject to the authority of a mayor, and governed by a legal system embodied in a sergeant at arms. A host of incidental allusions contribute to the actuality of the play world (e.g. the listing of the rich for purposes of taxation at 2.5.11–12, social distinctions in the consumption of alcohol at 2.5.26–37, the cost of hiring a post horse at 4.1.24–6), and unite audience and dramatis personae in a shared historical past (cf. Memphio's reference at 2.5.23 to 'Rufus, sometime king of this land'). At the same time, for all the familiarity of the setting, the plot is plainly structured on a non-native, Roman New Comedy, model, and is resolved by a classical device. The four aged fathers of the play clearly correspond with the authority figures of Terentian comedy, who oppose the amatory desires of their sons, while the young servants who outwit them look back to the witty slaves of the Roman genre, who work to further the young lovers' interests in the hope of securing manumission. The resolution of the plot through the recovery of lost children similarly derives from the Graeco-Roman literary stock, as does the confirmation of identity by means of significant birthmarks. Lyly has not simply imposed a classical formula upon the affairs of a sixteenth-century community, however, as in earlier plays by other writers engaged in 'Englishing' a non-native form (cf. *Gammer Gurton's Needle*).[44] The majority of the characters have names suggestive of Greece or Rome, rather than an English provincial town (e.g. Dromio, Sperantus, Rixula), and the boys who seek to deceive their masters are working to secure their freedom, like their classical predecessors, rather than simply attempting to improve their lot (cf. Memphio's promise to Dromio at 1.1.76 that if their plot succeeds he will be 'for ever set at liberty'). The leakage between the two societies evoked in the course of the work creates an imaginative arena ultimately divorced from any specific temporal reality, and thus comparable with the composite worlds of Lylian court comedy in which classical figures, English topography, sixteenth-century servants, and the topical concerns of Elizabethan England comfortably coexist.[45]

The figure of Mother Bombie probably provides the most striking example of the cultural ambivalence of the work. Cunning folk (i.e.

those credited with exceptional percipience, including the power to foretell the future), the social type with which the play's title-figure is insistently identified, were familiar figures in the landscape of sixteenth-century England, as the charting of the location of recorded practitioners reveals.[46] As Alan McFarlane has shown, 'nowhere in Essex was there a village more than ten miles from a known cunning man',[47] and there is no reason to suppose that the situation was any different in Kent.[48] The concerns on which cunning folk were consulted correspond, moreover, with the problems that bring clients to Mother Bombie's door, cementing the social realism of the piece. Advice was sought, as Macfarlane exhibits,[49] on sexual matters (cf. Silena's desire for clarification of her sexual status at 2.3.91ff.), on the recovery of lost property (cf. Rixula's request for information regarding a missing spoon at 3.4.159ff.), in cases of indecision (cf. Vicinia's need for help in determining upon a course of action at 5.2.1–9), and in resolving disputes between neighbours (cf. Mother Bombie's role in facilitating the resolution in the final act). Rather than being assertive in their pronouncements, they were characteristically gnomic or equivocal, merely affording the means of making a choice (cf. the cryptic nature of Mother Bombie's responses throughout), and were known for refusal of payment on the grounds that 'if they should take any thing they could doe no good'[50] (cf. Mother Bombie's assertion at 3.4.194 that 'I take no money, but good words').

The ambivalent status of Lyly's wise-woman also corresponds with the position occupied by cunning folk in the late Tudor period, as revealed by the historical record. On the one hand, they represented a major source of comfort and reassurance to the communities they served, were consulted for help when witchcraft was suspected, and supported by their neighbours for 'doing good',[51] while on the other hand their association with the occult was seen by some as pernicious, and laid them open to prosecution as witches themselves.[52] Though Serena reports at 3.1.28–9 that Mother Bombie is known as 'the good woman, who yet never did hurt', and Memphio confirms that she is 'cunning and wise, never doing harm, but still practising good' (5.3.366–7), Maestius suspects that her pronouncements 'are but false fires, to lead one out of a plain path into a deep pit' (3.1.62–3), while the young servants are terrified by her witch-like appearance, and fear that she will transform them into sub-human forms (3.4.88–9). Mother Bombie herself is quick to affirm that she is not among those engaged in the diabolic arts, implying her sensitivity to the misconstruction of the source of her powers. Confronted by Silena with the uncompromising pronouncement, 'They say you are a witch', she firmly locates herself within the arena of social acceptability with the equally trenchant 'They lie. I am a cunning woman' (2.3.98–9).

The play's title-figure does not merely conform, however, to a generalized sixteenth-century type. There is considerable evidence to suggest that in creating his cunning woman Lyly was drawing on a specific historical figure, or one reputed, at least, to have lived. Andreadis notes that the name 'Bombus' is listed in the 'Dictionarium Historicum & Poeticum' appended to Thomas Cooper's *Thesaurus Linguae Romanae & Britannicae* (1565), with the gloss, 'The name of a certain diuinour', and that a further seven references to a (Mother) Bungie, Bumbye, or Bumby occur in the course of the later sixteenth and early seventeenth centuries.[53] Though one of these almost certainly refers to Friar Bungay, rather than Mother Bombie,[54] and a further five post-date Lyly's play,[55] and may thus have been influenced by it,[56] the fact that Reginald Scot devotes a paragraph to the figure in his *The Discouerie of Witchcraft* (1584), prior to the composition of *Mother Bombie* itself, and locates her in the Rochester area, affords convincing evidence of the historical actuality of a cunning woman known by a name approximating to that of Lyly's creation in sixteenth-century Kent. The hostile account of the figure in Scot's work, while corresponding with the negative stance of later writers, is totally at variance, moreover, with the representation of the character in the Lylian play,[57] suggesting that knowledge of her reputed activities did not derive solely from the drama performed by Paul's Boys,[58] but was mediated via a different source.

Nevertheless, though Mother Bombie, like the aged fathers and mischievous servants of the play, is clearly at home in the landscape of sixteenth-century England, she too has Graeco-Roman anteced-ents, contributing to the cultural ambivalence of the work. Oracles and oracular figures occur elsewhere in the Lylian corpus, and are invariably located in contexts associated with classical myth. In *Endymion*, for example, the resolution is facilitated by recourse to a sacred fountain, which delivers a cryptic solution to Endymion's somnolent state, while the eponymous hero of *Midas* is relieved of his ass's ears through conformity to an oracle of Apollo, dismissed by one of the king's counsellors, in terms echoed by Serena and Maestius, as an 'old saw...without sense' (cf. *Midas*, 5.3.36–9 and

*Mother Bombie*, 3.1.51-4 and 61-3). It is the figure of Sibylla, the aged soothsayer of *Sappho and Phao*, however, who provides the closest parallel to the cunning woman of the later play. Like Mother Bombie, Sibylla is an isolated figure, who offers counsel to those in intractable situations, has the gift of foreknowledge, and the wisdom born of extreme old age. The history she relates to Phao at 2.1.43ff. serves to associate her with Cumean Sibyl, and thus with a style of prophecy that is cryptic and fragmentary by nature,[59] corresponding in its evasiveness to the enigmatic verses of Lyly's native seer. The suggestion that Mother Bombie may be seen as an English version of the classical figure is reinforced, furthermore, by a visual image linking the very different worlds of the two plays. The dialogue at the opening of Act 2 of *Sappho and Phao* implies that Sibylla is first revealed sitting on a stool at the mouth of her cave, and a similar stage spectacle is suggested when Mother Bombie encounters Silena at 2.3.93.1-2ff., and in the subsequent scenes in which she appears (see pp. 36-8 below).

Though the eclectic learning characteristic of Lylian comedy is less in evidence in *Mother Bombie* than elsewhere in the dramatist's work, the play is thus by no means as divorced from the context of sixteenth-century thought as its provincial setting and concerns might initially suggest, and a host of incidental exchanges and allusions serve to confirm its place within the culture of the educated Elizabethan elite. A knowledge of the emblem tradition and the works of Ovid is required, for example, for a full appreciation of the exchange between Candius and Livia at 1.3.131-68; Halfpenny makes fun of Risio and Dromio at 2.1.93-111 by means of a macaronic pun; William Lily's Latin grammar affords the basis for a joke between Dromio and Risio at 3.2.13-17; while some knowledge of both Latin and Ovid's *Heroides* is necessary for an understanding of Dromio's 'spurring' of Candius at 4.1.19ff. Candius himself is a scholar, and the neglect of scholarship in contemporary English society is alluded to at 4.1.19-26. In short, the world of the play is recognizably Elizabethan, not merely in its proximity to the concerns of sixteenth-century small-town life but in the assumed intellectual landscape of its more discerning spectators.

## STYLE AND STRUCTURE

At first glance, *Mother Bombie* appears to stand aside from the rest of the Lylian corpus not only in the provincial nature of its setting but its style. From the publication of *Euphues: The Anatomy of Wit* in 1578, Lyly was inexorably associated with the euphuistic mode, a highly stylized form of composition characterized by the insistent pairing of contrasting propositions, the pointing of oppositions by means of assonance and alliteration, syllabic patterning and word-play, and the use of illustrative analogies, turning on some species of duality, drawn from classical mythology and fabled aspects of the natural world. The dramatic language of *Mother Bombie*, by contrast, is far closer to the rhythms of contemporary speech, is insistently colloquial, and makes comparatively little parade of the wide reading that informs the Lylian corpus as a whole. Rather than drawing on the literary stock for its analogies, it depends far more heavily on proverbial sayings appropriate to the limited mental horizons of the provincial characters of the play, deploying at least ninety in the course of its 2,081 lines, and relying on their contemporary currency for much of the humour in scenes involving the two fools.

It would be a mistake to assume, for all that, that Lyly's character-istic style of composition is entirely absent from the work. The exchange between Candius and Livia at 1.3.74ff., for example, and their subsequent encounter with their fathers, exhibit all the familiar features of the euphuistic mode, including the see-saw oppositions (cf. Sperantus' complaint that 'What we get together with a rake, they cast abroad with a fork': lines 209–10), elaborate sound-patterning (cf. Prisius' assumption at lines 186–7 that his daughter believes him to be 'overgrown with ignorance because overworn with age'), classi-cal allusions (cf. the expounding of lines from Ovid by Candius at lines 146–68), and extensive references to the emblem tradition (cf. Livia's account of the items depicted in her sampler at lines 130–41). The syntactic patterning typical of the Lylian corpus is also evident from the outset of the work. The use of triplets, for example, a characteristic feature of Lyly's style,[60] is exemplified in Memphio's opening announcement that 'there are three things that make my life miserable: a threadbare purse, a curst wife, and a fool to my heir', and in the 'three medicines' that Dromio proffers in response, while antithetical balance invades the structuring of speeches not merely by the educated Candius but by speakers of every class (cf. Prisius' asser-tion to Sperantus that 'it becometh men of our experience to reason, not rail; to debate the matter, not to combat it': 1.3.31–2).

It is not only the syntactic habits of the dramatis personae, more-over, that echo Lyly's distinctive mode of composition. Though the generational conflict and servant–master relationships of the play are patently derived, as noted above, from Roman New Comedy, the structure of the drama conforms, in the patterned, antithetical nature of its development, to the paradigm of Lyly's more overtly non-naturalistic works. Just as the opening scenes of *Galatea* and *Love's Metamorphosis*, for example, evolve through a process of parallelism and contrast, amplified by further variations as the action unfolds,[61] so the exposition of *Mother Bombie* introduces a sequence of events structured upon an intricate series of repetitions and oppositions. The opening scene, for example, in which Memphio enlists Dromio's aid in marrying his simpleton son to Stellio's seemingly desirable daughter, is mirrored in the following scene in which Stellio invokes Risio's assistance in marrying his foolish daughter to Memphio's reputedly cosseted son; while the desire of both fathers to arrange wealthy marriages for their children stands in opposition to the determination of Prisius and Sperantus in the following scene to prevent a union between their offspring that would frustrate their social aspirations. The opening sequence of contrasting positions is further complicated at the start of Act 3 by the introduction of a fresh set of young lovers, Maestius and Serena, who correspond with the children of Prisius and Sperantus in the parental opposition they face, but stand in opposition to them through the nature of the barrier that divides them, while corresponding with the children of Memphio and Sperantus, with whom they contrast in their acuity, in being socially unacceptable sexual partners.

The parallels established in the course of the action are further multiplied by the dreams, real or supposed, reported by the boys. The use of dreams is a consistent feature of Lyly's work, functioning both as a metaphor for the experience afforded by a play and as a vehicle for commentary on a drama's concerns. The Prologue at the Court in *Sappho and Phao*, for example, dissolves the actuality of the play world by inviting the monarch to 'imagine yourself to be in a deep dream' (line 16),[62] while the 'visions' seen by Endymion in the course of his long sleep reflect allegorically on both his own situation and that of the ruler he loves (cf. *Endymion*, 5.1.77ff.).[63] In *Mother Bombie*, by contrast, the device is located in a comic context in that it is the mischievous young servant, Lucio, who claims to have been 'troubled with a vile dream' (3.4.75), and the impish Halfpenny who seeks to outgo him by narrating a dream of his own (cf. 3.4.132–44). Both accounts are ludicrous in the fantastic metamorphosis that they effect in the familiar fabric of daily life, and thus function on one level as a parody of the portentous visions of

other plays. At the same time, however, the dreams patently pertain
to the experience of the dreamers and consequently reflect on the
concerns of the work. Lucio's dream of a 'stately piece of beef'
(3.4.102) arises, as Mother Bombie points out, from the fact that
he went 'supperless to bed' (3.4.123), providing a further comment
on the hand-to-mouth existence of many of those caught up in the
action of the play (see pp. 25–6 below), while Halfpenny's dream
of a 'handful of currants' (3.4.136) swept up in the procedures of
the law looks forward to the boys' own endeavours to escape the
judicial process in the following act, and implies the impotence of
the poor in the face of oppressive institutions (cf. Memphio's threats
to the Fiddlers at 5.3.100–3 and the familiarity Bedunenus exhibits
with the law courts at 5.3.56–7).

The parallelism at work in the organization of the action is not
the only aspect of the drama that conforms to the structural paradigm of Lyly's work. Just as *Euphues* may be described as an anatomy
of wit, or *Love's Metamorphosis* as an anatomy of love, through their
patterned analysis of a complex state,[64] so *Mother Bombie* might be
seen as a lighthearted game with the nature of nature, in that the
situations of all of the play's lovers and their parents are both
'natural' and 'unnatural' in some sense, as those terms were understood when the work was composed. The fact that Accius and Silena
are both 'naturals' (i.e. fools incapable of an adult relationship), for
example, means that they are unnatural partners for one another;
the natural love between Candius and Livia (i.e. that between a
compatible couple) makes them unnatural children in their rebel-
lious stance towards their fathers; while the natural sibling affection
between Maestius and Serena is in violation of the laws of nature
by virtue of its sexual character. At the same time, the play's parents
are driven by their instincts to act in ways that run counter to socially
acceptable norms. The natural love of Memphio for his son, like
Stellio's for his daughter, leads to the proposal to effect a highly
unnatural marriage between unsuitable partners who are ignorant
of one another's limitations; the natural desire of Prisius and
Sperantus to better their children's condition results in their ruthless
opposition to a marriage between social equals that would promote
the happiness of both; while the intensity of Vicinia's desire to
improve her children's position in life gives rise not only to the
highly unnatural substitution of her own offspring for those of other
people but to the seemingly incestuous passion between Maestius
and Serena, and the proposed marriage between the fools.

Just as the assemblage of a series of contrasting perspectives serves to align the play with the structural methods characteristic of the Lylian canon as a whole, so the dramatis personae exemplify that duality and capacity for change present throughout the Lylian corpus. The location of 'doubleness' is a recurrent feature of Lyly's work, extending from the puns and word-play that destabilize meaning, through antithetical propositions exhibiting the instability of abstract ideas, to images illustrating the contrasting properties of natural phenomena and evoking an Ovidian universe in which a process of mutation is constantly at work.[65] For all the familiarity of its urban setting, *Mother Bombie* conforms to this pervasive fluidity in that the seeming stability and unchanging character of an English provincial town are progressively eroded as the action evolves. Memphio and Stellio, for example, reveal in the opening scenes that a sustained pretence, maintained over many years, has concealed their offsprings' imbecile condition, while Dromio and Risio promise not merely to uphold their masters' deceptions but to extend them into a wider sphere. The two simpletons on whom all four seek to build their fortunes might thus be said to be 'double' from the outset, in that their public and private selves are at odds, exciting both desire and derision depending upon the perspective from which they are viewed. Similarly, Memphio and Stellio exhibit one face to their servants and another to one another in seeking to advance the position of the children whom they wrongly assume to be theirs; Dromio and Risio simultaneously defer to their masters and mock them, while deceiving them to serve their own ends (cf. 2.1.1–11 and 33–40); Candius enacts a pretence in seeming to have abandoned his love for Livia in conformity with the wishes of his father (cf. 2.3.1–6); while the Fiddlers trust that their double mistake, in celebrating a marriage at two locations where none is thought to have taken place, will be ascribed to the town Waits, who will consequently be punished in their place (5.3.110–11). Halfpenny's diminutive stature is wholly at odds with the magnitude of his wit; Vicinia is not the mother of the children presumed to be hers; while Mother Bombie's witch-like appearance stands in opposition to her ultimate benevolence, causing her to be viewed with distrust by Maestius on the grounds of her hag-like state (cf. 3.1.61–3), and with approbation by Memphio for her wisdom and the goodness of her acts (cf. 5.3.366–7). The metaphorical façades consciously or unconsciously erected by the characters are literalized, moreover, by the disguises assumed, at the boys' prompting, by Candius and

Livia in 4.1, and by Accius and Silena in 4.2, with the consequent discrepancies between appearance and (presumed) reality leading Prisius and Sperantus to bestow their blessings on a marriage to which they have been inveterately opposed, and Memphio and Stellio to congratulate themselves on the success of their schemes, when the outcome, in fact, runs counter to their wishes.

The stable identities of all social groups, and the individual's related capability for coherent conduct, are further eroded in the course of the action by the resort of the majority of the play's characters to the tavern. The boys testify in their song at the close of 2.1 to the dehumanizing effect of the consumption of wine (illustrated on p.VI of the present edition),[66] and all social classes become subject its transformatory power. Dromio, Risio, Lucio, and Halfpenny are made physically sick by over-imbibing (cf. 2.4.19–20 and 3.2.44–50); while Memphio, Stellio, Prisius, and Sperantus, characteristically guarded in their stance towards one another and critical of their young servants, become garrulous after tippling, are amused by the impudent behaviour of their boys, and tricked into paying their bill (cf. 2.5 passim). Lured into a drinking bout by Dromio and Risio, the Hackneyman, the Scrivener, and the Sergeant lose all contact with reality, inhabiting imaginary worlds (cf. the Hackneyman's belief that the tavern is his stable at 5.1.6–9), endangering their positions (cf. the Sergeant's pawning of his mace at 5.1.2–3), and acting in ways that run counter to their own best interests (cf. the spurious bond the Hackneyman accepts at 5.1.10–11).

It is the revelation at the close of the play that Maestius and Serena are, in fact, the children not of Vicinia but of Memphio and Stellio, however, that produces the most radical transformation in the social landscape of the work, in that the identities and relationships of all the dramatis personae undergo some species of change. Memphio proves to be the father of a promising son, rather than of the imbecile youth he believed to be his; Sperantus finds himself the parent of a talented daughter, rather than the idiot child he has reared; Accius and Silena are abruptly transformed from potential marital partners to blood relatives, and removed from wealthy stations in life to a state of dependence; Maestius and Serena are metamorphosed from brother and sister into a marriageable couple, and from indigence to an affluent condition; while Prisius and Sperantus experience an inner change as a result of the events around them and bestow their blessings on their children's marriage in response to the stirrings of nature within them (5.3.264–71). The universal jubilation leads to the freeing of Vicinia from punishment and the burden of guilt she has borne, and an improvement in the positions of the Hackneyman, who is compensated for the losses he has sustained at Dromio's hands, and the Fiddlers, who receive double payment (appropriately) for their pains. The seemingly immutable social architecture of the play world is thus entirely transformed at the close of the play, not merely through the conventional comedic unravelling of a seemingly intractable knot but through a realignment of the familial circumstances of all the central figures of the work, none of whom proves to be precisely who or what he or she was presumed, or thought himself or herself, to be.

For all the domesticity of its setting and the colloquialism of its semantic field, *Mother Bombie* is thus closer in its procedures to other items in the Lylian canon than might well appear at first sight. Just as the structural patterns of *Galatea* or *Love's Metamorphosis* turn upon opposition and change, culminating in a reversal exhibiting the transformatory power of the gods, so *Mother Bombie* evokes the shifting character of a seemingly stable world, concluding with a metamorphosis as far-reaching as any of the transformations accomplished by the classical deities of the dramatist's more overtly Ovidian works. The surprise, incredulity, and awe that attend the mutations effected by the gods are echoed in Memphio's astonishment at Vicinia's revelation (cf. 'What monstrous tale is this?': 5.3.321), Accius' refusal to accept its truth (cf. 'I'll never believe it': 5.3.324), and the amazement and joy of the young lovers freed from their incestuous state ('How happy is Maestius, thou blessed, Serena': 5.3.350). The ordinariness of the play world is thus infused at the close with a sense of wonder, transforming a work seemingly rooted in the mundane concerns of small-town life into a further exhibition by the dramatist of a universal capacity for change.

### CUNNING AND FOLLY

The process of domestication at work in *Mother Bombie*, in the application of the structural methods of the dramatist's prose works and court comedies to the arena of English provincial life, is also evident in the play's focus on intelligence and degrees of knowledge or understanding. As the subtitle of his first published work, *Euphues: The Anatomy of Wit*, indicates, Lyly was interested in the relationship between wit and wisdom from the outset of his career, and oppositional figures embodying varieties or levels of perception may be found in the majority of his plays. In *Endymion*, for example, the vacuity of the huge Sir Tophas is set against the intelligence of his diminutive page, while the wisdom of the king's daughter in *Midas* stands in opposition to the folly of her father and his advisers' misguided positions. In *Mother Bombie*, all the inhabitants of the play world lay claim to some kind of 'cunning', while simultaneously betraying some species of folly to those either inside or outside the play world, embodying a spectrum of mental abilities ranging from the percipience of Mother Bombie at one extreme to the uncomprehending condition of the two simpletons at the other.

The pattern of the play's dance-like progression around the concept of 'wit' is initiated in the opening scenes, in which Memphio's lament over the folly of his son and gratification at his plan to outwit Stellio is mirrored in Stellio's concern at the foolishness of his daughter and self-satisfaction at the cunning of his device to deceive Memphio (cf. his enquiry to Risio at 1.2.10, 'How likest thou this head?'). At the same time, while the masters are congratulating themselves on their shrewdness, and are confident of the good faith of the young servants upon whom they rely to prosecute their plans, their boys mock them for their folly, and are determined, on their part, to delude them (cf. Risio's ironic comment on the departing Stellio at 1.2.49, 'If I come not about you, never trust me'). The introduction of Prisius and Sperantus in the following scene repeats the same pattern, with each man announcing that he has been scheming to secure an advantageous marriage for his child, and uniting in their opposition to their children's wishes, only to hear themselves derided by their offspring, who have no doubt that they are intellectually superior to their parents (cf. 'I'll ask him blessing as a father, but never take counsel for an husband': 1.3.88–9), and are quick to display their own knowledge (cf. 'Thou shalt be acquainted with case, gender, and number': 1.3.156–7). Candius is a scholar from Oxford, capable of quoting the classics, and with 'wit' according to his father 'at will' (1.3.41), while Livia 'knows her lerripoop' (1.3.142–3), as she shows in recounting the significance of the items depicted in her sewing. For all the types of learning they exhibit, however, Candius and Livia, in their turn, are by no means as astute as they suppose, abashed when overheard discussing their marriage, and obliged to trust to the wit of their servants in order to bring their union about. The boys to whom both parents and children turn for assistance regard themselves as the arch-manipulators of the play world, yet they undermine their own pretensions to cunning by participating in a joke turning on a macaronic pun (cf. 2.1.96–111), defeat their own schemes through their love of mischief (cf. 4.2.171), and act in ignorance throughout of Vicinia's deception which defeats both their own and their employers' machinations. Maestius and Serena, the presumed children of Vicinia, display their reflective natures in their discussion of the prohibition inhibiting their love (3.1.1–25), only to exhibit their lack of judgement in doubting the wisdom of Mother Bombie (cf. 3.1.47–54). The Hackneyman is sure of his position in declaring the boys to be fools (cf. 4.2.198), but demonstrates his own poor judgement in trusting to their good faith, and loses all contact with rational behaviour, in common with the Scrivener and the Sergeant, when lured by Dromio into the tavern. Even the old fiddler, Synis, at the very margin of the play world, exhibits his pride in his command of his 'faculty' (5.3.9), and irritation at the failings of his boy, only to find himself spurned by Sperantus as a 'twangler' (5.3.28); while his fellow musician, Nasutus, is obliged to hurriedly 'sheathe his science' (5.3.107) when threatened with the stocks as a 'jarring rogue' (5.3.101).

As noted above, Mother Bombie and the two simpletons, Accius and Silena, occupy opposite ends of the spectrum of mental abilities represented in the course of the play, but even they have links with one another, and those who assume the superiority of their own wit, through the misconceptions surrounding the former and the latter's misapprehensions. Though Mother Bombie defines herself as 'a cunning woman' (2.3.99), and Memphio confirms that she is both 'cunning and wise' (5.3.366), her responses to those who consult her seem to her visitors empty of sense, while she invites the sceptical Maestius and Serena to convict her of folly should her seemingly unfulfillable prophecy prove untrue (cf. 'If this be not true, call me old fool': 3.1.46). Maestius condemns both himself and his sister for seeking council from 'such an old fool' (3.1.49–50), while Serena, whose hopes are dashed at their meeting, declares the 'obscure words' of her prophecy to be 'but dreams of decayed brains' (3.1.51 and 53–4). The seemingly absurd, doggerel form of her utterances, emblematic of the confused and fragmentary nature of truth in the play world, aligns her linguistically with the two imbeciles, and Silena has no difficulty in imitating her when at a loss to understand her pronouncements (cf. 2.3.108–15).

Conversely, though Accius and Silena are defined as simpletons from the outset, the presumptuous nature of their folly associates them with that belief in their own wisdom common to the dramatis personae as a whole. Stellio, for example, who misguidedly congratulates himself on his shrewdness, notes that his daughter's folly consists in 'think[ing] herself subtle' (1.2.23), while Silena exhibits a confidence in her intellectual superiority (cf. 'Good God! I think gentlemen had never less wit in a year! We maids are mad wenches. We gird them, and flout them out of all scotch and notch, and they cannot see it': 2.3.88–91) that not only echoes her father's self-satisfied blindness but may be seen as a heightened version of that belief in their own 'cunning' displayed by all those who dismiss their fellow citizens as fools. Similarly, for all his own vacuity, Accius doubts the wisdom of his father (cf. his salutation to Memphio at 4.2.109–10, 'I perceive an old saw, and a rusty. No fool to the old fool'), while the garbled proverbs that make up his conversation reflect the reliance of all the inhabitants of the play world on time-honoured, empty formulations (cf. Stellio's meandering observation in 2.5 that 'I have heard my great-grandfather tell how his great-grandfather should say that it was an old proverb when his great-grandfather was a child, that it was a good wind that blew a man to the wine': lines 4–7). The song that the simpletons share between them at the start of 3.3 asserts that 'Fools in love's college / Have far more knowledge / To read a woman over / Than a neat prating lover' (3.2.9–12), and Accius' relative success in courting Silena in 4.2, in which he succeeds in engaging her in some species of tangential conversation (cf. the failure of Candius' Petrarchan courtship in 2.3), shows that in some fields, at least, wisdom and folly do not stand an immeasurable distance apart.

The rubbing off of the forged birthmarks that takes place in the final scene enacts the wider process of recognition that takes place at the close of the work as the folly of all the play's misguided claimants to acuity is revealed, and the wisdom of Mother Bombie is confirmed. The open acknowledgement by Memphio and Stellio of the imbecile condition of their heirs, following the bungling by the boys of their plot, brings their own unwise conduct into the public domain, while prompting Vicinia to reveal the ill-conceived device which initiated the seemingly aberrant love between Maestius and Serena. The open admission of their love by the last couple leads, in turn, to the renunciation by Prisius and Sperantus of their foolish opposition to their own children's match, allowing the secret marriage of Candius and Livia to be publicly avowed. At the same time, the universal acknowledgement by the characters of their folly is accompanied by an increase in understanding, reversing the relationship between wit and wisdom that existed at the start of the play. Though Mother Bombie alone proves to be both 'cunning and wise', all the dramatis personae gain some degree of perception, allowing the play to close on a harmonious note. Memphio and Stellio, for example, learn to forgive the servants who have tricked them and acknowledge the imbecile children they believe to be theirs (cf. 5.3.261ff.), Prisius and Sperantus yield to the stirrings of nature (cf. 5.3.264–71), Maestius implicitly admits his misjudgement of Mother Bombie in his echo of her prophecy (cf. 5.3.350–3), while the Sergeant discovers the dangers of falling foul of the boys (5.3.438–42). Even the two simpletons conform at the close to that universal capacity for change evident throughout the Lylian corpus. Accius recognizes that Silena's position is improved by being his sister rather than his wife (5.3.388–9), while Silena has sufficient wisdom to grasp the fact that she would 'have been but a bald bride' (5.3.391). Though the wise-woman is not present in person in the final scene, all the characters may thus be said to have 'been', in some sense, 'with Mother Bombie' (5.3.364).

## MARGINALIZATION

The homely, provincial character of *Mother Bombie*, indicated by the play's title, is reflected in the unusually large space afforded by the drama to figures conventionally situated on the margins of the social group. From the outset, Lyly's work exhibits an interest in those excluded from positions of influence by gender, mental attributes, or class, and affords a voice to one or more figures at variance with the ideology of the dominant set. The female figures of the court comedies, for example, are frequently at odds with patriarchal assumptions, and invite a degree of sympathy for the oppositional stances they adopt,[67] while a succession of figures from Diogenes and Lais in *Campaspe* to the shepherds of *Midas* advance views on the nature of power that have little bearing on the stances of those in authority positions. Similarly, Sybilla in *Sappho and Phao* is isolated from her society by the nature of her dwelling, her experience, and her extreme old age; the Alchemist and the Astrologer of *Galatea* occupy distinct mental worlds, divorced from the reality of the dramatist personae as a whole;

while Bagoa and Dipsas in *Endymion* stand aloof from those around them by virtue of their possession of supernatural power. Above all, the disempowered young servants, common to all but one of Lyly's dramatic works, inhabit a different mental sphere from that of their masters, in that their behaviour is governed by indigence, or a sceptical, irresponsible wit.

For all the dramatist's interest in those on the fringes of the social group, however, it is the concerns of elevated figures, accustomed to the exercise of power, that lie at the heart of the majority of his plays. The worlds of the court comedies are governed, in the main, by the gods,[68] and usually peopled by members of an aristocratic elite. The pastoral settings in which a number of the plays are located are entirely divorced from the harsh realities of everyday life,[69] and the shepherds and woodsman who inhabit them belong to the same intellectual universe as the sophisticated beings of the comedies more overtly directed towards courtly concerns.[70] Though some characters may adopt stances at variance with the world-view of the dominant group, it is that ideology which ultimately prevails, and which underpins the final resolution. The transgressive love between Galatea and Phillida in *Galatea*, for example, is resolved by Venus through the transformation of one of the maidens into a youth, while the nymphs' resistance to love in *Love's Metamorphosis* is overcome by Cupid through the ruthless exercise of his power. In *Mother Bombie*, by contrast, there are no all-powerful figures capable of resolving the complexities of the plot. The ultimate authority of the play world is neither a deity nor a monarch but the mayor of a provincial town, and, though Memphio claims to have pretensions to that office (cf. 5.3.101–3), the current incumbent of the position is merely a distant threat (cf. the Sergeant's fears at 5.3.438–9 of being removed from his post), and takes no part in the progress of events. The most influential figures who appear in the course of the drama are two wealthy, somewhat foolish, old men (Memphio and Stellio), while the majority of the dramatis personae have limited means (e.g. Prisius and Sperantus), or are barely capable of making a living (cf. Bedunenus' complaint at 5.3.15 that he could 'never get new shoes', and Vicinia's decision to exchange her children in order to improve their social lot). Of the play's twenty-three characters, Accius and Silena are fools incapable of governing their own affairs; Dromio, Risio, Lucio, Halfpenny, and Rixula are servants, entirely devoid of financial means; the Hackneyman makes a living hiring out horses; the Sergeant and the Scrivener hang on the fringes of the law; Synis, Nasutus, and Bedunenus are indigent fiddlers, who attach themselves to communal celebrations in the hope of payment; Maestius, Serena, and Vicinia exist in conditions of extreme poverty; while Mother Bombie is distanced from the social group by her age, witch-like appearance, and prophetic powers. Rather than being in a position to concern themselves with ideals of conduct or the exploration of abstract ideas, all the inhabitants of the play world, with the exception of Mother Bombie, are concerned in some way with financial gain, locked in the pursuit of money, if only by others, or in the form of redress for a loss. The aged fathers hope to buttress their fortunes through advantageous alliances for their heirs; the boys are enlisted to promote their employers' financial ambitions, and desire access to the purses that hang at their masters' belts; the Hackneyman seeks compensation for the gross mistreatment of a broken-down horse; and the Fiddlers look for a handsome reward for celebrating a marriage at the house of a wealthy man. Even the obstacles faced by the young lovers (Candius and Livia, and Maestius and Serena) derive from their parents' desire to enhance their social positions, while Candius briefly yields to his father's world view in succumbing to the double allure represented by Silena's beauty coupled with her wealth (cf. 2.3.6–17).

The low social station of the characters, together with their near-universal indifference to the higher abstractions, and the foolishness of their conduct outlined on pp. 21–4 above, invites interpretation of the play in terms of a gallery of comic grotesques. Memphio and Stellio, congratulating themselves on their cunning in their wholly misguided pursuit of one another's wealth; Prisius and Sperantus tricked into giving their blessing to their children's marriage on the basis of a change of clothes; the Hackneyman so befuddled with wine he signs an acquittance for the losses he is seeking to recoup (cf. 5.1.6–11); the old Fiddler, barely able to scrape a living, congratulating himself on the amount of spittle he is able to summon to moisten the hole of his instrument's peg (cf. 5.3.9–12) may all be constructed as farcical figures, exciting laughter or contempt. At the same time, a number of the characters exhibit some species of physical, emotional, or mental disability that serves to locate them beyond the parameters of human norms. Both Rixula and Mother Bombie, for example, are seen as exceptionally ugly (cf. 3.4.19–20 and 2.3.112–13); Prisius has the palsy, and is troubled by a persistent cough (cf. 1.3.24–5 and 70–1); Halfpenny is notably smaller than his companions; Maestius and Serena believe themselves to be locked in an incestuous love; while Accius and Silena are simpletons, incapable of coherent speech. Eleven of the play's characters succumb, moreover, at some point to the influence of wine, losing the ability to pursue their own interests (cf. the Hackneyman's unwitting release of Dromio from debt: 5.1.6–11), and conducting themselves in a manner that serves to equate them with beasts (cf. the boys' song on the dehumanizing effects of excessive drinking at 2.1.164ff.). Persistent references to physical abuse (e.g. branding at 2.1.158–61, hanging at 3.4.42–61, whipping at 4.2.173), and the grim preoccupations of those on the very fringes of power (e.g. imprisonment or consignment to the stocks (as at 4.2.217–18 and 5.3.114–15)) heighten the sense of disfigurement, while the contentious, vituperative nature of the exchanges contributes to the aggressive competitiveness of the play world (cf. the first encounter between Priṣius and Sperantus in 1.3. and the persistent wrangling between the boys).

For all their superficially grotesque nature, however, the misguided and socially disadvantaged figures of *Mother Bombie*, like the marginalized characters of the court comedies, are not presented as wholly unsympathetic objects of derision. Though Memphio and Stellio, for example, are ludicrous in their frenetic pursuit of one another's wealth, they are not entirely divorced from human feeling, or wholly incapable of change. Though they have concealed the folly of their children, they have reared them in a manner appropriate to their class (cf. Serena's comments on her clothes at 4.2.59–60), and are pained on their behalf when their follies are exposed, not merely frustrated by the defeat of their plans (cf. 4.2.97–139). Similarly, though Prisius and Sperantus hope to improve their social standing through the advantageous marriages they endeavour to engineer for their heirs, they do not regard their recalcitrant offspring simply as pawns in the advancement of their schemes. Both are proud of their children's accomplishments (cf. 1.3.33–145), while Prisius is hurt by his daughter's indifference to his wishes, and evokes the natural bond, when reproving her, between parent and child (cf. 1.3.183ff.). Similarly Sperantus' stance towards his cheeky young servant is surprisingly humane (cf. Stellio's attitude to Risio at 2.5.40–9), in that he is amused by his impudence, and admiring of his quickness of wit, rather than intolerant of his lack of respect (cf. 2.5.50–8). All four fathers, furthermore, are quick to forgive those who have deceived them when the boys' devices are revealed, and Memphio is ready to pardon Vicinia for her offence, 'though the law would see it punished' (5.3.379–80).

While the degree of humanity displayed the four fathers qualifies their seemingly straightforward presentation as antipathetic dramatic types standing in opposition to the happiness of the young, it is the sympathetic treatment accorded to those at the furthest remove from authority positions which constitutes the more striking aspect of the work. Though some characters are undoubtedly driven by avarice, for example, the pursuit of money is not the index of a covetous nature for the majority of the inhabitants of the play world but of the pressing financial imperatives that govern the behaviour of the poor. The boys who seek to exploit their gullible masters are entirely destitute of means, and know that beggary may well be their ultimate fate (cf. 3.4.179–82); Vicinia's decision to exchange her children is motivated by fear that her poverty will cost them their lives (cf. 5.3.303–5); while the Fiddler's boy, who hopes to glean a living by playing at rich men's doors, is too poor to replace his outworn shoes (5.3.13–15). The Hackneyman's attempt to seek compensation from Dromio is valid, however exploitative his own intents, in that Dromio is guilty of abusing his horse, and may well have hoped to profit from its sale (cf. 4.2.208–16), while the pathos evoked by the Sergeant's fear of losing his office qualifies his representation as an uncharacterized embodiment of an oppressive state (cf. 5.3.438–9). Similarly contentiousness and vituperation do not necessarily indicate a lack of fellow feeling. The angry rejection of Mother Bombie by Maestius and Serena, for example, is motivated by profound disappointment at a prophecy that appears painfully irrelevant to their seemingly incestuous state, while Bedunenus' petty tantrum at Synis' adverse reflections on his musicianship derives from his miserable condition, and is instantly repented (cf. 5.3.23–4). The physical disabilities of the characters are not represented, moreover, as either barriers to human interaction or external manifestations of an inner deformity of spirit. Though Rixula's ugliness is a constant theme of the boys' jokes, for example, her wit and courage are equal to theirs (cf. her verbal battle with Lucio and Halfpenny at 3.4.1–61, and comparable determination at 3.4.9 to 'set all on hazard'), and she believes herself to be as capable of finding a marital partner as any other member of her sex (cf. her comment at 3.4.14–15 that 'there's no goose so grey in the lake that cannot find a gander for her make'). Similarly, Halfpenny's physical size is wholly at odds with the scale of his mental abilities (cf. Dromio's insistence that 'Though bound up in *decimo sexto*...[he has] a wit in *folio* for cozenage': 2.1.49–50); his fellow servants are anxious to include him in their 'fellowship' (2.1.92); and his master is both amazed by and appreciative of his extraordinary quickness of mind (cf. 2.5.50–8).

It is the two simpletons, and Mother Bombie herself, however, who constitute Lyly's most notable departures in the representation of those fundamentally removed from societal norms. The fool is a stock figure on the Elizabethan and Jacobean stage, appearing in a number of guises – as the degenerate offspring of an aristocratic family (e.g. Bergetto in Ford's 'Tis Pity She's a Whore), the deranged inhabitant of a madhouse (e.g. the supposed fool of Middleton and Rowley's The Changeling), or a professional entertainer uttering truths in nonsensical form (e.g. the Fool in King Lear). In all three cases, though often percipient, the figure stands at a remove from society at large, threatened with whipping if too unruly,[71] and regarded as a source of amusement rather than treated as an object of respect.[72] The two fools of Mother Bombie patently conform in large measure to early modern representation of the type, in that they suffer a species of incarceration (both are locked away by their fathers), are seen by the boys as irresistibly funny (cf. 4.2.4–80), afford amusement to those outside the play world through their inanities (cf. 4.2.25ff.), and occasionally stumble, inadvertently, on truths (cf. Accius' observation at 4.2.14 that he 'never was so far as the proverbs of this city', and his derisive, 'No fool to the old fool' at 4.2.110 on seeing his father). Nevertheless, Lyly's simpletons are far from being the abused victims of a society intolerant of difference. Both have been reared, as noted above, in a manner appropriate to their class, and are regarded by their parents with pity rather than disgust. Confounded by the vacuity of Serena's response to a question at 4.2.126, for example, Stellio responds with sadness rather than derision (cf. 'Poor wench, thy wit is improved to the uttermost': 4.2.127), while Memphio comforts himself for the folly of his son with the reflection that there is much to be said for the simpleton state (cf. 'fools are fortunate; fools are fair; fools are honest': 5.3.120–1). Though both fathers are overjoyed at the close by the revelation that Accius and Silena are not, in fact, their heirs, each is quick to offer the other's supposed offspring a respectable place in their households (cf. 5.3.380–2), guaranteeing their future security, rather than returning them to the extreme poverty from which Vicinia sought initially to save them.

The stance of the two simpletons towards themselves and those around them further complicates their construction as targets for a now-uncomfortable mirth.[73] As Stellio notes at the start of the play, Silena's folly lies in the fact that 'she thinketh herself subtle...[and] over-weenth of herself' (1.2.23–5), and though the boys are amused by her intellectual limitations it is clear from the outset that she is both serenely unaware of the derision she excites and secure in the rightness of her judgements. At the close of her encounter with Candius in 2.3, for example, she congratulates herself on having trounced him by her quickness of wit (cf. 'I think gentlemen had never less wit in a year!...We gird them, and flout them out of all scotch and notch, and they cannot see it!': lines 88–91), while she makes fun of Mother Bombie's predictions in the course of the same scene by a parody of her prophetic style (cf. lines 108–15). Wooed by Accius, she is sufficiently confident of her own worth to require his father's name before considering the match (cf. 4.2.83), while she has enough wisdom to recognize that she 'should have been but a bald bride' (5.3.391) when the plan to match her with Accius fails. Though initially outraged at the prospect of being 'cozened of [her] father' (5.3.355), when her true identity is revealed, she is quick to recover her equanimity, happily resolving to 'eat as much pie' at the wedding feast 'as if [she] had been married' (5.3.391–2). Similarly, Accius is entirely unaware of himself as an inadequate member of the social group, resenting both the curtailment of his freedom (cf. 4.2.13–14) and the plot that obliges him to wear demeaning clothes (cf. 4.2.110–11). When Silena is revealed to be his sister, he blithely informs her, 'it's the better for you' (5.3.388–9), and is wholly content, at the close, in the knowledge that 'we shall have good cheer these four days' (5.3.443–4). The courtship between the couple prior to the revelation of their kinship exhibits a degree of understanding between them for all the nonsensical nature of the exchange, while it is Silena, her assurance unshaken, who speaks the play's final line, rather than one of the lovers whose amatory problems are resolved.

While the two simpletons, cocooned by their lack of percipience from any sense of their own limitations, evade classification as the pitiable objects of the unfeeling humour of an insensitive age, Mother Bombie defies the stereotype evoked by both her appearance and her profession by the probity of her reputation and the morality to which she adheres. Whereas witches and cunning folk on the early modern stage were conventionally marginalized figures, allied with the forces of evil (cf. the Weird Sisters in *Macbeth* and Mother Sawyer in *The Witch of Edmonton*), or exposed as charlatans exploiting the gullible for gain (cf. the title figure of *The Wise-Woman of Hogsdon*), Mother Bombie stands aloof from the social group, not by virtue of her malign disposition but by her distance from the values of her world. While the intentions of the dramatis personae are uniformly exploitative, she is known as 'the good woman, who yet never did hurt' (3.1.28–9), and refuses payment for her services, rather than being absorbed, like her neighbours, in the relentless pursuit of financial gain. Whereas the majority of the inhabitants of the play world scheme to outwit one another, she contributes to the healing of social divisions, affirming that she 'never spoke untruth once' (3.1.57), while those around her are uniformly embroiled in deception. Rather than tricking her visitants by her fake prophetic powers like the Wise-Woman of *The Wise-Woman of Hogsdon*, or leading them astray through deceptive half-truths like the Witches of *Macbeth*, she is genuinely gifted with foreknowledge, and firmly aligned with the social, natural, and spiritual orders throughout. When Silena comes to her declaring that she is 'One that would be a maid', she responds with the unequivocal, 'If thou be not, it is impossible thou shouldst be; and a shame thou art not' (2.3.96–7),[74] while she encourages Vicinia to 'discharge' her 'conscience' (5.2.21), and assures the troubled Maestius and Serena that they will be married in accordance with 'the laws of God, Nature, and the land' (3.1.42). It is her relationship to the events of the drama as a whole, however, that places her in a unique position among the witches and cunning folk of the drama of her age. Whereas she seems at first sight to be peripheral to the action prior to her exchange with Vicinia in the penultimate scene of the play, in fact, she has 'foretold all', as Lucio notes (5.3.365), and the events of the drama may therefore be seen as taking place, in some sense, in her mind. The new order, with its sociability and companionship, to which the play moves, is thus identified with her mental landscape, though she is physically absent from the celebrations at the close, and the recollection of her prophesies by her visitants (cf. 5.3.355–65) confirms her position as the highly unconventional presiding genius of the play.

The fascination exhibited in *Mother Bombie* with those at variance in some respect with societal norms, together with the degree of understanding accorded to their world-view, serves, once again, to qualify the notion of Lyly as an effete intellectual, wholly at ease with court panegyric but uncomfortable in the rough and tumble of a literary world exemplified by Greene's cony-catching pamphlets or the satirical polemic of Nashe (see pp. 8–9 above). The long line of figures stretching from Diogenes in *Campaspe*, through the Alchemist and Astronomer of *Galatea*, Sir Tophas in *Endymion*, Motto the barber in *Midas*, to the irreverent protagonist of *Pappe with an Hatchet*, and the pragmatic Gunophilus of *The Woman in the Moon*, exemplifies the fact that he was as delighted by the quirks and quiddities of human nature as his contemporaries, and was as much a Renaissance man in his embracing of the earthiness of human life (cf. Rixula's song at 3.4.42–61) as in his easy familiarity with the classics.

### DRAMATURGY, STAGING, AND THE STAGE HISTORY OF THE PLAY

As in so many other respects, *Mother Bombie* occupies a unique position in Lyly's work in its fusion of the staging conventions of classical drama with the theatrical practice of late sixteenth-century England. Whereas the majority of the dramatist's plays are set in pastoral arenas, divorced from any specific place or time,[75] with antithetical concepts implied through the juxtaposition of emblematic structures representative of contrasting positions or states of mind,[76] *Mother Bombie* adheres to Roman New Comedy conventions with events taking place in an urban setting, defined by a group of houses fronting a street. The number of doors required in the course of the action is far greater, however, than generally required by the inherited form, and there is consequently some disagreement over how the play was originally staged. Seven 'houses', one, at least, with a window opening above, are demanded by the exigencies of the plot, implying an uncomfortable degree of crowding given the limited dimensions of the playing space at Paul's.[77] Eleven of the characters enter a tavern (or emerge from it) at some point in the play; eight visit Mother Bombie, knocking in one instance on her door; Memphio, Stellio, Prisius, and Sperantus all summon their offspring from, or dismiss them into, their houses (the last berating the Fiddlers through a window); while the Scrivener is summoned by the Sergeant at the close of Act 4 from his 'shop' (4.2.261). Given the Terentian origins of the plot, Andreadis argues that the physical difficulties posed by the number of houses may have been resolved by a species of 'arcade façade', based upon 'early illustrated editions of Terence, especially that of Trechsel published at Lyons in 1493', which were understood in the Renaissance 'to portray authentic classical staging and were therefore imitated'.[78] She consequently posits a central 'arcade façade sectioned off by arches into compartments representing the dwellings of the various characters whose names would be displayed by placards indicating their respective doorways', flanked by three free standing 'houses' at either side of the stage – Mother Bombie's 'hut' (sic), stage right, and the Scrivener's shop, stage left, together with the tavern.[79] Attractive as the solution might appear at first sight, however, it does not resolve all the difficulties posed by the text. A series of curtained compartments would not allow Candius to enter from his father's house in 5.3, presumably through the curtains of the 'compartment', when Sperantus himself 'looks out', presumably through the same curtains, prior to his entry, and continues to observe what is taking place at his door, while a freestanding Scrivener's shop would prove an unnecessary impediment for much of the play, unless its introduction was delayed until the start of 4.2.

The possibility of the late introduction of a 'domus', implying that all seven 'houses' need not have been simultaneously present on stage, opens the door to an argument for some species of 'doubling'. Reavley Gair suggests that the play was staged 'using multiple-function houses...of which the principal is Mother Bombie's' and that they were 'placed in opposition to each other on the main acting area'. Three such houses, in his view, are sufficient to meet the needs of the plot. 'The house of Mother Bombie in the centre, separating the other two locales'; a structure 'which may have had a visible upper storey' and which 'served variously as "Stellio's house"...or that of Sperantus, Priscus [sic], Memphis [sic] or the Scrivener'; and the tavern 'a frequent point of exit' which stood opposite to it.[80] Though the concept of multiple-function houses is an attractive one, however, in that it frees the acting arena from an over-abundance of free-standing structures, the particular arrangement Gair postulates does not accord with either the performance indicators embedded in the dialogue or the priority afforded to the locations in the disposition of scenes. While the centrality afforded to Mother Bombie's house may accord with her position as the presiding genius of the play, it does not correspond with the prominence afforded to her in the action itself. Only four scenes take place at her door, and in each instance the dialogue implies that her house is not at the heart of the community but adjacent to the central locale. Serena, comments, for example, that the cunning woman resides 'hard by' (3.1.26), rather than at hand, while Dromio urges his companions to 'go quickly' (3.4.83), if they want to consult her prior to prosecuting their plot. The central positioning of her house runs counter, moreover, to her marginality in the world of the play, while displacing much of the action to either side of the stage. At the same time, a single house-front is insufficient to denote the dwellings of the four father figures and their offspring. Accius and Silena plainly emerge from separate houses at the start of 4.2 and are taken indoors by their fathers at the close of their exchange, while the Fiddlers play first at Memphio's door in 5.3 and then under Sperantus' window in the same scene, with no intermission to allow for the hanging of a placard to denote the change of place. Given that the majority of the action takes place in the immediate proximity of the dwellings of the four old men, it seems more likely that their houses were located at the centre of the stage, with the tavern at one side, and Mother Bombie's house, its antithesis in terms of social responsibility, at the other. Since the houses of Sperantus and Memphio and those of Prisius and Sperantus are not required at the same time, moreover, for much of the play, two doors with an opening above would have permitted the coherent representation of the majority of the action, without the unnecessary constrictions of an 'arcade façade' or too great an imposition on the imagination of the spectator. As Mother Bombie's house is utilized in only four scenes, her dwelling, whether a free-standing structure or a door at the back of the stage, could well have doubled as the Scrivener's shop, allowing the drama to be performed with no more than four 'houses', leaving a viable playing space for the relatively large cast.

Though a 'four-house' variation on Gair's 'multiple-function' locations thus has much to recommend it, it appears, unfortunately, to run counter to the sequence of events that takes place at the close of the play. After Sperantus and Memphio scold the Fiddlers from their houses at the opening of 5.3, Prisius and Sperantus enter, and encounter one another with their boys, leading to the revelation of the marriage between Candius and Livia, and the two outraged fathers requiring their children to 'come forth' (5.3.175 and 176–7). Since Candius and Livia then enter on being summoned, the scene appears to require three houses visible to the audience at the same time, that of Memphio, from which the Fiddlers are chased by Dromio, and those of Sperantus and Prisius, from which Livia and Candius emerge. The difficulty may not have been as great when the play was initially performed, however, as it now appears on the printed page. Following the exchange between Memphio and Dromio at 5.3.113–43, both characters leave the stage prior to the entrance of Sperantus and Prisius with their servants, suggesting that a new scene may have been intended at 5.3.144, dividing the now uncharacteristically lengthy final scene (see 5.3.143.SD.n.). A scene break would have allowed for the changing of a placard over Memphio's door to indicate that the location had shifted to Prisius' house, with two doors again sufficient for the representation of the plot. The issue is further complicated, however, by the exchange that then ensues, in which Memphio and Stellio also summon their children from within, suggesting either that their houses, too, are visible to the audience or that Accius and Silena enter through the same doors as Candius and Livia.[81] The structuring of the action thus appears to lead to an equally unsatisfactory choice between a plethora of locations, and multi-function houses, whose owners are denoted not by the use of placards but by the family members emerging from their doors.

While the play draws, to some degree at least, on Roman New Comedy conventions in the use of house-fronts denoting its urban location, the symbolic arrangement of the 'mansions' flanking the dwellings of the father figures looks back to the conceptual staging of medieval drama, and the emblematic settings of the comedies designed by Lyly for performance at court. The tavern, for all the classical origins of the ivy bush signalling its function, has a long history on the Tudor stage, representing the downfall of youth through the temptations of the flesh, and the song which precedes the boys' first drinking bout at the close of 2.1 invokes the location's traditional associations with the overthrow of reason, and the descent of man into beast. Similarly, Mother Bombie's house is not a neutral structure, but representative of a mental state. Though initially linked with the tavern through varieties of truth-telling (cf. 3.1.56–7 and 3.3.32–5), and by Maestius' warning that consorting with Mother Bombie could lead one 'out of a plain path into a deep pit' (3.1.63), the two locations emerge as opposing forces at work in human life, the one clouding human perceptions (cf. the boys' report of the irrational, self-destructive conduct of the Hackneyman, the Scrivener, and the Sergeant following their entry into the tavern at the close of Act 4),[82] and the other clarifying and enlarging moral understanding (cf. Mother Bombie's advice to Vicinia in 5.2 which promotes the well-being of all the inhabitants of the play world).

The fusion of the stylized staging of classical comedy with the conceptual arrangements of the sixteenth-century stage is mirrored in the handling of the plot. The clear articulation of Terentian drama, with its singleness of action, is overlaid with the intricate patterning characteristic of Lyly's work (see pp. 15–17 above), and amplified through that exuberant multiplication of classical devices characteristic of the Elizabethan stage (cf. the doubling of the Plautine plot in *The Comedy of Errors*). As Michael Pincombe points out, 'Lyly gives us not one *senex* (Old Man), but four; not one vexed liaison between *adulescens* and *virgo* (Youth and Maiden), but three…and there is a clutch of comic *servi* (Slaves) to complicate matters – with a witty *ancilla* (Serving-Woman) thrown in for good measure; there is even a *nutrix* (Nurse)'.[83] The type figures of Roman comedy are qualified by a degree of sympathy wholly at odds with the classical tradition (see pp. 27ff. above), while the action is complicated by the concerns of an admixture of figures drawn not from Roman models but from sixteenth-century English provincial life. The unities of time, place, and action thus give place to a highly complex sequence of events, set in a variety of locations, and requiring approximately twice the twenty-four hour time-span within which the action conventionally evolved in order to reach a resolution.[84]

The visual component of the drama, deducible from the characters' exchanges, serves to further the distance between the work and the classical form to which it looks back. In common with all Lyly's plays, meaning is generated by the use of significant spectacle, and not solely by verbal means, for all the dramatist's reputation as a wordsmith, exclusively concerned with stylistic effects. The deformity of the play world at the outset of the action, for example, is signalled by the physical peculiarities of the dramatis personae (e.g. the ugliness of Rixula, Prisius' palsy, and the over-large nose implied by the second fiddler's name), while extremes of wealth and poverty are denoted by the worn shoes of which Bedunenus complains, and the exchange of clothes between Accius and Silena and Maestius and Serena.

It is in the scenes that take place at Mother Bombie's door, that the drama comes closest to the type of visual effect characteristic of Lyly's plays for the court. Though there are very few stage directions in the two quartos, or Blount's collected edition of 1632 (see p. 2 above), indicating how these scenes were initially staged, the dialogue supplies some indications of the title-figure's

appearance and the way in which her encounters with her visitors
were originally performed. The comments of those who seek her
advice, for example, establish that she is old, ugly, and poorly
dressed. When she describes herself in 3.1, for instance, as 'The
dame of the house', Maestius responds, 'She might have said the
"beldame", for her face, and years, and attire' (lines 34–6), while
Halfpenny crosses himself, three scenes later, in fear at her looks,
and Dromio implies that her appearance is witch-like in his concern
that she might turn them into apes (cf. 3.4.88–9). The apprehen-
sions aroused by her physical appearance are intrinsic to her
ambivalent position in the play world (see pp. 12–13 above), and
the four occasions on which she appears, all of which turn upon
a prophecy, are carefully prepared for in the text. Though the
three early editions indicate that she 'enters', it is clear that she
is not the active agent in the four encounters in which she is
involved, in that she is sought out by her visitors, rather than
electing to intervene in the course of events, and is summoned
by those who consult her from her 'house'. Audience expectation
is aroused, furthermore, in each case by the dialogue and stage
business that accompany the opening of her door. Silena calls
'God be here' (2.3.93), with unwitting irony, before the witch-like
figure appears, while Maestius debates her status with his sister,
giving a larger meaning to his enquiry, 'Who is within?' (3.1.33).
The boys knock loudly to attract her attention, only to recoil
before her response, while Vicinia, having announced her decision
to seek her advice, signals her desire to speak to her with a greeting that supplies the play world with a spiritual dimension (cf.
5.2.10).

There is considerable evidence to suggest, moreover, that the
uncertainty surrounding her status, and thus the source of her
prophetic powers, is not simply a product of her personal appearance, but that a more striking stage spectacle is involved. When
Silena asks her to 'tell [her] something', Mother Bombie instructs
her to 'Hold up [her] hand', but the younger woman fails to grasp
her intention to tell her fortune by reading her palm, and holds it
too high for her to be able to inspect (cf. 2.3.100–2). No stage
directions are given in the three early editions to indicate the stage
business involved at this point, and William Tydeman is alone
among the play's twentieth-century editors in attempting to clarify
how the scene was originally played. Unfortunately, the stage direction that he supplies, 'SILENA *holds it above her head*', following

Mother Bombie's injunction to 'Hold up thy hand', is ambiguous, in that it fails to make clear whether Silena holds her hand above her own head, like an eager child clamouring to answer a question, or over that of the old woman, whose eye-line must thus be substantially lower than her own. The answer may be supplied in the following act in which Maestius and Serena also seek the cunning woman's advice. Angry at a prophecy which seems incapable of fulfilment, Maestius condemns her as 'an old fool' (3.1.50), while Serena declares, 'I would thou mightest sit on that stool till he and I marry by law' (3.1.54–5). The lines suggest that, rather than standing to converse with her visitors, Mother Bombie receives them sitting down, and that, when she is unable to see Silena's palm in the previous scene in which she appears, it is because she is seated, and Silena fails to allow for that fact. Tydeman notes, with reference to the stool that 'presumably this article remained on stage outside Mother Bombie's house door throughout the action',[85] but, leaving aside the logistical difficulties posed to the actors by having to negotiate an item redundant for much of the play on an already crowded stage, it seems more likely that it constituted part of the furniture of the old woman's household, contributing to the visual effect. In short, the sparse textual indicators suggest that what was intended was a stage spectacle designed to elicit surprise, and even a frisson of apprehension, among those both inside and outside the play world. Rather than simply entering when summoned, as the early editions imply, Mother Bombie may well have been disclosed, already seated upon her stool as her door opened, witch-like in both posture and attire. The discrepancy between her appearance and her true nature, realized in visual terms by the stage spectacle, would thus have corresponded with the obscured identities endemic throughout the play world, while her house would have become more overtly a gateway to supernatural forces, widening the mundane arena in which the inherited action is set.

The company for which the piece was designed further domesticates the work in the lack of concern that its personnel embodied with the verisimilitude implicit in the unities of the classical form. Like the rest of Lyly's plays, the drama was written for a juvenile troupe,[86] and thus draws attention in performance to its own artifice through the physique and vocal range of the cast. Opportunities are afforded to exhibit the musical accomplishments of the boys, with four songs in the course of the action, two accompanied by the on-stage playing of stringed instruments, and an opening for comic business turning on a youth's lack of mastery of a fiddle (cf. 5.3.8–12). The young actors' classical training is exhibited, as elsewhere in Lyly's work, through Latin quotations (e.g. at 1.3.152ff.) and macaronic word games (cf. 2.1.97–111) designed to appeal to an educated clientele, while the large number of juvenile and female roles minimizes the strains placed on the boys' ability to convincingly inhabit their parts.[87] The young company's capacity for quick-fire exchanges, evidenced throughout the dramatist's work, is exploited in the wrangling between Halfpenny and Risio in 2.1 and the sparring between the boys and Rixula in 3.4, while the rote learning that enabled the delivery of long passages of euphuistic prose is exemplified in the exchanges between Livia and Candius, and between the young lovers and their parents in 1.3. The play also yields some evidence of the 'star system' detected by Gair in the plays composed for performance by the troupe.[88] The role of Halfpenny clearly demands an exceptionally small but a precociously mature and quick-witted young actor, and his first appearance is heralded in a manner clearly designed to awaken audience expectation (cf. 2.1.44–50). Given that an equally diminutive boy was needed for the roles of Epiton in *Endymion* and Minutius in *Midas* it is probable that the part was written with a particular actor in mind, and that he was a favourite with the regular clientele at Paul's.[89] For all its Roman New Comedy origins, the play is thus very much a sixteenth-century repertory piece, designed for a specific company and with a particular set of playing conditions in mind.

Despite its probable success in its own day (see p. 40 below), *Mother Bombie* has rarely been performed in modern times. Its links with *The Comedy of Errors* prompted its inclusion, however, among the sixteenth-century plays revived at the Bristol Shakespeare Quartercentenary Festival in 1964, under the auspices of the Bristol University Drama Department in association with the Old Vic Trust.[90] The play, which was performed in Elizabethan costume, was directed by two Bristol Grammar School masters, C. P. Jenkins and J. M. Adams, while the company consisted of a group of boys from the school's Middle School Play Club, including J. M. Haddrell, whose 'excellent' performance of the part of Silena was notable for its 'persuasive charm', and A. D. Rees, who was 'outstandingly successful' in the role of Halfpenny. The performance was accompanied by 'period' music for the clavichord (composed

and played by C. R. Jones), contributing to the audience's enjoy-
ment (attested by reviews) of the occasion as a whole.[91] A further
production at the Other Place in Stratford was advertised in 1997
but subsequently cancelled without explanation. A staged reading
of the play will take place in December 2010, under the auspices of
the Education Department of Shakespeare's Globe (London), to
mark the publication of this edition.

## CRITICAL RECEPTION

Though *Mother Bombie* may well have been a theatrical success (cf.
Nashe's recollections, quoted above, of the laughter it induced, and
the title-page declaration that it was 'sundrie times plaied by the
Children of Powles'), it has posed problems for its readers from the
outset, and has not received a good press. The erroneous speech
prefixes at 4.2.90–6, common to all three early editions, may look
back to a misguidedly 'corrected' text, suggesting that the intricacies
of the plot may have proved baffling to a copyist (or stage-manager)
at a very early stage in the history of the work (see commentary
note). A handwritten attempt to construct a cast list in a copy of
the second quarto in the British Library is heavily corrected, indicating the writer's difficulty in determining familial relationships, and
a similar uncertainty is implied by Edmund Malone's emendations
and insertions in his list of the dramatis personae in his copy of the
first quarto. Marginal comments in the two early editions are also
far from appreciative. A reader has inscribed the word 'woeful' at
both the beginning and end of the British Library copy of *Q1*, while
an owner of the Houghton copy of *Q2* notes that the play is 'little
else than a tissue of absurd mistakes, arising from the confusion of
the different characters one with another. Most of them end in being
married to persons they specially dislike', a summary based on
William Hazlitt's remarks on the work in his *Lectures on the Literature
of the Age of Elizabeth* (1820).[92] The same comment by Hazlitt
formed the substance of Sir Paul Harvey's entry (under Bumby,
MOTHER) in *The Oxford Companion to English Literature* in 1932,
and has continued to be rehearsed in subsequent editions to the
present day,[93] perpetuating adverse criticism of the work, and an
erroneous account of the plot.

Hazlitt's extraordinary misreading of the conclusion (the four
lovers are, in fact, united and all the characters 'pleased': cf. 5.3.395)
is typical, moreover, of critical commentary on the piece. Though

it is Mother Bombie who triggers the final resolution, through her advice to Vicinia in 5.2, and is described by Andreadis as 'a normative figure... [reinforcing] the expectation that in a comedy all must turn out for the best',[94] she is pronounced by a number of commentators to be wholly superfluous, or incidental to the evolution of events. Violet Jeffery, for example, dismisses her as 'entirely unessential' and argues that she 'could well have been left out without any loss',[95] a position echoed by T. W. Baldwin,[96] while G. K. Hunter notes that 'her exact function is difficult to assess', and that her role in 'trip[ping] the switch for the catastrophe' could have been achieved by 'less clumsy' means.[97] The question of Mother Bombie's centrality to the plot is linked to a further uncertainty in relation to the young servants, and some equally dubious assertions regarding their role. Hunter's doubts, for example, about the wisewoman's position turn upon the assumption that it is the boys who are the prime movers of the action, and their wit that determines the progress of events. 'By forming a coherent group', he argues, 'the servants are able to fit together their individual fragments of knowledge, and so are able to manipulate... the whole course of the plot'.[98] The notion that the boys are in total control of the situation, and thus in a position to make 'all the other characters their victims',[99] is plainly at odds, however, with the course of events in the latter half of the play. Though their scheme to gain the consent of Sperantus and Prisius to the marriage of their children is successful, their plan to marry Accius and Silena fails (cf. Lucio's admission that he and Halfpenny have 'marred all': 4.2.171), while they are wholly ignorant of the essential piece of information that allows all the play's problems to be resolved. Joseph Houppert similarly argues that wit 'dominates' the drama, but disputes Hunter's position that it is the driver of events. Implicitly redefining the role of the boys in relation to the action, he designates the play a 'comedy of situation'[100] with wit arising from the positions of the characters, rather than being a means, as Hunter claims, 'of working towards a goal'.[101]

The role of the two simpletons has also given rise to conflict of opinion, and hostile criticism of a rather different kind from that attracted by the title-figure. Bond declares the 'ramblings of sheer idiocy' to be 'no proper subject for comic treatment',[102] a stance endorsed by Carter Daniel, who insists that 'a modern audience... will find no source of mirth either in the idea of retarded children in general or in the particular two portrayed here'.[103] The reviewer of the production of the play at the Shakespeare

Quartercentenary Festival at Bristol in 1964 (see pp. 39–40 above), by contrast, singled out the performance of the role of Silena not for its distasteful character but for its 'persuasive charm', suggesting that one member, at least, of a twentieth-century audience did not regard the character as the embodiment of a now outmoded 'source of mirth'. Even the old fathers of the play have been subject to widely differing, and sometimes surprising, accounts. While Tydeman sees them as merely the 'gulled fathers of the classical convention',[104] Houppert maintains that they 'put the claims of parenthood in a more humane fashion than...their Roman counterparts',[105] a view strikingly at odds with Daniel's contention that they are 'ruthlessly portrayed as stupid, greedy, materialistic, lacking in education, lacking in self-knowledge, lacking in moral principles, and lacking in human sympathy'.[106]

Disagreement and dissatisfaction are not merely confined to the play's characters, moreover, but extend to the entire structure of the work. While Hunter, Daniel, and Houppert agree, for example, that the play is a comedy of intrigue, emulating the 'order, regularity, neatness, and clarity of the Terentian mode',[107] they adopt very different positions in relation to its overall success. Whereas for Hunter the 'plot seems to move effortlessly, drawn by the feather-weight wit of the pages',[108] for Daniel its 'Terentian intricacy is...an insufficient support for so long a work',[109] while Houppert contends that Lyly 'attempts to pour too much into the plot', and that 'the initial intrigue is multiplied in such a labyrinthine fashion that suspense is soon sacrificed to confusion, and the comic catharsis is stillborn'.[110] Some critics, moreover, are far from persuaded that the organization of the play's action may be adequately described in New Comedy terms. Andreadis rejects the imposition of 'a rather rigid notion of "the Terentian formula"' on what is a more fluidly modulated, non-linear structure',[111] arguing that the play is comparable with the dramatist's court comedies in its evolution through a series of quasi-musical 'movements'.[112] Similarly Tydeman, while locating the work among a group of comedies engaged in 'Englishing' a non-native form, describes the development of the action in terms of 'a complex dance sequence in which, after a series of intricate figures, each of the company arrives in the correct position'.[113]

An equally striking division of opinion is evident in relation to the drama's concerns. Hazlitt's pronouncement that the comedy is 'very much what its name would import – old, quaint, and vulgar'[114] has largely given place to a more sophisticated approach, but the issues

explored in the course of the action, and the relative profundity of
the piece, continue to be matters of dispute. Hunter's characteristically subtle analysis, locating wit as 'the central area of value' in the
play,[115] has not been generally endorsed, and, though Andreadis and
Houppert are at one in finding marriage to be a major concern, there
is no agreement between them on the depth with which the subject
is explored. For Andreadis, *Mother Bombie* is 'Lyly's anatomy of
marriage', structured around a pattern of couples designed to exhibit
three kinds of union, those of 'love, labor, and grief' and firmly
rooted in the thought of 'Elizabethan popular moralists...con-
cerned to redefine marriage within a context of natural law and
mutual obligation'.[116] For Houppert, by contrast, the play 'sacrifices
romance to intrigue' and 'the analysis of love...is superficial'.[117] It
is Michael Pincombe, however, who probably offers the most star-
tling interpretation of the work. Aligning the play with the dramatist's court comedies, he argues that that 'Mother Bombie...acts as
a figurative link with Lylian panegyric; not by providing materials
for an Eliza [i.e. a mythical, idealized version of the Queen]...but
rather for her demonic or grotesque opposite: an "anti-Eliza"'.[118]
The play thus becomes a stepping-stone in the dramatist's own
stance towards the court, looking forward to the disillusionment
with the concept of a golden age displayed, in Pincombe's view, in
*The Woman in the Moon*.

Remarkably, even the tone of the work has occasioned dispute.
For all his reservations about the role of the simpletons, Bond
declares the play to be managed 'with humour and spirit',[119] while
Hunter finds it to be 'graceful and witty',[120] and Pincombe describes
it as 'merry', though 'written in anxious times'.[121] In Daniel's view,
by contrast, the 'satire is the strongest and most biting anywhere in
Lyly's works' and 'something of the same rage about parents and
children that informs Shakespeare's *King Lear* may have motivated
Lyly in writing this play'.[122] In short, though *Mother Bombie* differs
from the rest of the dramatist's works in a number of respects, it
has proved quintessentially Lylian in its capacity to yield 'divers
significations'.[123]

### THIS EDITION AND THE EDITORIAL HISTORY OF
### THE PLAY

*Mother Bombie* appeared in three early editions (see pp. 1–6 above),
and has been among the more frequently edited of Lyly's plays in

modern times. A lightly annotated modern-spelling edition, based on the second quarto but incorporating the songs published by Blount (see pp. 5–6 above), was included by Charles Wentworth Dilke in the first volume of his *Old English Plays* (1814), and was followed by a somewhat more extensively annotated old-spelling edition by F. W. Fairholt, again founded on the second quarto supplemented by Blount, in the second volume of his *The Dramatic Works of John Lilly* (1858). Five major editions followed in the course of the twentieth century, the first two of which were overtly directed towards an academic readership. R. W. Bond's old-spelling edition, in his *The Complete Works of John Lyly* (Oxford, 1902), was the first to be based on the first quarto, and to supply a detailed collation of the early editions together with an extensive commentary on the text, and it consequently remains a significant landmark in the publication history of the play; while a typographical facsimile of the first edition, edited by Kathleen M. Lea with the assistance of D. Nichol Smith, published by The Malone Society in 1948 (as the society's 1939 volume), provided an important aid to scholarly investigation of the text. Two of the three subsequent twentieth-century editions were directed towards making the play accessible to a wider audience. William Tydeman, in his old-spelling *Four Tudor Comedies* (Harmondsworth, 1984), included the work among a group of sixteenth-century plays exhibiting the transference of the conventions of classical comedy to the Tudor stage, while Carter A. Daniel, in *The Plays of John Lyly* (Lewisburg, 1988), published the entire corpus of Lyly's comedies in a lightly annotated, one-volume, modern-spelling edition in order to make the work of a largely neglected dramatist more 'conveniently available to the modern reader'.[124] The remaining edition to be published in the course of the twentieth century, that by Harriette Andreadis in the Elizabethan and Renaissance Studies Series (Salzburg Studies in English Literature, 1975), stands apart from the rest, in that it is the only one-volume, modern-spelling edition, with a full scholarly apparatus, to have appeared prior to the publication of this work.

Though the present edition is based, as noted above (p. 6), on the first quarto, augmented by the songs published by Blount, all the surviving copies of the two quartos (1594 and 1598), together with both issues of Blount's *Sixe Court Comedies* (1632) and the seven modern editions listed above, have been collated in the course of its preparation. The play is edited in accordance with the practices set out in the General Editor's Preface, with the on-page collation notes recording substantive editorial interventions and divergences between the three early editions only, but a full historical collation (including minor typographical discrepancies between the early editions) has been supplied, in this instance, in an Appendix in view of the relatively extensive editorial history of the work. Though spelling has been modernized in line with the practice of the Revels series, some sixteenth-century forms have been retained (e.g. 'hether', 'thether') where they are insistently employed in the earliest edition. Direct indebtedness to the work of previous editors is acknowledged as far as possible in the commentary, but it would be impossible to record every instance in which a predecessor's observation has informed an editorial choice, or stimulated a fresh line of thought.

The volume brings to completion the project to publish Lyly's complete dramatic works in the Revels Plays series.

### NOTES

1 Greg, i, p. 11. Greg notes, 'The words "Mother Bumbye" are inserted by the same hand in a space originally left blank'.

2 In total, sixteen plays were published by him or entered to him in *SR* between 1594 and 1600 including *Love's Labour's Lost*, *Romeo and Juliet*, and *Every Man in His Humour*. See Greg, iii, pp. 1498–9.

3 Both copies are defective. That in the British Library has suffered damage to the title-page, lacks I4, and has lost text and/or catchwords through cropping at the foot of E–G1r, while the Bodleian Library copy has been mutilated by the insertion of songs from Blount's 1632 edition of Lyly's plays.

4 Loose type has led to the displacement of a comma and the final letters of the concluding words of the first eight lines of B2r in the BL copy, while the second 'e' of 'thee' has been lost from the Bodleian copy at the end of the first line of H4v. The spacing of '*Sub leuabo*' on A3v also appears to differ between the two copies.

5 The misnumbering of scenes is a recurrent feature of Lylian quartos, possibly arising from some ambiguity in authorial practice. Three mistakes occur, for example, in the numbering of scenes in *Love's Metamorphosis*, while 'Actus terius [*sic*], Schaena prima' appears for 'Actus tertius, Schaena quarta' in the first quarto of *Sappho and Phao*.

6 Andreadis, p. 7. For a fuller discussion of the bibliographical features summarized here, see Andreadis, pp. 7–11.

7 Andreadis, p. 9.

8 For a detailed analysis of the evidence relating to broken type, see Andreadis, pp. 10–11.

9 See Bevington, in Hunter and Bevington, eds, *Galatea: Midas*, p. 112, and Scragg, ed., *Love's Metamorphosis*, p. 2. *The Woman in the Moon* is an exception, with a number of features implying a greater proximity

to the production process than is the case with the majority of Lyly's plays (see Scragg, ed., *The Woman in the Moon*, p. 2).

10  The erroneous stage direction on E2v (3.3.01 this ed.), '*Memphio and Stellio singing*', which appears to fall into this category of error, may arise from eye-skip on the part of the compositor given the proximity of the direction to the entrance of Memphio and Stellio at the start of the next scene, and the omission from the quarto of the intervening song.

11  Three editions of *Campaspe* were published by Thomas Cadman in 1584 and a fourth by William Broome in 1591, while two editions *Sappho and Phao* were published by Cadman in 1584, and a third by Broome in 1591.

12  The appearance of *The Woman in the Moon* in 1597 and *Love's Metamorphosis* in 1601, together with the transfer of the rights to another five of Lyly's plays to George Potter in 1601, presumably with a view to publication, supports the suggestion that the revival of the juvenile troupes at the turn of the century triggered a fresh interest among publishers in the commercial possibilities of Lyly's work.

13  A framed device of Truth being scourged by a hand from the clouds, with the motto '*Viressit vulnere veritas*'.

14  In the British Library (C34.d.16 and C.34.f.32); Victoria and Albert Museum (Dyce 26, Box 25/5)); Bodleian Library (Mal. 195 (2) and Mal. 212 (2)); Magdalene College, Cambridge (Pepys Library, PL. 939 (1)); National Library of Scotland (Bute 326); Boston (Mass.) Public Library (G.3873.29); Folger Shakespeare Library (two copies: STC 17085); Harry Ransom Humanities Research Center, University of Texas at Austin (PFORZ 634 PFZ); Houghton Library, Harvard (STC 17085), and Huntington Library (62384). A residual trace of a fourteenth copy survives in an unbound duplicate leaf of G1r in the Houghton Library copy, which may have been acquired to replace the existing leaf, damaged by a tear (now repaired). One of the two Folger Library copies has suffered the loss of a substantial proportion of the text (replaced, in part, by a transcript, incorporating sung material from Blount's 1632 edition (see note 18 below)).

15  Greg, i, p. 210.

16  Though Andreadis argues (p. 12) that some variant readings (e.g. 'foule words' for 'foule speeches'on E2r (3.4.28 this ed.), and 'wine and beere' for 'sacke and beere' on E3r (3.4.108 this ed.)) may be the product of 'intervention by a printing house editor', it seems more likely that they are compositorial errors.

17  BL. C34.f.32, Boston (Mass.) Public Library (G.3873.29), and the defective Folger Library copy.

18  The defective Folger Library copy is an exception, in that the relevant page is missing and replaced by an inaccurate transcript incorporating the song from Blount's 1632 edition.

19  The defective Folger Library copy is again the exception, in that E3v is among the pages missing from the text.

20  Of the thirteen extant copies, that in the Boston Library has all three pages in their uncorrected states, with the ornament on A2r inverted and the textual errors on E1v and E3v. The Huntington Library copy

has A2r in its corrected state but the uncorrected E1v and E3v; BL
C34.f.32 has E1v and E3v in their corrected states, but the uncorrected
A2r; while the defective Folger Library copy has the uncorrected A2r
but lacks E1v and E3v. The other nine copies have all three pages in
their corrected states.

21 Greg, i, p. 36.

22 Greg, iii, p. 1088. As Greg notes, the general title-page is found in a
number of states of correction.

23 For the significance of Blount's edition in relation to Lyly's biography
and critical reputation, see Leah Scragg, 'Edward Blount and the
History of Lylian Criticism', *RES*, XLVI (1995), 1–10.

24 The duet between Accius and Silena in 3.3 is wrongly assigned, however,
to Memphio and Stellio, and the sung interventions by Lucio and
Halfpenny in Rixula's song in 3.4 are oddly assigned to '4. Pag. / 4 Pa.'.

25 For a detailed discussion of the authenticity of the songs in Blount's
edition of Lyly's plays, see Hunter, pp. 367–72, and Tiffany Stern,
*Documents of Performance in Early Modern England* (Cambridge, 2009),
pp. 135–9.

26 See Leah Scragg, 'Edward Blount and the History of Lylian Criticism',
pp. 7–9.

27 The relevant passage reads: 'Then we neede neuer wish the Playes at
*Powles* vp againe, but if we were wearie with walking, and loth to goe
too farre to seek sport, into the Arches we might step, and heare him
[Gabriel Harvey] plead; which would bee a merrier Comedie than
euer was old Mother *Bomby*' (quoted from McKerrow, ed., *Nashe*, iii,
p. 46).

28 The term 'Jost there', attributed to the Hackneyman at 5.1.8, may also
be of Kentish origin (see 5.1.8n.).

29 Wilson, p. 114. Similar doubts are expressed by Violet Jeffery, who
argues that 'It would be hard to find a play of the time more unlike the
rest of Lyly's work' (Jeffery, p. 114).

30 Quoted from Hunter, p. 76.

31 'An Aduertisement for Papp-hatchett, and Martin Mar-prelate', in
*Pierces Supererogation* (1593), quoted from Alexander B. Grosart, ed.,
*The Works of Gabriel Harvey* (Huth Library, 1884), ii, p. 213.

32 Hunter, for example, assumes Lyly's 'ineptitude in polemic' (p. 80).

33 The pamphlet was twice republished in the year of publication, while
Nashe commented in 1593 that if Lyly were to enter the lists against
Gabriel Harvey again, 'there woulde more gentle Readers die of a merry
mortality...than haue done of this last infection. I my self...inioy but
a mite of wit in comparison of his talent' (*Strange News*, quoted from
Bond, i, p. 59).

34 The relevant passage reads, 'He shall not bee brought in as whilom he
was, and yet verie well, with a cocks combe, an apes face, a wolfs bellie,
cats clawes, &c. but in a cap'de cloake, and all the best apparell he ware
the highest day in the yeare....Would it not bee a fine Tragedie, when
*Mardocheus* shall play a Bishoppe in a Play, and *Martin Hamman* and
that he that seekes to pull downe those that are set in authoritie aboue
him, should be hoysted vpon a tree aboue all other' (quoted from Bond,
iii, p. 408).

35 Dover Wilson, for example, describes the play as 'an experiment in the drama of realism' (p.114).

36 For examples of echoes of the two former, see p. 7 above. Links with all three plays are noted in the commentary.

37 For the circumstances surrounding the late publication of the other two Lylian plays not published by William and Joan Broome, see Scragg, ed., *Love's Metamorphosis*, pp. 7–10, and Scragg, ed., *The Woman in the Moon*, pp. 3–9.

38 Bond, iii, p. 168.

39 Andreadis, p. 18. For a full discussion of the tenuous evidence for the continued existence of Paul's Boys in the provinces subsequent to the closure of their London theatre, see Andreadis pp. 16–17. The proposition is convincingly discounted by Chambers (ii, p. 19n.).

40 Hunter, p. 81.

41 The specificity of the title-page announcements of all five plays published by William and Joan Broome regarding the date and place of performance before the Queen support the contention that performance before the monarch constituted a significant selling point.

42 For the similar uncertainty surrounding the transmission history of *Love's Metamorphosis* and *The Woman in the Moon*, see Scragg, ed., *Love's Metamorphosis*, pp. 7–8, and Scragg, ed., *The Woman in the Moon*, pp. 3–9.

43 *Love's Metamorphosis* is an exception in that relies heavily on Ovid's *Metamorphoses*, bk. viii, for one strand of the plot. See Scragg, ed., *Love's Metamorphosis*, pp. 10ff.

44 For a detailed discussion of the play in the context of a succession of works marrying English subject matter to a format derived from Roman New Comedy, see Tydeman, pp. 9–31.

45 Compare *Galatea*, which is set on the banks of the river Humber, governed by classical deities, and peopled by human figures with both English and classical names.

46 See Macfarlane, pp. 116 and 119.

47 Macfarlane, p. 120.

48 The incidence of cunning folk was probably much higher, moreover, than the records suggest, in that only the more notable practitioners will have come to the attention of the authorities, and so entered the historical record.

49 For documentary evidence of the concerns addressed by sixteenth-century cunning folk, see Macfarlane, pp. 115–34.

50 Richard Bernard, *A Guide to Grand Jury Men* (1627), p. 131, quoted by Macfarlane, p. 126.

51 John Stearne, *A Confirmation and Discovery of Witchcraft* (1648), p. 11, quoted from Macfarlane, p. 115.

52 See Macfarlane, pp. 129–30.

53 Andreadis, pp. 243–8. The extract from Cooper quoted by Andreadis is from the edition of 1584, rather than the earlier edition of 1565, as here.

54 See Thomas Randolph's 'An Apologie for his False Prediction' (*Poems*, 1638), where the name appears in conjunction with those of learned men (including Friar Bacon) rather than cunning folk. Compare, 'Are

then the *Sibils* dead? What is become / Of the lowd Oracles? are the
Augurs dumbe? / Live not the *Magi* that so oft reveald / Natures intents?
Is Gipsisme quite repeald? / Is Friar Bacon nothing but a name? / Or
is all witchcraft braind with Doctor *Lambe*? / Does none the learned
*Bungies* soul inherit?' (G3r).

55  See Thomas Heywood, *The Wise-Woman of Hogsdon* (1604?, pub. 1638),
    B4r; William Rowley, Thomas Dekker, and John Ford, *The Witch of
    Edmonton* (1621, pub. 1658), G2v; Thomas Middleton and William
    Rowley, *The Spanish Gipsie* (1623, pub. 1653), C3v; Thomas Deloney,
    *The Gentle Craft, Part 1* (1627, 2nd ed. 1637), C3v; Michael Drayton,
    'The Moone-Calfe', in *The Battaile of Agincovrt* (1627), Y1v.

56  Evidence that *The Wise-Woman of Hogsdon*, at least, looks back to Lyly's
    play is furnished on B4r by an echo of Silena's decision to ask Mother
    Bombie 'whether I be a maid or no' (2.3.91–2 this ed.). Compare:
    '*Wisewo[man]*. And what's your suit, Lady? / *Kitchin* [*maid*]. Forsooth,
    I come to know whether I be a Maid or no'.

57  Scot records that 'mother *Bungie*' was 'registred and chronicled by the
    name of the great witch of *Rochester*' and reputed to be 'the cheefe
    ringleader of all other witches' but was found to be 'a meere cousener',
    confessing on her death-bed that 'hir cunning consisted onlie in delud-
    ing and deceiving the people', and that she did not know 'how to worke
    anie supernaturall matter, as she in hir life time made men beleeve she
    had and could doo' (bk. xvi, chapter 3: Mm5r–v).

58  It is possible, in fact, that Lyly is consciously pitting local knowledge
    against an ideological position.

59  The fragmentary nature of the Cumean prophecies derived from the
    fact that they were written on leaves placed at the mouth of the Sibyl's
    cave and subject to dispersal by the wind, while six of the nine books
    of her prophecies were burned by the Sibyl herself when Tarquin II
    refused the price asked for them.

60  For a fuller discussion of the use of the use of triplets as a structural
    feature of Lyly's work, see Scragg, ed., *Love's Metamorphosis*, pp. 18 and
    20–1).

61  In *Galatea*, Tityrus' decision to disguise his daughter as a boy in 1.1
    is mirrored in Melebeus' similar decision in 1.3, while Cupid reverses
    the gender disguise in the following act by adopting the form of a
    girl. Similarly the action of *Love's Metamorphosis* opens with three
    foresters doing honour to Ceres and announcing their dedication to
    love, while scene 2 simultaneously echoes and reverses the process
    with three maidens doing honour to Ceres but devoting themselves
    to chastity.

62  Compare the similar emphasis on the unreality of the play world in the
    Prologus to *The Woman in the Moon* in which the spectators are enjoined
    to remember that 'all is but a poet's dream' (line 17).

63  Compare the dreams related by Sappho and her ladies in *Sappho and
    Phao* (4.3. *passim*), which reflect on both the situations and the psy-
    chologies of the narrators.

64  For an account of *Love's Metamorphosis* in terms of an 'anatomy' of a
    multi-faceted condition, see Scragg, ed., *Love's Metamorphosis*, pp.
    16–21.

65 For a detailed account of the range of antithetical devices employed in
   Lyly's work, see Jonas Barish, 'The Prose Style of John Lyly', *English
   Literary History*, 23 (1956), pp. 14–35, from which the term 'doubleness'
   is drawn.

66 The English version of the Latin verses accompanying the illustration
   reads (with modernized spelling and punctuation): 'Calves, goats, swine,
   asses, at a banquet set, / To grasp healths in their hooves, thou seest here
   met; / Why wondrest thou, oh drunkard, to behold / Thy brothers, in
   whose ranks thou art enrolled? / When thou (so oft as tox't at any feast) /
   Canst be no better held than such a beast; / Since, like Circean cups, wine
   doth surprise / Thy senses, and thy reason stupifies. / Which foe, would
   war-like Britain quite expel, / No nation like it could be said to excel'.

67 Campaspe's resistance to the pressure placed upon her by Alexander
   to bow to his authority and accept his love, for example, is an index
   of her virtue, while the refusal of the three nymphs of *Love's
   Metamorphosis* to accede to the wishes of their lovers, both before and
   after their transformation by Cupid, exhibits both their own rationality
   and the circumscribed nature of female choice (see Scragg, ed., *Love's
   Metamorphosis*, pp. 22–6).

68 Of the six court comedies, four (*Sappho and Phao*, *Galatea*, *Love's
   Metamorphosis*, and *Midas*) are resolved by some interaction between
   the human and the divine, while a fifth (*Endymion*) is comparable with
   them in that the governing figure occupies an ambiguous position
   between human and divine. *The Woman in the Moon*, not generally
   classed among the court comedies, takes place in a universe wholly
   governed by Nature and the Planets.

69 *Galatea* is set in a woodland location, adjacent to a river, while the
   action of *Love's Metamorphosis* takes place in Arcadia. Similarly, *The
   Woman in the* Moon (see previous note) is set in Utopia.

70 Compare the focus on the tension between love and chastity common
   to *Sappho and Phao*, in which the action largely takes place in Sappho's
   court, and *Love's Metamorphosis*, which is set in an Arcadian landscape
   of woods and seashore.

71 Even Bergetto, the son of a wealthy father engaged, like Memphio, in
   securing a marriage for his heir, is warned by Poggio to 'take heed of
   whipping' (Derek Roper, ed., *'Tis Pity She's a Whore*, 2.4.48).

72 Ralph Simnell, the fool in Greene's *Friar Bacon and Friar Bungay*, is of
   interest here, in that, though he is treated with amused affection, and
   allowed to impersonate the Prince, he contributes to the dangerous
   subversion of order in the play as his master accedes, in part, to his
   plans.

73 See p. 41 below for a discussion of modern discomfort with the comedy
   deriving from the conduct of the fools.

74 Again, the Wise-Woman of Hogsdon offers a useful comparison here,
   in that she is actively engaged in prostitution and the disposal of the
   unwanted products of illicit unions.

75 *Campaspe* may seem, at first sight, to be an exception in that it turns
   on the choices faced by a historical personage (Alexander the Great),
   but it is nevertheless ahistorical in its anachronistic inclusion of non-
   contemporaneous figures, while the staging is conceptual rather than
   representational (see following note).

76 In *Campaspe*, for example, the workshop of the painter, Apelles, stands in opposition to the tub of the philosopher, Diogenes, embodying the celebration of the senses as against their suppression, while in *Love's Metamorphosis* a tree dedicated to Ceres and the temple of Cupid represent the opposition between chastity and love.

77 See note 27 above for evidence that the play was performed in the playhouse at Paul's, and Gair, pp. 54ff., for the structure and location of the theatre. Discussion of the staging of the play has been clouded by comparison with comedies designed for performance at court, where different playing conditions obtained. Chambers, for example, in a chapter devoted to 'Staging at Court', concludes his discussion of Lyly's plays with the comment that '*Mother Bombie* is an extreme example of the traditional Italian comic manner. The action comes and goes, rapidly for Lyly, in an open place, surrounded by no less than seven houses, the doors of which are freely used' (iii, pp. 34–5). For a fuller discussion of critical commentary on the staging of the play than is appropriate here, see Andreadis, pp. 31–40.

78 Andreadis, p. 35.

79 See Andreadis pp. 35 and 40. There is no evidence to support the concept of Mother Bombie's house as a 'hut'.

80 Gair, p. 107.

81 Though it is, of course, possible that they merely enter from opposing wings.

82 The function of the tavern thus differs from its role in classical drama in which it figures as a site of Saturnalian release, leading to reconciliation.

83 Pincombe, p. 164.

84 See Bond, iii, p. 168. Bond argues that the first two acts take place on one day, concluding with the boys' decision, to meet again the following morning (cf. 2.4.24–5), and their masters' re-entrance from the tavern. Acts 3 and 4, together with the first scene of act 5, take up the next day, with the meeting between Accius and Silena taking place that night (cf. 3.2.39–40), while the Fiddlers initiate the resolution at dawn on the third day. There is no evidence, however, to support his accompanying assertion that the days of the week are specified (i.e. that the action takes place 'from the middle of Monday to the middle of Wednesday'), and Halfpenny's declaration that the wine 'wrought' in him for 'two days' (3.2.46) following the drinking bout in Act 2 calls in doubt some aspects of his time scheme.

85 Tydeman, p. 417.

86 See Scragg, ed., *The Woman in the Moon*, pp. 3–5, for a counter-argument to the proposition that Lyly's last play may have been designed for an adult troupe.

87 Eight of the play's twenty-three characters are boys or young men, while a further six are women (conventionally performed on the Elizabethan-Jacobean stage by boys).

88 See Gair, pp. 85–6 and 99.

89 The occurrence of the three similar parts in this group of plays also serves to support the contention that *Mother Bombie* belongs to the same period of Lyly's career as *Endymion* and *Midas* (see p. 9 above).

90 I am indebted for my information on this production to *The Stage Archive* (14 May, 1964), p. 15, and to *The Bristol Grammar School Chronicle*, XXIX (1964), pp. 244–5, kindly supplied by Anne Bradley. All the subsequent quotations are drawn from these publications.

91 Though *The Bristol Grammar School Chronicle* prints two photographs of the production, one of which shows a number of doors, it is impossible to deduce from them how many entrances were used (see pp. 32–5 above). The fact that the music was played on the 'minstrels' gallery of the Elizabethan set' (*Bristol Grammar School Chronicle*, p. 245) suggests, however, that the space allowed for an entry 'above'.

92 See Hazlitt, p. 38.

93 See the sixth edition, ed. Margaret Drabble (2000, revised 2006). Other adverse comments on the overall success of the work include Dover Wilson's assertion that it is 'undeniably tedious', though 'clever in construction' (Wilson, p. 114).

94 Andreadis, p. 61.

95 Jeffery, p. 113.

96 Baldwin declares her to be 'a wholly superfluous piece of atmosphere so far as the necessary plot machinery is concerned', arguing that 'her only real contribution [is] to advise the mother of the cradle-changed idiots to confess the substitution, and even at that the advice was not needed' (p. 530).

97 Hunter, p. 223.

98 Hunter, p. 226.

99 Hunter, pp. 221–2.

100 See Houppert, p. 129.

101 Hunter, p. 227.

102 Bond, ii, p. 277.

103 Daniel, p. 285.

104 Tydeman, p. 31.

105 Houppert, p. 132.

106 Daniel, p. 285.

107 Hunter, p. 220. Baldwin similarly asserts that 'the play is an excellent illustration of the Terentian formula as interpreted in the sixteenth century' (Baldwin, p. 532).

108 Hunter, p. 221.

109 Daniel, p. 285. Daniel's reservations regarding the plot and his belief that the presentation of the simpletons is at odds with contemporary taste appear to run counter to his assertion that the play is notable for its 'stageworthiness' (p. 285).

110 Houppert, p. 136.

111 Andreadis, p. 44.

112 Interestingly, though Hunter aligns the play with Terentian comedy, it is his analysis of the court comedies in terms of Bach's *Brandenburg Concertos* ('the formal perfection with which the expected elements are arranged, organized, combined, the skill in utilizing the different parts, the unfailing resource in counterpoint': Hunter, p. 159) that Andreadis draws on in support of her position (p. 45).

113 Tydeman, p. 31.

114 Hazlitt, p. 36.

115 The term 'wit' is defined by Hunter as encompassing in this context
both 'the cleverness which enables the servants to play off one master
against another' and 'the love of fun and conviviality for its own sake,
a good which no one in the play is prepared to question, and which in
the end carries the work to a denouement of feasting and marriage and
good-fellowship' (p. 226).
116 Andreadis, pp. 54 and 51. For a fuller account of the argument that the
play reflects sixteenth-century concerns with the marital state, see
Andreadis, pp. 50–60. The extent of critical disagreement over the play
may be measured by the discrepancy between Andreadis's views here
and Hunter's assertion that 'In *Mother Bombie*...love is not treated as
an emotion at all; it is an animal impulse, thinly disguised as a social
duty' (Hunter, p. 227).
117 Houppert, pp. 107 and 128.
118 Pincombe, p. 158. It is hard to reconcile this view of Mother Bombie
with the writer's earlier suggestion that it may have been 'to scotch or
trivialise [accusations of witchcraft against himself] that Lyly wrote...[a]
play featuring a harmless – indeed, benevolent – old crone: *Mother
Bombie*' (p. 85).
119 Bond, ii, p. 277.
120 Hunter, *Lyly and Peele*, p. 35.
121 Pincombe, p. 173.
122 Daniel, p. 285.
123 *Campaspe*, 3.2.24.
124 Daniel, p. 25.

# MOTHER

## BOMBIE

As it was sundry times played by
the Children of Paul's.

LONDON,

Imprinted by Thomas Scarlet
for Cuthbert Burby.
1594.

# [Characters in Order of Appearance

MEMPHIO, *a wealthy old man, supposed father of Accius.*
DROMIO, *his young servant.*
STELLIO, *a wealthy old man, supposed father of Silena.*
RISIO, *his young servant.*
PRISIUS, *an old man of modest means, father of Livia.*                    5
SPERANTUS, *an old man of modest means, father of Candius.*
CANDIUS, *son of Sperantus, in love with Livia.*

---

Characters...Appearance] *Not in Q1, 2, Bl. Handwritten lists, their numerous corrections and erasures testifying to the complex relationships of the dramatis personae, appear in a number of early editions, including Malone's copy of Q1 in the Bodleian library. No two modern editions agree on the information supplied and / or the form or ordering of the characters' names. The first printed list was attempted by Dilke.*

---

1. MEMPHIO] a name evocative through its form of the classical tradition from which the structure of the play derives (see p. 11 above), and of antiquity from its association with the ancient city of Memphis.

2. DROMIO] a variant of *Dromo* (from Latin *dromos* = runner), a type name used by Terence for a slave-driver in *Andria* and for witty slaves in *Heauton Timorumenos* and *Adelpoe*. The name is adopted by Shakespeare for the twin servants of the Antipholus brothers in *The Comedy of Errors*.

3. STELLIO] a newt or gecko (Latin), used metaphorically in classical literature to denote one of a knavish or crafty disposition.

4. RISIO] The name appears as both 'Risio' and 'Riscio' in *Q1, 2, Bl*, and no agreement exists among modern editors over which form to employ. 'Risio' is preferred here for its association with Latin *risio* (laughter) in view of the character's mischievous nature.

5. PRISIUS] possibly a derivative of Latin *priscus* (old). Bond (iii, p. 172n.) assumes him to be a fuller (one who cleans and thickens cloth) from references at 2.5.69–70 and 5.3.159–60.

6. SPERANTUS] one who flatters himself with hopes (from Latin *spero*). Prisius' marriage proposals at 1.1.95–6, and the punishments he himself intends for his disobedient son (1.3.206ff.), support Bond's assumption (iii, p. 172n.) that he is a farmer.

7. CANDIUS] derived from Latin *candor* (integrity), and indicative of the moral status of the figure.

56

LIVIA, *daughter of Prisius, in love with Candius.*
HALFPENNY, *young servant to Sperantus.*
LUCIO, *young servant to Prisius.*                                    IO
SILENA, *a simpleton, supposed daughter of Stellio.*
MOTHER BOMBIE, *an aged 'cunning woman', or soothsayer.*
MAESTIUS, *supposed son of Vicinia, in love with Serena.*
SERENA, *supposed daughter of Vicinia, in love with Maestius.*
ACCIUS, *a simpleton, supposed son of Memphio.*                      15
RIXULA, *a servant-girl in Prisius' household.*

---

8. *LIVIA*] a classical female proper name, appropriate to the Roman New Comedy ethos of the play.

9. *HALFPENNY*] a coin worth half of one penny in pre-decimalization English currency, and thus indicative of small size. Only the farthing (worth one quarter of a penny) was of lower value (see the joking at 4.2.178–81).

10. *LUCIO*] variously represented as 'Lucio', 'Luceo', 'Linceo', and 'Linceo' in *Q1*, *2*, *Bl.* The form 'Lucio' is preferred here as the more familiar form of the name (cf. Latin *Lucius*), and for its connotations of mischief-making (cf. Lucifer) and brightness (cf. Latin *lucinus* = light-bringing).

11. *SILENA*] probably derived from Latin *sileo* (to be silent) and thus appropriate to one her father does not wish to be heard. The name also carries echoes, however, of 'Selene' (Greek goddess of the moon) and may thus be designed to hint at a lunatic condition.

12. *MOTHER BOMBIE*] a sixteenth-century Kentish-woman credited with supernatural powers (defined in 3.1.27–8 as the ability to 'tell fortunes, expound dreams, tell of things that be lost, and divine of accidents to come'). For a detailed discussion of the historicity of the play's title-figure and the powers attributed to those classed as 'wise-women' or 'cunning folk', see pp. 11–13 above.

13. *MAESTIUS*] derived from Latin *maestus* (sorrowful, afflicted), and consequently in accordance with the seemingly intransigent situation of a man in love with a woman he believes to be his own sister.

14. *SERENA*] a classical female proper name with connotations of brightness, and associated with the coming of fair weather. The similarity with the name Silena (see line 11 above) hints at the interchangeability of the two young women.

15. *ACCIUS*] a variant of 'Macchius', a clownish stock figure in classical farce, and thus appropriate to both the Roman New Comedy ethos of the play and the intellectual limitations of the character himself. Andreadis (p. 146) suggests that the name may also be designed to recall the simpleton Acco, cited by Thomas Cooper in his *Thesaurus Linguae Romanae & Britannicae* (1565): 'A woman whiche was so foolishe, that she woulde speake and talke to hir owne image in a glasse, whereof commeth *Accissare*, to playe the idiote: and suche fooles be called *Acci*' (*Dictionarium Historicum et Poeticum*, A1v). Plautus adopted 'Maccius' as his middle name.

16. *RIXULA*] derived from Latin *rixa* (dispute), and indicative of a quarrelsome nature.

SERGEANT.

HACKNEYMAN.

SCRIVENER.

VICINIA, *an old nurse, supposed mother of Maestius and Serena.*     20

SYNIS,

NASUTUS,     } *fiddlers (Synis an old man, Bedunenus a boy).*

BEDUNENUS,

SCENE: *Rochester, Kent. A street.*]

SCENE] *Not in Q1, 2, Bl; Rochester, Kent. / first supplied by Fairholt and amplified by Bond, who (omitting / Kent /) adds / an open square or street.*

17. SERGEANT] an officer of law, responsible for the arresting of offenders and the summoning of malefactors to court, rather than the holder of a military rank.

18. HACKNEYMAN] one who keeps horses or hackney carriages for hire.

19. SCRIVENER] a scribe, specifically one engaged in the drawing up of legal documents.

20. VICINIA] Latin for 'neighbourhood', but used here as a proper name to denote 'a woman of the district'. The name also appears as 'Vicina' in *Q1, 2, Bl.*

21. SYNIS] possibly derived from the Latin prefix '*syn-*' (together). The name may be designed to suggest the co-ordinator of the trio.

22. NASUTUS] one with a big nose (Latin).

23. BEDUNENUS] obscure. No explanation has been offered by previous commentators for the choice of name, which also appears in *Q1* as 'Bedunens'. Tydeman emends to Beduneus.

# A Pleasant Conceited Comedy called
## *Mother Bombie*
## Act I

Actus primus, Scena prima

[*Enter*] MEMPHIO [*and*] DROMIO.

*Memphio.* Boy, there are three things that make my life
miserable: a threadbare purse, a curst wife, and a fool to
my heir.

*Dromio.* Why then, sir, there are three medicines for these
three maladies: a pike-staff to take a purse on the highway,　5
a holly wand to brush choler from my mistress' tongue,

---

HT. *Pleasant Conceited*] Amusing Witty.　0.1.] *Stage directions derive from Q1,
unless otherwise indicated, with editorial amplification signalled by square brackets.
The following collation notes record substantive changes only, as when new stage
directions or portions of stage directions have been added. The collation notes do
not record routine amplifications, such as the supplying of an [Enter] where the
entry is clearly implied in the Quarto by the listing of the characters' names, or an
[and] in a series of names. Where a direction is not original to this edition, or
differs from that of a previous edition, the first intervention by a previous editor is
recorded in the notes and a full collation supplied in the Appendix.*　6. holly] Q2,
B1; holy Q1.

---

0.1.] The action takes place throughout in Rochester, in a street flanked by
the residences of the play's four father figures (Memphio, Stellio, Prisius, and
Sperantus), and by Mother Bombie's house, a Scrivener's shop, and a tavern
(signalled by a branch of ivy over the door: see 2.1.153n.). Entrances take place
from either end of the street (i.e. either side of the stage) unless otherwise
indicated. For a detailed discussion of the staging of the play, and the problems posed by the multiple 'houses' required by the plot, see pp. 32–5 above.

2. *threadbare purse*] lack of money (literally, a fabric purse from which the
nap has been worn away by use). The subsequent action makes plain that
Memphio is not, in fact, a poor man, but a rich one with pretensions to be
Mayor (cf. 5.3.101–3).

*curst*] cantankerous. Compare the description of Katherina in *Shrew* as
'curst and shrewd' (1.1.179).

*to*] for.

5. *pike-staff...highway*] heavy wooden shaft of a pike (spear-like weapon)
to enable you to become a highwayman.

6. *holly wand*] slight prickly branch.

*choler*] anger.

and a young wench for my young master; so that as your
worship, being wise, begot a fool, so he, being a fool, may
tread out a wise man.

*Memphio.* Ay, but Dromio, these medicines bite hot on great          10
mischiefs; for so might I have a rope about my neck,
horns upon my head, and in my house a litter of fools.

*Dromio.* Then, sir, you had best let some wise man sit on
your son, to hatch him a good wit. They say if ravens
sit on hens' eggs, the chickens will be black, and so          15
forth.

*Memphio.* Why boy, my son is out of the shell, and is grown
a pretty cock.

*Dromio.* Carve him, master, and make him a capon, else all
your breed will prove coxcombs.          20

---

10. Ay] *Andreadis;* I *Q1, 2, Bl (also at line 47).*

7-9. *as your worship…wise man*] The comment turns on the proverb, 'A
wise man commonly has a fool to his heir' (Tilley, M421).

9. *tread out*] beget. The metaphor, drawn from the mating habits of birds,
initiates the sequence of images turning on the breeding of poultry in the
following lines.

10. *bite hot on*] put one in dangerous proximity to. As Tydeman notes
(p. 407), Bond's 'border close upon' (iii, p. 537) is not supported by *OED*
(Bite, *v.* 9 a: cause a sharp smarting pain), and the same objection may be
made regarding the gloss proposed here. Both the *OED* definition and
Tydeman's 'smart painfully', however, pose syntactic problems in this
context.

11. *so*] in that way.

12. *horns upon my head*] be cuckolded (in revenge for my mistreatment
of my wife).

13-14. *let some…son*] The image sustains the metaphor turning on the
breeding of birds initiated by Dromio in his previous speech.

14-15. *if ravens…black*] i.e. the child will take after the parent. The
saying counters the proverbial maxim, 'A black hen lays a white egg' (Tilley,
H418), i.e. a bad parent may have a good child, but no comparable example
has been traced.

17. *out of the shell*] grown up.

17-18. *is grown a pretty cock*] (*a*) has become a handsome young man
(Memphio's meaning); (*b*) has developed a fine penis (the sense Dromio
plays on in the following line).

19. *Carve*] Geld.
*capon*] castrated cock.

20. *breed*] descendants.
*coxcombs*] fools (from the cap resembling a cock's comb worn by professional jesters).

*Memphio.* I marvel he is such an ass. He takes it not of his
    father.

*Dromio.* He may, for anything you know.

*Memphio.* Why villain, dost thou think me a fool?

*Dromio.* Oh, no, sir! Neither are you sure that you are his     25
    father.

*Memphio.* Rascal, dost thou imagine thy mistress naught of
    her body?

*Dromio.* No, but fantastical of her mind; and it may be, when
    this boy was begotten she thought of a fool, and so     30
    conceived a fool, yourself being very wise, and she
    surpassing honest.

*Memphio.* It may be, for I have heard of an Ethiopian that,
    thinking of a fair picture, brought forth a fair lady, and
    yet no bastard.                                              35

*Dromio.* You are well read, sir. Your son may be a bastard,
    and yet legitimate; yourself a cuckold, and yet my
    mistress virtuous. All this in conceit.

*Memphio.* Come, Dromio, it is my grief to have such a son
    that must inherit my lands.                                  40

*Dromio.* He needs not, sir; I'll beg him for a fool.

---

21. *takes it not of*] doesn't get it from.

27–8. *naught of her body*] to be a wanton (*naught* = wicked).

29–35.] Bond (iii, p. 537) cites Heliodorus' *Aethiopica*, iv. 8, in which
'Persina, queen of Ethiopia, tells her white daughter, Chariclea, that
when she was begotten a picture of Perseus leading away the naked
Andromeda hung in her view' as an example of both the beliefs, and
the kind of tale, rehearsed here. For a further reference to the popular
notion that the thoughts of the parents at the moment of conception
have a bearing on the nature of the child, see 4.2.49–54 below. Compare Shylock's tale of Jacob's device to increase his flock in *MV*
(1.3.66–82).

34. *lady*] Bond (iii, p. 537) notes a suggestion by P. A. Daniel that *Q1*
'ladie' (*Q2/Bl* 'Lady') should be emended to 'babie', but the change is both
unnecessary, in that the word makes sense as it stands, and without textual
support.

38. *conceit*] imagination.

41. *beg...fool*] proverbial (Tilley, F496). Those deemed intellectually
incapable of managing their estates in the sixteenth century were made wards
of court and interested parties could petition for their guardianship. The
proposal is thus a comic bid for self-advancement on Dromio's part. The
phrase is echoed at 4.2.121–2 below.

*Memphio.* Vile boy! Thy young master?

*Dromio.* Let me have in a device.

*Memphio.* I'll have thy advice, and if it fadge, thou shalt eat
    till thou sweat, play till thou eat, and sleep till thy bones    45
    ache.

*Dromio.* Ay, marry, now you tickle me. I am both hungry,
    gamesome, and sleepy, and all at once. I'll break this
    head against the wall but I'll make it bleed good matter.

*Memphio.* Then this it is. Thou knowest I have but one son,    50
    and he is a fool?

*Dromio.* A monstrous fool.

*Memphio.* A wife, and she an arrant scold.

*Dromio.* Ah, master, I smell your device. It will be excellent.

*Memphio.* Thou canst not know it till I tell it.    55

*Dromio.* I see it through your brains. Your hair is so thin, and
    your skull so transparent, I may sooner see it than hear it.

*Memphio.* Then, boy, hast thou a quick wit and I a slow
    tongue. But what is't?

*Dromio.* Marry, either you would have your wife's tongue in    60
    your son's head, that he might be a prating fool, or his
    brains in her brain pan, that she might be a foolish scold.

---

45. till thou¹] *Bond;* thou shalt *Q1, 2* (shalr*), Bl.*   53. arrant] *Dilke;* arrand
*Q1, 2, Bl.*

43. *have in a device*] devise a stratagem.

44. *fadge*] works.

45. *till thou¹*] Bond's emendation of *Q1, 2, Bl* 'thou shalt' (see collation
note) is adopted here as it both improves the sense of an otherwise obscure
passage, and is supported by a comparable formulation in an earlier work.
Compare: 'Neither was I much unlike these abbey-lubbers in my life (though
far unlike them in belief), which laboured till they were cold, eat till they
sweat, and lay in bed till their bones ached' (*Anatomy*, p. 92).

47. *tickle me*] excite my interest.

48. *break*] cut open. Compare *MWW*: 'Slender, I broke your head: what
matter have you against me?' (1.1.114–15).

49. *bleed good matter*] bring forth some worthwhile idea.

53. *arrant*] thorough-going.

54. *smell*] have an inkling of (*OED, v.* 2).

61. *prating*] chattering.

62. *brain pan*] skull, head.

*Memphio.* Thou dreamst, Dromio, there is no such matter.
Thou knowest I have kept them close, so that my neighbours think him to be wise, and her to be temperate,      65
because they never heard them speak?
*Dromio.* Well?
*Memphio.* Thou knowest that Stellio hath a good farm, and
a fair daughter; yea, so fair that she is mewed up, and
only looketh out at the windows, lest she should by some   70
roisting courtier be stolen away?
*Dromio.* So, sir?
*Memphio.* Now, if I could compass a match between my son
and Stellio's daughter, by conference of us parents, and
without theirs, I should be blessed, he cozened, and thou  75
for ever set at liberty.
*Dromio.* A singular conceit.
*Memphio.* Thus much for my son. Now for my wife, I would
have this kept from her, else shall I not be able to keep
my house from smoke; for let it come to one of her ears    80
and then woe to both mine. I would have her go to my
house into the country whilst we conclude this; and this
once done, I care not if her tongue never have done.
These if thou canst effect, thou shalt make thy master
happy.                                                     85

---

64. them] *Dilke;* him *Q1, 2, Bl.*

64. *them]* Though without textual authority, Dilke's emendation of the
'him' of *Q1, 2, Bl* (see collation note) is adopted here, as Memphio is plainly
referring to both his son and his wife.
*close]* shut away.
65. *temperate]* mild mannered, equable.
69. *mewed up]* shut up, confined (image drawn from the practice of
caging hawks when 'mewing', i.e. moulting).
71. *roisting]* obsolete form of 'roistering' (riotous).
73. *compass a match]* bring about a marriage.
75. *theirs]* their participation.
*cozened]* tricked.
76. *for ever…liberty]* See Introduction, p. 11, for a discussion of the play's
conflation of classical (here the implication that Dromio is a slave) and
sixteenth-century social conditions.
77. *singular conceit]* extraordinary idea.
79–80. *keep…smoke]* avoid trouble at home. Andreadis (p. 74) cites
Tilley, S574: 'Smoke, rain, and a very curst wife make a man weary of house
and life'.

*Dromio.* Think it done. This noddle shall coin such new
device as you shall have your son married by
tomorrow.

*Memphio.* But take heed that neither the father nor the maid
speak to my son, for then his folly will mar all.                    90

*Dromio.* Lay all the care on me. *Sublevabo te onere*: I will rid
you of a fool.

*Memphio.* Wilt thou rid me for a fool?

*Dromio.* Tush, quarrel not.

*Memphio.* Then for the dowry, let it be at least two hundreth        95
ducats, and after his death the farm.

*Dromio.* What else!

*Memphio.* Then let us in, that I may furnish thee with some
better counsel, and my son with better apparel.

*Dromio.* Let me alone. [*Aside*] I lack but a wag more to make      100
of my counsel, and then you shall see an exquisite cozenage, and the father more fool than the son. [*To Memphio*]
But hear you, sir; I forgot one thing.

*Memphio.* What's that?

---

91. care] *Q2, Bl;* eare *Q1.*   97. What else!] *This ed.;* What else? *Q1, 2, Bl.*
100. SD.] *Bond.*   102. SD.] *This ed.*

---

86–7. *noddle…device as*] head shall mint such a novel scheme that.

89. *maid*] daughter.

91. Sublevabo te onere] I shall lift this burden from you.

91–2. *rid you of a fool*] deliberately ambiguous, through a pun on *rid* =
relieve/ride: (*a*) relieve you of this fool (the sense Dromio purports to
intend); (*b*) exploit your folly (the meaning Memphio adduces in the following line). Compare Falstaff's exclamation, 'Am I ridden with a Welsh goat
too', on discovering that Evans has been a party to his deception (*MWW*,
5.5.136), and Sir Toby's aside regarding Sir Andrew, 'Marry, I'll ride your
horse as well as I ride you' (*TN*, 3.4.287–8).

95. *hundreth*] archaic form of hundred.

96. *ducats*] gold or silver coins, of variable value, used in a number of
European countries. The term contributes to the play's conflation of periods
and customs, and should probably be taken to signify 'pounds'.

98. *furnish*] supply.

100. *Let me alone*] Leave it to me.

100–1. *a wag…counsel*] another mischievous boy to conspire with me.

101–2. *you shall see…cozenage*] Directed towards the audience, the
comment initiates an alignment between the boys and those outside the play
world. *cozenage* = piece of deception.

*Dromio.* Nay, *Expellas furca licet, usque recurret.*                    105
*Memphio.* What's the meaning?
*Dromio.* Why, though your son's folly be thrust up with a pair
    of horns on a fork, yet being natural, it will have his
    course.
*Memphio.* I pray thee, no more; but about it.                    110
              *Exeunt [into Memphio's house].*

Act[us] 1, Sce[na] 2

[*Enter*] STELLIO [*and*] RISIO.

*Stellio.* Risio, my daughter is passing amiable, but very simple.
*Risio.* You mean a fool, sir.
*Stellio.* 'Faith, I imply so much.
*Risio.* Then I apply it fit. The one she takes of her father, the
    other of her mother. Now you may be sure she is your                    5
    own.

---

110.1. SD.] *Bracketed material this ed.*

0. Act[us] 1] *Fairholt (*ACTUS PRIMUS*);* Act. 2 *Q1, 2;* Actus secundus *Bl.*

---

105. Expellas furca...recurret] Though you cast nature out with a pitch-
fork, it will always return. The saying derives, as Bond notes (iii, p. 538),
from Horace (*Epi.*, 1.10.24), but had become proverbial by the sixteenth
century. Compare Erasmus, *Adagia*, 617B ('*Naturam expellas furca, tamen
usque recurrit*') and Tilley, N50 ('Though you cast out Nature with a fork it
will still return').

107–9. *though your son's...course*] obscure. Tydeman proposes 'though
your son's folly is exalted by marrying him and making a cuckold of him,
yet his idiocy being native to him will eventually manifest itself' (p. 408),
while Daniel suggests 'Even if you entirely cast out your son's foolishness,
it will return, since he is a "natural", i.e. an idiot' (p. 377). It is unclear,
however, what Tydeman's 'exalted' means in this context, while Daniel's
explanation does not account for the allusion to horns. Dromio may merely
intend that marriage, and the cuckoldry that will inevitably follow, will
simply bring Accius' folly further to light, but that nothing can be done about
that because it is intrinsic to him.

110.1.] Though there is no direction in *Q1, 2, Bl* (or any subsequent
edition) indicating that the characters exit into Memphio's house, the direction given here is supported by lines 98–9 above.

1.2.0. *Sce[na] 2*] For the misnumbering of scenes here and at 3.2 and 5.1
below (see collation notes), see Introduction, n. 5.

1. *passing amiable*] extremely beautiful.

5–6. *Now...own*] The comment implies that Risio regards his master as
a fool (paralleling Dromio's stance towards Memphio in the previous scene),

*Stellio.* I have penned her up in a chamber, having only a
window to look out, that youths seeing her fair cheeks
may be enamoured before they hear her fond speech.
How likest thou this head?                                    10

*Risio.* There is very good workmanship in it, but the matter
is but base. If the stuff had been as good as the mould,
your daughter had been as wise as she is beautiful.

*Stellio.* Dost thou think she took her foolishness of me?

*Risio.* Ay, and so cunningly that she took it not from you.      15

*Stellio.* Well, *quod natura dedit tollere nemo potest.*

*Risio.* A good evidence to prove the fee-simple of your daughter's folly.

*Stellio.* Why?

*Risio.* It came by nature, and if none can take it away it is      20
perpetual.

---

though the phrasing is sufficiently ambiguous to allow Stellio to regard it as
a reflection on his good looks.

7. *penned*] shut.

9. *fond*] foolish.

10. *How likest...head*] What do you think of this device? Bond's suggestion (iii, p. 538), supported by later editors, that rather than seeking Risio's
approbation he might be referring to a miniature of his daughter which he
produces at this point, runs counter to the fact that he has been engaged in
outlining his own plans; while his question to Risio at line 14, confirms that
he is speaking of himself. Risio's response at lines 11–13 constitutes a deliberate misunderstanding of the term that his master employs (*head*), in that he
comments not on the cleverness of Stellio's scheme but the appearance and
intellectual limitations of the man who devised it. For a comparable use of
'head' to denote cleverness or wit, see 2.1.34 below.

11–12. *There is...base*] It's well made, but material itself is of poor quality
(i.e. your brains are not as good as your looks).

12. *stuff*] filling.

15.] I.e. you remain a fool even though you have passed your folly on to
your daughter. Risio's low opinion of his master's intelligence is confirmed
by the fact that Stellio seems oblivious of the insulting nature of his servant's
remarks.

16. quod natura...potest] what came by nature no man can take away
(see lines 20–1 below). Andreadis (p. 77) cites Hans Walther, *Proverbia
Sententiaeque Latinitatis Medii Aevi* (Göttingen, 1966), IV, No. 92a ff., for
the medieval sources and variants of the proverb.

17. *fee-simple*] inherited character (legal term used of an estate held by
the owner and his heirs in perpetuity).

*Stellio.* Nay, Risio, she is no natural fool, but in this consisteth
      her simplicity, that she thinketh herself subtle; in this her
      rudeness, that she imagines she is courtly; in this the
      over-shooting of herself, that she over-weeneth of herself.      25
*Risio.* Well, what follows?
*Stellio.* Risio, this is my plot. Memphio hath a pretty stripling
      to his son, whom with cockering he hath made wanton.
      His girdle must be warmed, the air must not breathe on
      him, he must lie abed till noon, and yet in his bed break      30
      his fast. That which I do to conceal the folly of my daugh-
      ter, that doth he in too much cockering of his son. Now,
      Risio, how shall I compass a match between my girl and
      his boy?
*Risio.* Why, with a pair of compasses. And bring them both      35
      into the circle, I'll warrant they'll match themselves.
*Stellio.* Tush, plot it for me, that, never speaking one to
      another, they be in love one with another. I like not

---

23. subtle; in this] *Dilke;* subtile in this *Q1, 2, Bl.*   24. courtly; in
this] *Dilke;* courtly, in this *Q1;* courtlie: in this *Q2, Bl* (courtly).   35. compasses. And] *Punctuation as Andreadis;* compasses, and   *Q1, 2, Bl.*
36. they'll] *Andreadis;* the'il *Q1, 2, Bl.*

22. *Nay...fool*] No, Risio, she is not simply a congenital idiot.
22–5. *in this...of herself*] her folly consists in believing herself to be clever;
her vulgarity in thinking herself to be sophisticated; her over-reaching in
having too high a regard for her own abilities. Dilke's punctuation of the
passage is adopted here (see collation note) in that it clarifies the oppositions
obscured by the pointing of all three early modern editions.
27. *pretty stripling*] good-looking youth.
28. *with cockering...wanton*] he has been spoiled with over-indulgence.
29. *His...warmed*] an extreme example of Memphio's pampering of his
son (*girdle* = sash).
30–1. *yet in...fast*] have his breakfast while still in bed.
32. *cockering*] pampering.
33. *compass*] bring about.
35. *pair of compasses*] scientific instrument for drawing circles (with a play
on *compass* in line 33).
35–6. *And bring...circle*] If you bring them into proximity with one
another (with a possible pun on *circle* = vulva).
37–8. *never speaking...with another*] they fall in love without exchanging
a word.

solemn wooing; it is for courtiers. Let country folks
believe others' reports as much as their own opinions.          40
*Risio.* Oh, then, so it be a match you care not?
*Stellio.* Not I, nor for a match neither, were it not I thirst after
my neighbour's farm.
*Risio.* [*Sardonically*] A very good nature. – Well, if by flat wit
I bring this to pass, what's my reward?                         45
*Stellio.* Whatsoever thou wilt ask.
*Risio.* I'll ask no more than by my wit I can get in the bargain.
*Stellio.* Then about it.                                    *Exit.*
*Risio.* If I come not about you, never trust me. I'll seek out
Dromio, the counsellor of my conceit.              [*Exit.*]    50

Act[us] 1, Sce[na] 3

[*Enter*] PRISIUS [*and*] SPERANTUS.

*Prisius.* It is unneighbourly done to suffer your son, since he
came from school, to spend his time in love, and unwisely
done to let him hover over my daughter, who hath
nothing to her dowry but her needle, and must prove a
sempster, nor he anything to take to but a grammar, and     5
cannot at the best be but a schoolmaster.

44. SD.] *This ed.*   50. SD.] *Bond.*

---

39–40. *Let country...opinions*] The comment alludes to the custom of
arranging marriages by taking soundings regarding their propriety, and
through discussions between authority figures, rather than in accordance
with the feelings of the parties.
  44. *flat wit*] sheer ingenuity.
  48. *about it*] get on with it.
  48. SD.] Though there is no textual justification for a direction indicating
that Stellio exits into his house, the parallel structure of the play's two
opening scenes suggests that his exit corresponds with Memphio's at
1.1.110.1 above.
  49. *come not about you*] don't deceive you.
  49–50. *I'll seek out...conceit*] The comment echoes Dromio's need for 'a
wag more to make of my counsel' at 1.1.100–1 above, and suggests that,
rather than following his master, Risio exits by a different route.
  50. *counsellor of my conceit*] my imagination's right-hand man.

  1. *suffer*] allow.
  2. *school*] university.
  4. *to her...needle*] for her marriage portion but her ability to sew.
  5. *sempster*] seamstress.
  *take to but a grammar*] follow as his profession except learning.
  6. *at the best be but*] be anything better than.

*Sperantus.* Prisius, you bite and whine, wring me on the
withers, and yet winch yourself. It is you that go about
to match your girl with my boy, she being more fit for
seams than for marriage, and he for a rod than a wife.          10
*Prisius.* Her birth requires a better bridegroom than such a
groom.
*Sperantus.* And his bringing up another gate marriage than
such a minion!
*Prisius.* Marry gup! I am sure he hath no better bread than is     15
made of wheat, nor worn finer cloth than is made of wool,
nor learned better manners than are taught in schools.
*Sperantus.* Nor your minx had no better grandfather than a
tailor, who (as I have heard) was poor and proud; nor a
better father than yourself, unless your wife borrowed          20
a better to make her daughter a gentlewoman.

---

9. your girl] *Q2* (girle), *Bl;* my girle *Q1.*   13. another gate] *Q1;* another
gates *Q2, Bl;* another gate's *Fairholt;* another-gate *Andreadis.*   21. her] *Q1;*
your *Q2, Bl.*

---

7. *bite*] snap.

7–8. *wring me on the withers*] irk me (image turning on the discomfort
caused to a horse by an ill-fitting saddle).

8. *winch yourself*] you are the one who kicks (and hence causes problems
for others). The retort develops the previous image, drawing on the proverb,
'Touch a galled horse on the back and he will wince' (Tilley, H700).
Compare *Ham.* (First Folio): 'let the gall'd iade winch; our withers are
vnrung' (Hinman, TLN 2110).

10. *for a rod*] to be disciplined like a child (i.e. beaten).

12. *groom*] low-class fellow.

13. *another gate*] a very different kind of.

14. *minion*] hussy.

15. *Marry gup*] contraction of 'Marry come up', an expression of
derision.

15–17. *he hath...schools*] has no claims to be thought of as a man of rank.
To eat better bred than is made of wheat is proverbial for one of overly
fastidious tastes (Tilley, B622); the wearing of specific materials under
sumptuary law denoted the class to which one belonged; while cultivated
manners were associated with the court rather than the university. Lyly refers
to social pretensions in similar terms in the Dedicatory Epistle to *Anatomy*:
'It is a world to see how Englishmen desire to hear finer speech than the
language will allow, to eat finer bread than is made of wheat, to wear finer
cloth than is wrought of wool' (p. 29).

20–1. *your wife...gentlewoman*] an insulting taunt implying an adulterous
relationship between Prisius' wife and a member of a higher social class.

*Prisius.* Twit not me with my ancestors, nor my wife's honesty.
    If thou dost –                    [*He threatens Sperantus.*]
*Sperantus.* Hold thy hands still, thou hadst best! And yet it is
    impossible, now I remember, for thou hast the palsy.                    25
*Prisius.* My hands shake so, that wert thou in place where, I
    would teach thee to cog!
*Sperantus.* Nay, if thou shake thy hands, I warrant thou canst
    not teach any to cog! [*He calms himself.*] But neighbour,
    let not two old fools fall out for two young wantons.                    30
*Prisius.* Indeed, it becometh men of our experience to reason,
    not rail; to debate the matter, not to combat it.
*Sperantus.* Well then, this I'll tell thee friendly. I have, almost
    these two years, cast in my head how I might match my
    princox with Stellio's daughter, whom I have heard to be                    35
    very fair, and know shall be very rich. She is his heir, he
    dotes; he is stooping old, and shortly must die. Yet by
    no means, either by blessing or cursing, can I win my son
    to be a wooer, which I know proceeds not of bashfulness
    but stubbornness, for he knows his good, though I say it.                    40

---

23. If thou] *Q1;* for if thou *Q2, Bl.*    SD.] *Bond (subst.).*    29. SD.] *This
ed.*    35. princox] *Andreadis;* princockes *Q1, 2;* princocks *Bl.*    40-1. good,
though I say it. He] *Punctuation as Daniel;* good though I saie it, he *Q1, 2*
(thogh*), Bl.* (say it, hee*).

---

22. *Twit not me*] Don't taunt me.
*honesty*] chastity.
25. *palsy*] a blanket term for a number of neurological conditions characterized by uncontrolled shaking of the limbs (specifically the hands).
26. *wert thou in place where*] were you somewhere more appropriate.
27. *cog*] (*a*) play fast and loose with the truth (the meaning Prisius
intends); (*b*) cheat by sleight of hand (Sperantus' derisive play on the term
at lines 28-9 below).
30. *young wantons*] wayward children.
32. *debate...combat it*] talk things through, not fight over them.
34. *cast in my head*] deliberated.
35. *princox*] saucy young man. Compare *R&J*: 'You are a saucy boy.../
You are a princox, go / Be quiet' (1.5.83-7).
37. *stooping old*] bent with age.
40. *knows his good*] understands courteous behaviour. Compare the claim
of the Merchant in *Love's Metamorphosis* that 'merchants know their good
as well as gentlemen' (3.2.81), and the description of the manner in which
Euphues responds to a gentle reproof in *England*: 'Euphues, as one that knew
his good, answered her in this wise' (p. 297).

He hath wit at will. As for his personage, I care not who
sees him. I can tell you, he is able to make a lady's mouth
water, if she wink not.

*Prisius.* Stay, Sperantus, this is like my case, for I have been
tampering as long to have a marriage committed between          45
my wench and Memphio's only son. They say he is as
goodly a youth as one shall see in a summer's day, and
as neat a stripling as ever went on neat's leather. His
father will not let him be forth of his sight, he is so tender
over him. He yet lies with his mother for catching cold.        50
Now my pretty elf, as proud as the day is long, she will
none of him. She, forsooth, will choose her own husband!
Made marriages prove mad marriages! She will choose
with her eye, and like with her heart, before she consent
with her tongue! Neither father nor mother, kith nor kin,       55

---

41. *He hath wit at will*] He has every intellectual gift at his command
(proverbial: Tilley, W552).

*personage*] personal appearance. Compare *MND*: 'And with her personage, her tall personage, / Her height, forsooth, she hath prevail'd with him'
(3.2.292–3).

43. *if she wink not*] unless she has her eyes closed.

45. *tampering*] scheming (*OED, v.* II. 2).

*committed*] put together (*OED, v.* III. e).

47. *as one...day*] proverbial for a protracted length of time (Tilley,
S967). Compare *MND*: 'Pyramus is a sweet-faced man; a proper man as
one shall see in a summer's day' (1.2.80–3).

48. *neat...neat's leather*] trim a young man as ever trod on cow-hide (i.e.
leather-soled shoes). Compare the Cobbler's claim in *JC* that, 'As proper
men as ever trod upon neat's leather' have worn his handiwork (1.1.26). The
comparison, which is proverbial (Tilley: M66), is among the hodge-podge
of sayings garbled by Silena in 2.3 below (lines 21–3).

49. *forth of*] out of.

50. *yet lies*] still sleeps.

*for*] for fear of. Compare *The Woman in the Moon*: 'Beware, she sleeps!
No noise, for waking her' (1.1.178).

51. *elf*] term for a mischievous child (*OED, sb.* 3. b).

52–7. *She, forsooth...likes best*] Livia's stance here echoes that of a number
of female characters in Lylian drama, who resist the traditional role of
authority figures in the arranging of marriages (cf. Lucilla in *Anatomy*,
Semele in *Endymion*, and Celia in *Love's Metamorphosis*).

53. *Made marriages...marriages*] The formulation suggests the contention
is proverbial, but no comparable example has been traced.

55. *kith nor kin*] fellow countrymen nor blood relatives (proverbial: Tilley,
K117).

shall be her carver in a husband; she will fall to where
she likes best! And thus the chick scarce out of the shell
cackles as though she had been trodden with an hundreth
cocks, and mother of a thousand eggs.

*Sperantus.* Well then, this is our best, seeing we know each          60
other's mind, to devise to govern our own children. For
my boy, I'll keep him to his books, and study shall make
him leave to love. I'll break him of his will, or his bones
with a cudgel.

*Prisius.* And I'll no more dandle my daughter. She shall prick          65
on a clout till her fingers ache, or I'll cause her leave to
make my heart ache. But in good time, though with ill
luck, behold if they be not both together. Let us stand
close and hear all, so shall we prevent all.

                              [*They conceal themselves.*]

*Enter* CANDIUS [*with a book*] *and* LIVIA [*with a sampler*].

*Sperantus.* [*Aside to Prisius*] This happens pat. Take heed you          70
cough not, Prisius.

---

62. him] *Q1; not in Q2, Bl.*  69.1.] *This   ed.; They   stand   aside.   /
Dilke.*  69.2.] *Bracketed   material / Tydeman (subst.).*  70. SD.] *This ed.;
aside / Bond.*

56. *be her carver in*] the one to allot her (proverbial metaphor (Tilley,
C110), drawn from the apportioning of meat at the family table by the head
of the household).
  *fall to*] make her meal (sustaining the metaphor initiated in the previous
clause), i.e. act on her own behalf (with the implication of satisfying her own
desires).
  58–9. *had been…eggs*] was a sexually experienced woman with numerous
children.
  58. *hundreth*] archaic variant of hundred.
  60. *best*] most appropriate course.
  61. *For*] As for.
  63. *leave*] cease.
  65. *dandle*] indulge.
  65–6. *prick on a clout*] sew cloth.
  66–7. *or I'll…heart ache*] but I'll make her stop causing me grief.
  67. *in good time*] at an appropriate moment.
  68–9. *stand close*] conceal ourselves.
  69.2. *sampler*] See 1.3.96n.
  70. *pat*] opportunely.
  71, 72. *cough…spit*] unattractive habits conventionally associated with
old men.

*Prisius.* [*Aside to Sperantus*] Tush, spit not you, and I'll
    warrant, I, my beard is as good as a handkerchief.
*Livia.* Sweet Candius, if thy father should see us alone, would
    he not fret? The old man, methinks, should be full of       75
    fumes.
*Candius.* Tush, let him fret one heart string against another,
    he shall never trouble the least vein of my little finger.
    The old churl thinks none wise unless he have a beard
    hang dangling to his waist. When my face is bedaubed          80
    with hair as his, then perchance my conceit may stumble
    on his staidness.
*Prisius.* [*Aside*] Ay? In what book read you that lesson?
*Sperantus.* [*Aside to Prisius*] I know not in what book he read
    it, but I am sure he was a knave to learn it.                 85
*Candius.* I believe, fair Livia, if your sour sire should see you
    with your sweetheart, he would not be very patient.
*Livia.* The care is taken. I'll ask him blessing as a father, but
    never take counsel for an husband. There is as much
    odds between my golden thoughts and his leaden advice         90
    as between his silver hairs and my amber locks. I know

72. SD.] *This ed.; aside / Tydeman.*   73. warrant, I, my] *Punctuation
as Bond;* warrant I my *Q1;* warrant I, my *Q2, Bl.*   83. SD.] *Bond.*
Ay] *Andreadis; I Q1, 2, Bl.*   84. SD.] *This ed.; aside / Tydeman.*

72–3. *spit not...handkerchief*] don't you spit, and I assure you that my
beard will prove as effective as a handkerchief (for smothering my cough).
For a further reference to Prisius' cough, see line 92 below.
    75. *fret*] (*a*) chafe (Livia's meaning); (*b*) part of the fingerboard of a
stringed instrument (initiating Candius' punning application of the word at
line 77 below).
    76. *fumes*] noxious vapours, thought to rise from the stomach to the brain
(cf. modern English, 'fuming with anger').
    79. *old churl*] miserable old man.
    80. *bedaubed*] festooned (literally, 'plastered').
    81–2. *perchance...staidness*] perhaps my imagination may be almost as
sober as his.
    83. *In what...lesson?*] Where did you get that idea from?
    88. *The care is taken*] I'm prepared for that.
    89–91. *There is...amber locks*] The opposition between the conditions of
youth and age (a conventional literary motif) is formulated in similar terms
in *Love's Metamorphosis*. Petulius informs the supposed Ulysses, who has
warned him against the Siren, that 'Thy silver hairs are not so precious as
her golden locks, nor thy crooked age of that estimation as her flowering
youth', while the Siren declares that 'That old man measureth the hot assault

he will cough for anger that I yield not, but he shall cough
me a fool for his labour.

*Sperantus.* [*Aside to Prisius*] Where picked your daughter that
work out of broad stitch?                                                95

*Prisius.* [*Aside to Sperantus*] Out of a flirt's sampler. But let us
stay the end; this is but the beginning. You shall hear two
children well brought up.

*Candius.* Parents in these days are grown peevish; they rock
their children in their cradles till they sleep, and cross      100
them about their bridals till their hearts ache. Marriage
among them is become a market. 'What will you give
with your daughter?' 'What jointure will you make for
your son?' And many a match is broken off for a penny
more or less, as though they could not afford their      105
children at such a price, when none should cheapen such
ware but Affection, and none buy it but Love!

94. SD.] *Bond.*   95. work out of] *Punctuation this ed.; worke, out of Q1,
2, Bl.*   96. SD.] *This ed.; aside / Tydeman.*

---

of love with the cold skirmishes of age' (4.2.81–5). The same contrast in
attitudes is developed more extensively in *Anatomy* (p. 40). *odds* =
difference.

92–3. *cough me a fool*] make a fool of himself (proverbial: *OED*, Cough
*v.* 6; Tilley, F508). Compare Tydeman (ed.), *Roister Doister*: 'Goe say that
I byd him keepe him warme at home / For if he come abroade he shall cough
me a mome [fool]!' (lines 889–90).

94–5. *Where picked...stitch?*] an ironic play on terms used in sewing: (*a*)
Where did your daughter take that design from a piece of sewing by unpick-
ing stitches?; (*b*) Where did she derive that idea from?

95. *broad stitch*] possibly a variant, as Tydeman suggests, of 'brede-
stitch', an 'inter-linked stitch like braid' (p. 410), with a pun on 'broad'
(i.e. 'coarse' or 'immodest'). Though unrecorded elsewhere, Bond's suggestion that the stitch may have been 'imagined to suit the occasion'
(iii, p. 539) seems unlikely given the precise nature of the other sewing
terms employed (cf. 'picked', 'work', 'sampler'). Linthicum notes, somewhat unhelpfully, that 'the "broad-stitch" of *Mother Bombie*...[is] self-
explanatory' (p. 147).

96. *sampler*] a piece of needlework designed to perfect (or exhibit) the
skill of the sewer in a variety of stitches and thus, in this instance, her skills
as a flirt.

99–107.] The speech reflects contemporary arguments in favour of
'companionate', as against arranged, marriage (cf. Fenton's observations
in *MWW* (5.5.213ff.) on the marriage-market conducted over Anne Page).

99. *peevish*] perverse.

103. *jointure*] property held jointly by husband and wife during the former's lifetime, but reserved for the latter's maintenance after his death.

106–7. *cheapen such ware*] ask a price for such a commodity.

*Sperantus.* [*Aside*] Learnedly and scholarlike!

*Livia.* Indeed, our parents take great care to make us ask blessing and say grace whenas we are little ones, and growing to years of judgement they deprive us of the greatest blessing and the most gracious things to our minds, the liberty of our minds. They give us pap with a spoon before we can speak, and when we speak for that we love, pap with a hatchet. Because their fancies being grown musty with hoary age, therefore nothing can relish in their thoughts that savours of sweet youth. They study twenty years together to make us grow as straight as a wand, and in the end, by bowing us, make us as crooked as a cammock. For mine own part, sweet Candius, they shall pardon me, for I will measure my love by mine own judgement, not my father's purse or peevishness. Nature hath made me his child, not his slave. I hate Memphio and his son deadly, if I wist he would place his affection by his father's appointment.

*Prisius.* [*Aside*] Wittily, but uncivilly.

108. SD.] *Bond.*　110. whenas] *Q1* (when as); when *Q2, Bl.*　119. make us] *Q1; not in Q2, Bl.*　126. SD.] *Bond.*

108. an ironic reflection on the use Candius has made of his learning.
110. *whenas*] when.
113. *pap*] soft food designed for a baby.
115. *pap with a hatchet*] proverbial for harsh treatment under a show of kindness or where kindness might have been expected (Tilley, P45). The phrase was used by Lyly in 1589 for the title of his satirical pamphlet in support of the bishops in the Martin Marprelate controversy (see p. 9 above).
115-16. *being grown*] have become.
116. *hoary*] grey (as with frost).
116-17. *relish in*] be agreeable to (literally, 'tastes good in').
117. *savours*] has the flavour.
*study*] endeavour solicitously.
118-19, 119-20. *straight as a wand...crooked as a cammock*] upright as a stick...bent as a crook. The opposition is used metaphorically at a number of points in Lyly's work, cf.: 'If my fortune be so ill that searching for a wand I gather a cammock...I must be content' (*England*, pp. 303-4).
120-1. *they shall pardon me*] I must decline to comply with their wishes.
124. *wist*] thought.
*he*] Accius.
124-5. *place his...appointment*] lodge his love in accordance with his father's directions.
126.] Cleverly, but not according to mannerly behaviour.

*Candius.* Be of that mind still, my fair Livia. Let our fathers
lay their purses together; we our hearts. I will never woo
where I cannot love. Let Stellio enjoy his daughter. [*He
looks at her sampler.*] But what have you wrought here?          130
*Livia.* Flowers, fowls, beasts, fishes, trees, plants, stones, and
what not. Among flowers, cowslops and lilies, for our
names, Candius and Livia. Among fowls, turtles and
sparrows, for our truth and desires. Among beasts, the
fox and the ermine, for beauty and policy, and among          135
fishes, the cockle and the tortoise, because of Venus.

---

129-30. SD.] *Tydeman (subst.).* 136-7. Venus. Among trees, the]
*Punctuation as Bond;* Venus among trees, the *Q1; Venus* among trees: the
*Q2, Bl.*

---

129. *enjoy his daughter*] marry his daughter himself. An ironic reflection
on the marriage market in which the play's parents are engaged.

131. *fowls*] birds.

132-3. *Among flowers...Livia*] Bond notes: 'the yellow cowslip representing the stem *liv-*, the white lilies the stem *cand-*' (iii, p. 539). As Tydeman
points out, however, though 'the link with Candius' name is obvious, that
with Livia [is] obscure' (p. 410), in that Latin *lividus* denotes bluish rather
than yellow. The initial letters of the flowers' names may simply form a
coded reference to those of the lovers, but the link between Candius and
white suggests that more may be involved.

132. *cowslops*] archaic variant of 'cowslips'.

133-4. *turtles and sparrows*] both birds conventionally associated with
love; the turtle (turtle dove), as Livia indicates, emblematic of constancy,
and the sparrow of amorous desire. Compare Cupid's readiness in *Love's
Metamorphosis* to accept an offering from Ceres who 'feedeth my [i.e.
Cupid's] sparrows with ripe corn, my pigeons [i.e. turtle doves] with whole-
some seeds' (2.1.97–8), and Sappho's reproach to Venus in *Sappho and Phao*,
'O Venus, have I not strewed thine altars with sweet roses, kept thy swans
in clear rivers, fed thy sparrows with ripe corn, and harboured thy doves in
fair houses?' (3.3.89–92).

135. *fox*] proverbial for cunning ('policy'). See Tilley, F629: 'As wily
(crafty) as a fox'.

*ermine*] member of the weasel family, noted for the beauty of its white
winter coat.

136. *cockle and the tortoise*] both traditionally associated with the goddess
of love. Venus was believed to have emerged from the sea off the coast of
Cyprus in a cockle (scallop) shell (cf. the representation of her birth by
Botticelli, circa 1485), while she is frequently depicted with one foot on a
tortoise shell, signifying either the need for women to remain in the home
or that 'Loue creepeth on by degrees' (Greene, *Menaphon*, p. 63) and is 'slow
to harms' (*England*, p. 241). For a full account of the sources of the two
emblems, see Bevington, ed., *Sappho and Phao*, 3.3.92–4n.

Among trees, the vine wreathing about the elm, for our
embracings. Among stones, abeston, which being hot will
never be cold, for our constancies. Among plants, thyme
and heart's ease, to note that if we take time we shall ease        140
our hearts.
*Prisius.* [*Aside to Sperantus*] There's a girl that knows her
lerripoop.
*Sperantus.* [*Aside to Prisius*] Listen, and you shall hear my
son's learning.                                                     145
*Livia.* What book is that?

---

138. abeston] *Bond;* Abestor *Q1, 2, Bl.*    139. thyme] *Andreadis;* Time *Q1,*
*2, Bl.*    142. SD.] *This ed.; aside / Bond.*    144. SD.] *This ed.; aside / Bond.*

---

137. *the vine…elm*] proverbial (Tilley, V61) for enduring, supportive
relationships between marital partners, friends etc. Compare *Errors:* 'Thou
art an elm, my husband, I a vine, / Whose weakness married to thy stronger
state, / Makes me with thy strength to communicate' (2.2.173–5). Andreadis
(p. 91) cites Henkel and Schone, *Emblemata*, col. 259, for the traditions
informing the image.
138. *abeston*] legendary stone associated with Venus and reputed, once
heated, never to cool (cf. *Anatomy*, Bond, i, p. 191: 'the stone *Abeston*
being once made hotte will neuer be made colde'). Bond (i, p. 332) quotes
Barthol. Anglicus: 'Abeston is a stone of Archadia with yron colour: and
hathe [*sic*] that name of fire. If it be ones kyndlyd [*sic*], it neuer quencheth',
but omits the association with Venus in the passage that follows: 'Of that
stone is made that craftye ingin, of the which nations taken with sacriledge
wondred. For in a temple of Venus was made a candlestick, on which
was a lanterne so bright burning, that it might not be quenched with
tempest, nether with raine' (Stephen Bateman, *Batman vppon Bartholome,
his booke De proprietatibus rerum*, 1582, xvi, 12: Xxiiii). Though historically
a variant of 'asbestos', the properties associated with the two terms are
now diametrically opposed.
139. *thyme*] shrubby plant with aromatic leaves (chosen here solely to
enable the following play on words).
140. *heart's ease*] pansy (again chosen to enable the pun).
143. *lerripoop*] Bevington notes: 'originally the long tail of a university
graduate's academic and clerical hood, thence coming to mean a lesson or
role to be learned and spoken or acted' (ed., *Sappho and Phao*, 1.3.7n.). The
term is used by Lyly on a number of occasions in the course of his career,
cf: 'Thou mayst be skilled in thy logic but not in thy liripoop' (*Sappho and
Phao*, 1.3.6–7), and 'I am not al tales, and riddles, and rimes, and iestes,
thats but my Liripoope' (*Pappe with an Hatchet*, Bond, iii, p. 407, lines 30–1).
Bond (i, p. 483, line 7), notes an occurrence of the word in the Entertainment
at Sudeley, which he believes to be Lyly's work.

*Candius.* A fine, pleasant poet, who entreateth of the art of
    love, and of the remedy.
*Livia.* Is there art in love?
*Candius.* A short art, and a certain. Three rules in three lines.    150
*Livia.* I pray thee, repeat them.
*Candius. Principio, quod amare velis, reperire labora,*
    *Proximus huic labor est placidam exorare puellam,*
    *Tertius, ut longo tempore duret amor.*
*Livia.* I am no Latinist, Candius; you must conster it.    155
*Candius.* So I will, and parse it too. Thou shalt be acquainted
    with case, gender, and number. First, one must find out
    a mistress, whom before all others he voweth to serve.
    Secondly, that he use all the means that he may to obtain
    her. And the last, with deserts, faith, and secrecy, to study    160
    to keep her.
*Livia.* What's the remedy?
*Candius.* Death.
*Livia.* What of all the book is the conclusion?
*Candius.* This one verse: *Non caret effectu, quod voluere duo.*    165
*Livia.* What's that?
*Candius.* Where two are agreed, it is impossible but they must
    speed.
*Livia.* Then cannot we miss. Therefore give me thy hand,
    Candius.    170

---

153. *exorare*] *Dilke; euorare* / *Q1, 2, Bl.*    154. *duret*] *Dilke; ducet* / *Q1, 2,*
*Bl.*    156. *parse*] *Dilke;* pace *Q1, 2, Bl.*    165. *effectu*] *Dilke; effertu* / *Q1, 2,*
*Bl.*    167. *are*] *Q1;* is *Q2, Bl.*

147–8. *A fine....love*] Ovid (43 BC–18 AD).
147. *pleasant*] amusing.
*entreateth of*] is concerned with.
152–4.] The lines are taken from Ovid's *Ars am.*, I, 35–8 (with the omission of the second line of the original). The Loeb translation reads: 'First,
strive to find an object for your love...The next task is to win the girl that
takes your fancy; the third, to make love long endure'. The Loeb edition
reads 'placitam' for 'placidam' (line 153, this ed.). For Candius' translation,
see lines 157–61 below.
155. *conster*] construe.
156. *parse it*] describe it grammatically in terms of its component parts.
160. *study*] find the means, strive.
165. *Non caret...duo*] What two have willed lacks not accomplishment
(Ovid, *Am.*, II.iii.16). For Candius' translation, see lines 167–8 below.
167–8. *but...speed*] that they will not be successful.
169. *miss*] fail.

*Prisius.* [*Coming forward*] Soft, Livia, take me with you. It is
not good in law without witness.

*Sperantus.* [*Coming forward*] And, as I remember, there must
be two witnesses. God give you joy, Candius! I was worth
the bidding to dinner, though not worthy to be of the    175
counsel.                          [*Candius and Livia are abashed.*]

*Prisius.* I think this hot love hath provided but cold cheer.

*Sperantus.* Tush, in love is no lack. But blush not, Candius;
you need not be ashamed of your cunning. You have
made love a book case, and spent your time well at    180
school, learning to love by art and hate against nature.
But, I perceive, the worser child the better lover.

*Prisius.* And my minion hath wrought well, where every
stitch in her sampler is a pricking stitch at my heart.
You take your pleasure on parents; they are peevish,    185

---

171. SD.] *Bond (subst.).*    173. SD.] *Tydeman (subst.).*    176. SD.] *This
ed.*    177. hath] *Q1;* have *Q2, Bl.*    179. You have] *Q1;* and haue *Q2, Bl.*

---

171. *Soft...you*] Just a moment, Livia, let me be included in the
discussion.

171–2. *It is...witness*] No witnesses were required, in fact, in Elizabethan
law, a simple agreement to marry by the two parties (without the presence
of a priest) being sufficient to validate the union. See Ernest Schanzer, 'The
Marriage-Contracts in *Measure for Measure*', *Shakespeare Survey*, 13
(Cambridge, 1960), p. 83. The informality of marital arrangements in the
period led to a range of problems surrounding the legality of marriages.

174. *God give you joy*] conventional formula marking the conclusion of a
marriage ceremony (see 5.3.170–4 below), or used to offer good wishes to a
bride or groom.

174–6. *I was worth...counsel*] I am good enough to be asked to the
wedding breakfast, even if I wasn't thought fit to be a party to the
agreement.

177. *cold cheer*] (*a*) little joy; (*b*) dismal hospitality (literally 'cold food').
The ironic comment plays on the proverb 'Hot love is soon cold' (Tilley,
L483). For a further reference to the saying, see lines 222–3 below.

178. *in love is no lack*] proverbial expression (Tilley, L485), denoting the
self-sufficiency of love.

179. *cunning*] learning, cleverness.

180. *book case*] a subject of study.

181. *school*] university (as at 1.3.2).
*hate against nature*] repudiate natural bonds (i.e. hate your own father).

183. *minion*] hussy.

184. *sampler*] See 1.3.96n. above.

185–98. *You take...their bridals*] The passage as a whole echoes Ferardo's
lament over the undutiful behaviour of his daughter, Lucilla, in *Anatomy*

fools, churls, overgrown with ignorance because overworn with age. Little shalt thou know the case of a
father before thyself be a mother, when thou shalt breed
thy child with continual pains, and bringing it forth with
deadly pangs, nurse it with thine own paps, and nourish        190
it up with motherly tenderness; and then find them to
curse thee with their hearts, when they should ask blessing on their knees, and the collop of thine own bowels
to be the torture of thine own soul. With tears trickling
down thy cheeks, and drops of blood falling from thy           195
heart, thou wilt in uttering of thy mind wish them rather
unborn than unnatural, and to have had their cradles
their graves rather than thy death their bridals. But I
will not dispute what thou shouldst have done, but
correct what thou hast done. I perceive sewing is an idle       200
exercise, and that every day there come more thoughts
into thine head than stitches into thy work. I'll see
whether you can spin a better mind than you have

---

189–90. pains…pangs] *Text and punctuation as Q1;* paines, and with
deadly pangs *Q2, Bl.*    193. collop] *Q1;* collops *Q2, Bl.*    194. soul. With]
*Punctuation as Andreadis;* soul, with *Q1, 2, Bl.*    200. sewing] *Dilke;* sowing
*Q1, 2, Bl.*    201. come] *Q1;* comes *Q2, Bl.*

---

(pp. 85–6). Compare, for example, *With tears trickling down thy cheeks, and
drops of blood falling from thy heart* (lines 194–6) and Ferardo's allusion to
'The tears which thou seest trickle down my cheeks, and my drops of blood
(which thou canst not see) that fall from my heart' (p. 86).

186. *churls*] miserable old men.

187. *the case of*] what it is to be.

190. *paps*] teats.

193. *collop…bowels*] offspring of your own loins. The term 'collop' (literally a thick slice of flesh) was used figuratively as a term of endearment in
the early modern period to denote the bond between parent and child (cf.
'flesh of my flesh'). Compare the terms in which Leontes addresses Mamillius
in *WT*: 'Come, sir page, / Look on me with your welkin eye: sweet villain!
/ Most dear'st, my collop!' (1.2.135–7).

196. *uttering…mind*] speaking your thoughts.

197. *unnatural*] lacking in filial piety.

197–8. *their cradles…bridals*] them die in infancy rather than occasion
your death by their marriages.

200. *idle*] fruitless, unprofitable. Compare *R3*: 'idle weeds are fast in
growth' (3.1.103).

stitched, and if I coop you not up, then let me be the
capon.                                                    205
*Sperantus.* As for you, sir boy, instead of poring on a book,
you shall hold the plough. I'll make repentance reap what
wantonness hath sown. But we are both well served. The
sons must be masters, the fathers gaffers. What we get
together with a rake, they cast abroad with a fork, and   210
we must weary our legs to purchase our children arms.
Well, seeing that booking is but idleness, I'll see whether
threshing be any occupation. Thy mind shall stoop to my
fortune, or mine shall break the laws of nature. How like
a micher he stands, as though he had truanted from        215
honesty! Get thee in, and for the rest, let me alone. In,
villain!

---

205. *capon*] castrated cock (used to denote an ineffectual man, or fool).
The birds were confined in order to fatten them for the table. Hence the
preceding, *if I coop you not up*.
   206. *sir boy*] an imperious term of address denoting an assertion of
authority.
   207. *hold the plough*] be set to ploughing. Compare *LLL*: 'I have vowed
to Jaquenetta to hold the plough for her sweet love three year'
(5.2.874-5).
   209. *gaffers*] Though glossed (in varying terms) as an aged countryman
by all previous editors in accordance with *OED*, it is more likely that the
word is used in this context as a disrespectful term for grandfather (cf. the
etymology proposed by *SOED*). Thus, in seeking to usurp the position of
their fathers, sons are forcing them into the role of incapacitated
grandsires.
   209–10. *What we...fork*] a proverbial metaphor for improvidence (Tilley,
R25). Lyly uses the saying on a number of occasions, cf. *England*: 'When
wealth cometh into the hands of youth before they can use it, then fall they
to all disorder that may be, tedding [spreading] that with a fork in one year
which was not gathered together with a rake in twenty' (p. 168).
   211. *arms*] armorial bearings (indices of elevation to a higher social class),
capable of being purchased, during this period, by those not born into the
nobility.
   212. *booking*] academic study.
   213–14. *stoop to my fortune*] conform to my situation in life.
   214. *break the laws of nature*] violate parental ties.
   215. *micher*] truant.
   216. *let me alone*] leave things to me.

*Prisius.* And you, pretty minx, that must be fed with love
upon sops, I'll take an order to cram you with sorrows.
Get you in, without look or reply!                                      220
                *Exeunt* CANDIUS [*into Sperantus' house*] *and*
                            LIVIA [*into Prisius' house*].
*Sperantus.* Let us follow; and deal as rigorously with yours as
I will with mine, and you shall see that hot love will wax
soon cold. I'll tame the proud boy, and send him as far
from his love as he is from his duty.
*Prisius.* Let us about it, and also go on with matching them    225
to our minds. It was happy that we prevented that
by chance which we could never yet suspect by
circumstance.
                *Exeunt* [*one following his son, the other his daughter*].

---

220.1–2.] *Bracketed material this ed.*    228.1.] *Bracketed material this ed.*

219. *sops*] cakes steeped in some form of liquid (e.g. milk or wine), specifically here, as Andreadis notes (p. 96), a delicacy offered to a bride at her
wedding.
*take an order to*] put arrangements in hand to.
222–3. *hot love...cold*] proverbial (Tilley, L483). Lyly plays on the same
proverb at line 177 above.
226. *to our minds*] in accordance with our wishes.
*happy*] fortunate.
227–8. *by circumstance*] on the evidence available to us.

# Act 2

[*Enter*] DROMIO [*and*] RISIO [*from different directions,
and initially unaware of one another*].

*Dromio.* Now, if I could meet with Risio, it were a world of
waggery.

*Risio.* Oh, that it were my chance *obviam dare Dromio*, to
stumble upon Dromio, on whom I do nothing but dream.

*Dromio.* His knavery and my wit should make our masters    5
that are wise, fools; their children that are fools, beggars;
and us two that are bond, free.

*Risio.* He to cozen, and I to conjure, would make such altera-
tions that our masters should serve themselves; the idiots,
their children, serve us; and we to wake our wits between    10
them all.

---

0.1–2.] *and initially...another* / *this ed.; Dromio. Risio.* / *Q1, 2, Bl (subst.);
Enter from different directions* DROMIO *and* RISIO. / *Tydeman.*

---

0.1–2. from...another] It is clear from the opening speeches, in which
Dromio and Risio express their desire to meet, that they are unaware of one
another's presence, and must therefore enter the stage by different routes.

1–29.] Some similarities have been noted between these lines and the
initial encounter between Toxilus and Sagaristio (lines 1–17) in Plautus' *Persa*
(see *Bryn Mawr Classical Review* (e-journal), 2004.4.23). There are no verbal
correspondences, however, between the two scenes and, though it is possible
that Lyly was influenced by the classical play, the parallels are insufficiently
close to warrant the Plautine comedy being regarded as a probable source.

1–2. *it were...waggery*] our mischief would be wonderful to see.

3. *chance*] luck.

*obviam dare Dromio*] for Dromio to cast himself in my way (translated
more colloquially by Risio in the following words). Bond suggests (iii, p.
540) that Lyly 'meant *obviam ire* or *fieri*, or intended a mistake'.

7. *bond*] bondmen, slaves. See 1.1.75–6 and n. for an earlier conflation of
Roman and sixteenth-century social conditions.

8. *cozen*] cheat.

*conjure*] (*a*) conspire, plot (*OED*, *v*. 1). Compare Spenser's *The Faerie
Queene*: 'When those gainst states and kingdomes do conjure, / Who then
can thinke their hedlong ruine to recure' (V.X.XXVI); (*b*) summon up (some
clever device).

9. *serve themselves*] become servants in our place.

10. *wake our wits*] put our brains to work.

*Dromio.* [*Seeing Risio*] *Hem quam opportune!* Look if he drop
    not full in my dish!
*Risio.* [*Seeing Dromio*] *Lupus in fabula!* Dromio, embrace me,
    hug me, kiss my hand! I must make thee fortunate!            15
*Dromio.* Risio, honour me, kneel down to me, kiss my feet! I
    must make thee blessed.
*Risio.* My master, old Stellio, hath a fool to his daughter –
*Dromio.* Nay, my master, old Memphio, hath a fool to his son –
*Risio.* I must convey a contract –            20
*Dromio.* And I must convey a contract –
*Risio.* Between her and Memphio's son without speaking one
    to another.
*Dromio.* Between him and Stellio's daughter, without one
    speaking to the other.            25
*Risio.* Dost thou mock me, Dromio?
*Dromio.* Thou dost me, else.
*Risio.* Not I, for all this is true.
*Dromio.* And all this.
*Risio.* Then are we both driven to our wits' ends; for if either    30
    of them had been wise, we might have tempered, if no
    marriage, yet a close marriage.
*Dromio.* Well, let us sharpen our accounts. There's no better
    grindstone for a young man's head than to have it whet

---

12. SD.] *Tydeman.*    14. SD.] *Tydeman.*    15. kiss my hand] *Q1* (kisse);
not in *Q2, Bl.*

---

12. Hem quam opportune] Well, what luck.
    14. Lupus in fabula] The wolf in the fable, a proverbial expression
(Tilley, W607) for the arrival of one spoken about by others (cf. 'Speak of
the devil'). The saying is recorded by Erasmus (*Adagia*, 916A) and occurs
in 4.1 of Terence's *Adelpoe*, when Ctesipho and Syrus are unexpectedly
interrupted by the appearance of the subject of their discussion.
    16–17. The lines develop the acknowledgement of a favour (*kiss my hand*)
in the previous speech into an act of homage to a priest-like figure bestowing
a blessing.
    20. *convey a contract*] engineer a marriage (with connotations of secrecy).
    22–3. *without…another*] without allowing either to speak to the other.
    27. Or you are mocking me.
    31. *tempered*] plotted clandestinely, secretly devised (obsolete variant of
'tampered', *OED, v.* II. 2).
    32. *close*] contracted privately rather than publicly celebrated.
    33. *sharpen our accounts*] reckon things up more precisely.
    34–5. *head…purse*] wit than to be sharpened (*whet*) by thoughts of an
old man's money (image drawn from the sharpening of knives).

upon an old man's purse. Oh, thou shalt see my knavery    35
shave like a razor!

*Risio.* Thou for the edge, and I the point, will make the fool
bestride our mistress' backs; and then have at the bag
with the dudgeon haft – that is, at the dudgeon dagger
by which hangs his tantony pouch.                         40

*Dromio.* These old huddles have such strong purses with
locks, when they shut them they go off like a snaphance.

*Risio.* The old fashion is best, a purse with a ring round about

---

37. *Thou for...point*] The comment sustains the suggestion that the boys
are knife-like in their sharpness, initiated by Dromio in the preceding speech
and culminating in the notion of them cutting their masters' purses at lines
38–9 below.

37–8. *make the fool...backs*] obscure. Possibly, 'make Accius (*the fool*)
straddle Silena's (*our mistress'*) buttocks (*backs*)', i.e. bring about a
marriage.

38–40. *then have at...pouch*] having brought about the marriage between
Silena and Accius, we may go after our masters' money. As Fairholt explains,
the lines allude 'to the constant custom, from the fourteenth to the seventeenth century, of carrying the purse ['tantony pouch'] at the girdle, and the
dagger thrust between the straps or cords by which it hung' (ii, p. 272).
*Dudgeon*, a wood favoured by craftsmen for the straightness of its grain, and
equated with boxwood in Gerard's *Herball* (1597), was frequently used for
the handles of high-quality knives (cf. *Mac.*, 2.1.33–47), while *tantony*, a
contraction of St Anthony, probably denotes pigskin, in that St Anthony was
the patron saint of swine, and frequently depicted accompanied by a pig.
Both the passage itself and the lines that follow are fraught with sexual
innuendo from *bag* (suggestive of testicles) through *dagger* (a term with
phallic overtones), to the *ring* and *circle* requiring defence from male assault.

41. *huddles*] disrespectful term for a person of advanced years. Compare
*Anatomy*: 'But as to the stomach quatted [satiated] with dainties all delicates
seem queasy...so these old huddles, having overcharged their gorges with
fancy, account all honest recreation mere folly' (p. 41).

42. *snaphance*] an early form of flint-lock (hammer and flint mechanism),
used in muskets and pistols. The term derives from Dutch *snap* + *haan* =
snap-cock.

43–4. *The old...from it*] Purses in the sixteenth century usually consisted
of a pouch fastened by a drawstring, and were hung from the belt (see lines
38–40 and n. above), affording an easy target for a cutpurse. Fairholt (ii, p.
272) notes that the ring around the purse was frequently engraved with a
moral exhortation, and cites 'a curious engraving' of a fifteenth-century
example in the *Journal of the British Archaeological Association* (vol. i, 1845,
p. 251). *A circle to course* [chase] *a knave's hand from it* may thus refer to the
metal ring with its spiritual admonition, though the type of pouch illustrated
does not precisely accord with one closed by means of a drawstring.

it, as a circle to course a knave's hand from it. But
Dromio, two, they say, may keep counsel if one be away,                45
but to convey knavery, two are too few, and four too
many.
*Dromio.* And in good time, look where Halfpenny, Sperantus'
boy, cometh. Though bound up in *decimo sexto* for
carriage, yet a wit in *folio* for cozenage. – Single Halfpenny,       50
what news are now current?

*Enter* HALFPENNY.

*Halfpenny.* Nothing, but that such double coistrels as you be
are counterfeit!

---

44. as] *Q1;* is *Q2, Bl.*    45. if] *Q2, Bl;* is *Q1.*

45. *two…away*] proverbial (Tilley, T257) for the dangers of confiding a
secret. Compare *Anatomy*: 'If I had not loved thee well, I would have swal-
lowed mine own sorrow in silence, knowing that in love nothing is so dangerous as to participate the means thereof to another, and that two may keep
counsel if one be away' (p. 59). Aaron uses a variant of the same proverb in
*TA* to justify the killing of the nurse who witnessed the birth of his child
(4.2.145–6). See also *R&J*, 2.4.195.
46. *convey*] carry out (with connotations of secrecy).
49–50. *Though…cozenage*] Though small in size, he is huge in terms of
his skill in deception. The terms 'decimo sexto' and 'folio' refer to printed
books of contrasting size, the former produced by folding a sheet of paper
four times to produce sixteen small leaves, the latter by folding a sheet only
once. The same metaphor is used in the Induction to Marston's *The
Malcontent* (lines 78–9) with reference to the discrepancy in size between the
boy players who originally staged the play and the adult actors who subsequently performed it.
50–1. *Single…current*] Though the greeting suggests that Halfpenny may
already be visible to the audience, the placement of his entry at line 51.1
follows the printing convention adhered to in *Q1* of signalling an entrance
immediately prior to the arriving character's first speech. For a similar
example of this practice, see 5.3.210–14 below.
50. *Single Halfpenny*] The greeting initiates the word play on 'double' that
follows, and emphasizes the small size denoted by the character's name (see
Characters, 9n.), in that had there been two of him he would have been a
penny.
51. *current*] (*a*) in circulation (Dromio's primary meaning); (*b*) valid
currency (the sense on which Halfpenny plays in the following line).
52–3. *such double…counterfeit*] two scoundrels (*coistrels*) such as you are
worthless and false. The response depends upon a play upon *double*: (*a*) two
in number; (*b*) given to doubling (i.e. cheating).

*Risio.* Are you so dapper? We'll send you for an halfpenny
        loaf.                                                    55
*Halfpenny.* I shall go for silver, though, when you shall be
        nailed up for slips.
*Dromio.* Thou art a slipstring, I'll warrant.
*Halfpenny.* I hope you shall never slip string, but hang steady.
*Risio.* Dromio, look here. [*He catches hold of Halfpenny.*] Now    60
        is my hand on my halfpenny.
*Halfpenny.* Thou liest, thou hast not a farthing to lay thy
        hands on. I am none of thine. [*He frees himself.*] But
        let me be wagging. My head is full of hammers, and

---

60. SD.] *This ed.; Tydeman supplies /* RISIO *grabs* HALFPENNY. / *following*
steady *(line* 59 *this ed.)*.   63. SD.] *This ed.*

54. *dapper*] smart.
54–5. *send...loaf*] dispatch you on an errand from which you won't come
back (in that Halfpenny will be exchanged for the bread).
56–7. *go for silver...slips*] be recognized as of value when you shall be
exposed as frauds.
56. *silver*] Bond notes (iii, p. 541) that silver halfpennies were coined
in the reigns of Henry VIII, Edward VI, and Elizabeth I, indicating
the considerably greater value of coins worth less than a penny than
their twentieth-century equivalents prior to the decimalization of English
currency.
57. *nailed up*] Counterfeit coins were commonly nailed by tradesmen to
their counters both as a warning and to remove them from circulation.
*slips*] counterfeit coins. Compare Greene's *A Disputation Betweene a Hee
Conny-catcher, and a Shee Conny-catcher* (1592): 'He went & got him a cer-
taine slips, which are counterfeyt peeces of mony being brasse, & couered
ouer with siluer' (Grosart, x, p. 260).
58. *slipstring*] (*a*) one who has slipped his leash (Dromio's meaning);
(*b*) one who deserves to be hanged (the sense on which Halfpenny plays
in the following line).
59. *slip string*] escape the noose.
60–1. *Now...Halfpenny*] a literalization of proverbial expressions denoting avarice or preoccupation with personal gain (cf. 'I will lay my hand on
my halfpenny ere I part with it', and 'His heart (mind, hand) is on his halfpenny': Tilley, H80 and 315). Given the common equation between the
scrotum and an old-fashioned purse, however, a bawdy implication may also
be intended here.
62. *farthing*] the coin of lowest value in pre-decimalization English
currency, worth one quarter of a penny (i.e. half a halfpenny).
62–3. *to lay thy hands on*] at your disposal.
64. *wagging*] going, on my way (*OED, v.* I. 7).
*My head...hammers*] Tydeman (p. 413) notes Surrey's lines on the death

they have so malleted my wit that I am almost a      65
malcontent.
*Dromio.* Why, what's the matter?
*Halfpenny.* My master hath a fine scholar to his son; Prisius
a fair lass to his daughter.
*Dromio.* Well?                                       70
*Halfpenny.* They two love one another deadly.
*Risio.* In good time.
*Halfpenny.* The fathers have put them up, utterly disliking the
match, and have appointed the one shall have Memphio's
son, the other Stellio's daughter. This works like wax,   75
but how it will fadge in the end, the hen that sits next
the cock cannot tell.
*Risio.* If thou have but any spice of knavery, we'll make thee
happy.
*Halfpenny.* Tush, doubt not of mine. I am as full for my pitch   80
as you are for yours. A wren's egg is as full of meat as a
goose egg, though there be not so much in it. You shall find
this head well stuffed, though there went little stuff to it.

---

of Sir Thomas Wyatt for a comparable example of the notion of the mind
being full of hammers that beat ideas into shape: 'A hed.../Whose hammers
bet styll in that liuely brayn / As on a stithe'. The metaphor of the mind
hammering when engaged in intense mental activity is still current in modern
English.
   65. *malleted*] beaten.
   66. *malcontent*] a type figure in late sixteenth- and early seventeenth-
century literature, associated with melancholia and a surly unresponsiveness
or antagonism to others.
   71. *deadly*] to the point of death (*OED*, adv. 2).
   72. *In good time*] Very well.
   73. *put them up*] shut them away.
   75. *works like wax*] proverbial (Tilley, W138) for something readily
manipulated or easily done. For a further use of the saying, see 3.2.2 below.
   76. *fadge*] work out.
   76-7. *the hen...tell*] i.e. even the person with the best access to information cannot predict. The formulation suggests that the metaphor is proverbial, but no comparable example has been traced.
   78-9. If you have the least love of mischief in you, you will be delighted
by what we are about to say.
   80. *pitch*] size.
   81. *meat*] edible matter.

*Dromio. Laudo ingenium*: I like thy sconce. Then hearken.
Memphio made me of his counsel about marriage of his        85
son to Stellio's daughter; Stellio made Risio acquainted
to plot a match with Memphio's son. To be short, they
be both fools.
*Halfpenny.* [*Flaring up*] But they are not fools that be short.
If I thought thou meantst so, *senties qui vir sim*: thou        90
shouldst have a crow to pull.
*Risio.* Be not angry, Halfpenny. For fellowship we will be all
fools, and for gain all knaves. [*Halfpenny laughs.*] But why
dost thou laugh?
*Halfpenny.* At mine own conceit and quick censure.                95
*Risio.* What's the matter?
*Halfpenny.* Suddenly methought you two were asses, and that
the least ass was the more ass.
*Risio.* Thou art a fool. That cannot be!
*Halfpenny.* Yea, my young master taught me to prove it by        100
learning, and so I can, out of Ovid, by a verse.
*Risio.* Prithee, how?
*Halfpenny.* You must first, for fashion sake, confess your-
selves to be asses.
*Dromio.* Well.                                                   105
*Halfpenny.* Then stand you here, and you there.
            [*They take up the positions he indicates.*]
*Risio.* Go to.

89. SD.] *This ed.*   93. SD.] *Tydeman.*   106.1.] *This ed.*

84. Laudo ingenium] literally, 'I praise your mode of thought' (translated
more colloquially in the second half of the sentence).
   *sconce*] head (i.e. wit).
   87. *they*] i.e. the marriageable children.
   90. senties qui vir sim] a quotation from Terence (*Eunuchus*, 1.1.21),
translated in the Loeb edition (which reads '*sentiet qui vir siem*') as '[you]
shall realize what sort of man I am' (TLN, line 66).
   90–1. *thou shouldst...pull*] you would have a quarrel to settle (proverbial:
Tilley, C855). Compare Dromio of Ephesus' threat to his alter ego in *Err.*:
'If a crow [i.e. a crowbar] help us in...we'll pluck a crow together' (3.1.83).
   93. *gain*] profit.
   95. At my own imagination and sharpness of judgement.
   98. *the least ass...ass*] The mock syllogism is explained at lines 108–11
below.
   103. *for fashion sake*] as a matter of form.
   107. *Go to*] abbreviated form of 'Go to it' (i.e. begin).

*Halfpenny.* Then this is the verse as I point it: *Cum mala per*
  *longas* [*He points to the taller of the two boys*] *invaluere moras*
  [*He points to the smaller boy*]. So you see, the least ass is     110
  the more ass.
*Risio.* We'll bite thee for an ape, if thou bob us like asses. But
  to end all, if thou wilt join with us, we will make a match
  between the two fools, for that must be our tasks,
  and thou shalt devise to couple Candius and Livia, by     115
  overreaching their fathers.
*Halfpenny.* Let me alone. *Non enim mea pigra juventus*: there's
  matter in this noddle.

*Enter* LUCIO.

  But look where Prisius' boy comes, as fit as a pudding
  for a dog's mouth!                                        120
*Lucio.* Pop three knaves in a sheath, I'll make it a right
  Tonbridge case, and be the bodkin.

---

109. SD.] *This   ed.*   110. SD.] *This   ed.*   112. thee] *Q1;   not   in   Q2,*
*Bl.*   117. *juventus*] Bond *n.; iuuentus* / *Q1, 2; inuentus* / *Bl.*

---

108. *point it*] (*a*) punctuate it; (*b*) indicate its meaning through gesture.

108–9. Cum mala…moras] macaronic quip depending not upon the
meaning of the words ('when the disease has gained strength by long delay')
but upon their sound (i.e. longas = long ass: moras = more ass). The line
derives from Ovid (*Rem. am.*, 92). LCL reads '*convaluere*'.

112. *bite thee…asses*] revile you as a fool if you belabour us as if we were
donkeys. The retort puns on the proverb 'with a bit and a bob, as they feed
apes' (Tilley, B420).

116. *overreaching*] outwitting.

117. *Let me alone*] Leave it to me.

Non…juventus] adapted from Ovid, *Met.*, x, 396: '*non est mea pigra
senectus*' ('my old age is not without resources'). Halfpenny substitutes
'juventus' (youth) for Ovid's '*senectus*' (old age).

118. *noddle*] head.

119–20. *as fit…mouth*] a variant of the proverb, 'As fit as a pudding for
a friar's mouth' (Tilley, P620), denoting something apt for a specific occasion or purpose.

119. *pudding*] the stomach or entrails of a pig, sheep etc., stuffed with a
mixture of minced meat, suet, oatmeal, and seasoning, boiled and stored
until required.

121–2.] The greeting depends on a pun on knaves/knives. Together
Dromio, Risio, and Halfpenny make up an assemblage of knaves/knives of
a variety of kinds, requiring only a bodkin (see below) to complete the set
(cf. William Percy, *The Cuck-queanes and Cuckolds Errants*: 'Three Kniues
do make vp the Sheathe of a Tunbridge [*sic*] dagger' (ed. J. A. Lloyd,

*Risio.* Nay, the bodkin is here already. [*He indicates Halfpenny.*]
You must be the knife.
*Halfpenny.* I am the bodkin! Look well to your ears; I must    125
bore them!
*Dromio.* Mew thy tongue, or we'll cut it out. [*Halfpenny looks
aggrieved.*] This I speak representing the person of a
knife, as thou didst that in shadow of a bodkin.
*Lucio.* I must be gone. *Taedet*, it irketh; *oportet*, it behoveth.    130
My wits work like barm, *alias* yeast, *alias* sizing, *alias*
rising, *alias* God's good.

---

123. SD.] *This ed.* 127–8. SD.] *This ed.* 130. irketh] *Q1;* liketh *Q2,*
*Bl.* 130–1. behoveth. My] *Punctuation as Andreadis;* behoueth, my *Q1, 2,*
*Bl.* 131. wits work] *Q1 (*worke*);* wits to worke *Q2, Bl.*

---

Roxburghe Club, 1824, 5.3)). The area around Tonbridge (a town on the
Medway in Kent, approximately 20 miles from Rochester) appears to have
been known for the production of knives (cf. Edward H. Sugden, *A
Topographical Dictionary to the Works of Shakespeare and His Fellow Dramatists,*
Manchester, 1925, p. 528). Christopher Chalklin notes in his *Seventeenth-
Century Kent: A Social and Economic History* (1965), 'An occasional cutler
was often to be found in the small market town or village, but the number
in Tonbridge parish between 1550 and 1620 suggests that production was
probably greater than local needs required' (p. 138). The claim by the rogue,
Mendax, in William Bullein's 'A Dialogue…against the Fever Pestilence'
(1564), that 'I was borne nere unto Tunbridge, where fine kniues are made'
(folio 75), turns on the same pun on knaves/knives as the Lylian allusion,
and may indicate, as Chalklin suggests that 'the little industry…had a reputation far outside the district' (p. 138). The allusion to Tonbridge is among
a series of references contributing to the topographical actuality of the play
(see Introduction, p. 7).
   122. *bodkin*] term used for both a short pointed knife and a needle-like
instrument used for boring holes in cloth. Compare *Ham.*: 'When he himself
might his quietus make / With a bare bodkin' (3.1.75–6).
   123–4.] The objection rests upon the fact that, as the smallest of the boys,
Halfpenny must be the bodkin, and Lucio must therefore be the knife.
   125–6. *Look well…them*] The warning alludes to the punishing of
some misdemeanours by the boring of a hole through the ear (cf. 4.2.216
below).
   127. *Mew thy tongue*] Keep your mouth shut (cf. 1.1.69n.).
   129. *in shadow*] like one playing the part. Compare *MND*, 'If we shadows
have offended' (5.1.417), for a comparable use of shadow for player.
   130. *Taedet…oportet*] it goes against the grain (*irketh*)…is necessary
(*behoveth*).
   131. *work*] ferment. Compare the *Entertainment at Sudeley* (ascribed by
Bond to Lyly): 'My wits worke like new beare, and they will break my head,
vnlesse it vent at the mouthe' (Bond, i, p. 483).
   131–2. *barm…sizing…rising…God's good*] all synonyms for yeast.

*Halfpenny.* The new wine is in thine head, yet was he fain to
take this metaphor from ale. And now you talk of ale, let
us all to the wine.                                                    135
*Dromio.* Four makes a mess, and we have a mess of masters
that must be cozened. Let us lay our heads together; they
are married and cannot.
*Halfpenny.* Let us consult at the tavern where, after to the
health of Memphio, drink we to the life of Stellio. I       140
carouse to Prisius, and brinch you Mas. Sperantus. We
shall cast up our accounts and discharge our stomachs,
like men that can disgest anything.
*Lucio.* I see not yet what you go about.
*Dromio.* Lucio, that can pierce a mud wall of twenty foot    145
thick, would make us believe he cannot see a candle
through a paper lanthorn. His knavery is beyond *ela*, and
yet he says he knows not *gam ut*.

---

142. up] *Bl;* us *Q1, 2.*

---

133–4. *The new wine...ale*] The new wine has made you loquacious,
though you were obliged (by the poverty of your imagination) to take your
imagery from the brewing of ale. The shift from *thine* to *he* in the course of
the sentence may suggest that the first clause is addressed to Lucio and the
second to Dromio and Risio.

136. *mess...mess*] a company of four people eating together (cf. *LLL*,
4.3.203: 'You three fools lacked me fool to make up the mess')...dishful.

137. *cozened*] tricked.

137–8. *Let us...cannot*] joke depending upon a pun on 'head': (*a*) part of
the body; (*b*) antlers of a stag. The comment implies that the four old men
are cuckolds, and hence cannot lay their heads together, as the boys can,
because of the horns conventionally associated with the cuckolded state.

141. *brinch you*] you propose a toast to (from Italian *brins, brinsi*: I drink
to you). *You* probably refers to Lucio here, with Halfpenny arranging for the
boys to toast one another's masters in turn.

*Mas.*] Master.

142. *cast up our accounts*] (*a*) calculate our position; (*b*) vomit up what we
spend.

*discharge our stomachs*] (*a*) unburden our valiant spirits; (*b*) spew up what
we drink.

143. *disgest*] (*a*) arrange (cf. *A&C*: 'We haue cause to be glad, that
matters are so well disgested' (Hinman: TLN, 886–7)); (*b*) consume.

144. *go about*] are plotting.

147–8. *ela...gam ut*] the highest and lowest notes in the hexachord scale,
and hence a register of levels of accomplishment. The metaphor is used at
a number of points in Lyly's work (cf. *Midas*, The Prologue at Court, lines

*Lucio.* I am ready. If any cozenage be ripe, I'll shake the tree.

*Halfpenny.* Nay, I hope to see thee so strong to shake three     150
trees at once.

*Dromio.* We burn time, for I must give a reckoning of my
day's work. Let us close to the bush *ad deliberandum.*

*Halfpenny.* Indeed. *Inter pocula philosophandum*: it is good to
plea among pots.                    [*They approach the tavern.*]     155

*Risio.* Thine will be the worst. I fear we shall leave a halfpenny
in hand.

*Halfpenny.* [*Flaring up*] Why sayest thou that? Thou hast
left a print deeper in thy hand already than a halfpenny

---

154. *philosophandum*] *Bl; philosophundum* / *Q1,* 2. 155. SD.] *This
ed.* 158. SD.] *This ed.* Why…Thou] *Punctuation as Bond;* Why, sayest
thou that thou *Q1, 2 (*saiest*), Bl.*

---

7–8), while Hortensio, disguised as a musician in *Shrew,* uses instruction in
the gamut as a vehicle for declaring his love for Bianca. *OED* notes that the
names of the six notes are derived from certain initial syllables of a sapphic
stanza in a Latin hymn for the feast day of John the Baptist (24 June): **Ut**
*queant laxis /* **re***sonare fibris, /* **Mi***ra gestorum /* **fa***muli tuorum, /* **Sol***ve polluti /*
**la***bii reatum, / Sancte Iohannes* (So that your servants may, with loosened
voices, resound the wonders of your deeds, clean the guilt from our stained
lips, O St John).

150–1. *three trees at once*] Bond suggests (iii, p. 542) that the reference
may be to the three timbers used in the construction of a gibbet, but it seems
more likely that the reference is to the three plots that the boys have in hand,
i.e. the marriages of Accius, Silena, and the lovers (Candius and Livia).

153. *close to*] approach.

*bush*] synonym for a tavern, from the practice of displaying an ivy bush
(sacred to Bacchus) over the door to advertise the sale of wine. The reference
prepares for the exit into the tavern at the close of the scene.

ad deliberandum] in order to deliberate.

154. Inter pocula philosophandum] to philosophize among the cups. The
quotation probably derives as Bond notes (iii, p. 542) from Plutarch's *Questio
convivium,* i. I, '*An philosophandum sit inter pocula*' ('Whether it is possible
to philosophize among drinking vessels').

155. *plea among pots*] debate (variant of 'plead': *OED, v.* I 1b) with drinking cups around us.

156. *Thine*] Your position.

156–7. *I fear…hand*] The joke turns on the proverb, 'He drank till he
gave up his halfpenny' (Tilley, H50), used of drinking until intoxicated. Risio
implies that Halfpenny will get drunk, and have to be left behind.

158–61.] The riposte turns on the practice of punishing malefactors by
branding, and implies that Risio already has an imprint considerably larger
than a halfpenny in his hand (i.e. that he is a convicted felon).

can leave, unless it should singe worse than an hot    160
iron!

*Lucio.* [*Calming him*] All friends. And so let us sing. 'Tis a
pleasant thing to go into the tavern clearing the throat.

SONG

| | |
|---|---|
| *Omnes.* | Io Bacchus! To thy table |
| | Thou callst every drunken rabble.          165 |
| | We already are stiff drinkers, |
| | Then seal us for thy jolly skinkers. |
| *Dromio.* | Wine, O wine! |
| | O juice divine! |
| | How dost thou the noll refine.          170 |
| *Risio.* | Plump thou mak'st men's ruby faces, |
| | And from girls canst fetch embraces. |
| *Halfpenny.* | By thee our noses swell, |
| | With sparkling carbuncle! |
| *Lucio.* | Oh, the dear blood of grapes          175 |
| | Turns us to antic shapes. |
| | Now to show tricks like apes. |

---

160. singe] *Dilke;* sing *Q1, 2, Bl.*  162. SD.] *This ed.*  163.1–183.] *Bl; not
in Q1, 2.*  170. noll] *Andreadis; Nowle / Bl.*

163.1–83.] The song, like those at 3.3.1–14, 3.4.42–61, and 5.3.65–84
below, does not appear in *Q1, 2* (see collation note), but is included in
Blount's collected edition of Lyly's works (*Sixe Court Comedies,* 1632). See
Introduction, pp. 5–6.

164. SP. Omnes] All (also at line 182).

*Io Bacchus*] Hurray for the god of wine.

166. *stiff*] stout, hard.

167. *skinkers*] tapsters.

170. *noll*] (*a*) head; (*b*) drunkard (*OED,* 1b).

174. *carbuncle*] literally a precious stone, fiery red in colour, but used
metaphorically to denote the facial eruptions commonly associated with
those addicted to alcohol.

176. *antic*] grotesque.

177–81. *Now to show...i'th' fire*] As Andreadis notes (pp. 236–7), the
types of behaviour alluded to here correspond with generally recognized
stages of inebriation. Compare Nashe's account of the drunkard in *Peirce
Penilesse His Supplication to the Divell* (1592): 'Nor haue we one or two kinds
of drunkards onely, but eight kindes. The first is Ape drunke, and he leaps,
and sings, and hollowes, and daunceth for the heauens: the second is Lion
drunke, and he flings the pots about the house, calls his Hostesse whore,

| | |
|---|---|
| *Dromio.* | Now lion-like to roar. |
| *Risio.* | Now goatishly to whore. |
| *Halfpenny.* | Now hoggishly i'th' mire. 　　　　180 |
| *Lucio.* | Now flinging hats i'th' fire. |
| *Omnes.* | Io Bacchus! At thy table, |

　　　　　　　Make us of thy reeling rabble!

　　　　　　　　　　　　*Exeunt [into the tavern].*

Act[us] 2, Sce[na] 2

*Enter* MEMPHIO *alone.*

*Memphio.* I marvel I hear no news of Dromio; either he slacks
　the matter, or betrays his master. I dare not motion
　anything to Stellio till I know what my boy hath done.
　I'll hunt him out. If the loitersack be gone springing into
　a tavern, I'll fetch him reeling out! *Exit [into the tavern].* 　5

*Enter* STELLIO *alone.*

*Stellio.* Without doubt, Risio hath gone beyond himself in
　casting beyond the moon. I fear the boy be run mad with

---

183.1.] *Bracketed material* / *Bond (subst.).*

5. SD.] *Bracketed material* / *Bond.*

---

breakes the glasse windowes with his dagger, and is apt to quarrell with any
man that speaks to him: the third is Swine drunke, heauy, lumpish, and
sleepie, and cries for a little more drinke, and a fewe more cloathes…the
seuenth is Goate drunke, when in his drunkennes he hath no minde but on
Lechery' (quoted from Harrison, pp. 79–80). Thomas Young's *Englands
bane: or, the description of drunkennesse* (1617) describes the stages in very
similar terms, while the frontispiece of Thomas Heywood's *Philocothonista*
(1635) depicts a party of drunkards with animal heads (see p. vi above).
　179. *goatishly to whore*] The goat is one of a cluster of animals commonly
associated with lechery. Compare Tilley, G167: 'As lecherous as a goat'.
　183. *reeling*] staggering (with drunkenness). Compare *A&C*: 'Let's grant
it is not / Amiss…/…to sit / And keep the turn of tippling with a slave, /
To reel the streets at noon' (1.4.16–20.)
　1. *marvel*] am surprised.
　2. *motion*] broach.
　4. *loitersack*] idle fellow.
　5. *reeling*] staggering (from blows rather than wine as at 2.1.183).
　6. *gone beyond*] overreached.
　7. *casting beyond the moon*] proverbial for engaging in wild speculation
(Tilley, M1114). Compare *Anatomy*: 'Pardon me, Euphues, if in love I cast
beyond the moon, which bringeth us women to endless moan' (p. 67).

studying, for I know he loved me so well that for my
favour he will venture to run out of his wits. And it may
be, to quicken his invention he is gone into this ivy-bush,            10
a notable nest for a grape owl. I'll ferret him out, yet in
the end use him friendly. I cannot be merry till I hear
what's done in the marriages.            *Exit [into the tavern].*

*Enter* PRISIUS *alone.*

*Prisius.* I think Lucio be gone a-squirrelling, but I'll squirrel
him for it. I sent him on my errand, but I must go for an            15
answer myself. I have tied up the loving worm, my
daughter, and will see whether fancy can worm fancy out
of her head. This green nosegay I fear my boy hath smelt
to, for if he get but a penny in his purse, he turns it
suddenly into *argentum potabile.* I must search every place            20

13. SD.] *Bracketed material / Bond.*   15. errand] *Dilke;* arrande *Q1;* arrand
*Q2, Bl.*   20. suddenly] *Q1;* so suddainely *Q2, Bl* (suddenly).

8. *studying*] racking his brains.
9. *venture…wits*] risk his sanity.
10. *quicken his invention*] stimulate his mental processes.
*ivy-bush*] tavern (see 2.1.153n.).
11. *grape owl*] one who spends the night drinking wine. The relationship
between the owl and the ivy-bush is proverbial (Tilley, O96), conventionally
denoting ridiculous behaviour.
14. *a-squirrelling…squirrel*] hunting squirrels (i.e. engaging in a childish
pastime rather than attending to his master's concerns)…use him like a
squirrel (i.e. hunt him out in turn). Compare Memphio's earlier determination to 'hunt [Dromio] out' (line 4).
16. *tied up*] confined.
*loving worm*] indulgent or patronizing term for someone in love. The
phrase occurs on a number of occasions in Lyly's work: cf. Euphues'
comment in *England*, 'What can be the cause of these loving worms but only
idleness?' (p. 314), and Alexander's description of Apelles and Campaspe in
*Campaspe* as 'Two loving worms' (5.4.141). Shakespeare uses a similar
phrase in *Temp.* when Prospero observes Miranda's feelings for Ferdinand:
cf. 'Poor worm, thou art infected' (3.1.31).
17–18. *fancy can…head*] one notion can drive out another.
18. *green nosegay*] the ivy bush denoting the tavern.
18–19. *smelt to*] sniffed. Compare *Love's Metamorphosis*, 'Take thou these
few ears of corn, but let not Famine so much as smell to them' (2.1.36–7).
Daniel's emendation, 'smelt too' (see Appendix), is unnecessary and runs
counter to the sense of the passage.
20. *argentum potabile*] quaffable silver, i.e. alcohol. The phrase may
designed to suggest *aurum potabile*, a highly prized elixir, derived by alche-
mists from gold (see Bond, iii, p. 542), the indigent Lucio having only silver
pennies rather than gold coins.

for him, for I stand on thorns till I hear what he hath
done.　　　　　　　　　　　*Exit [into the tavern].*

*Enter* SPERANTUS *alone.*

*Sperantus.* Well, be as be may is no banning. I think I have
charmed my young master. A hungry meal, a ragged coat,
and a dry cudgel have put him quite beside his love and　　25
his logic too. Besides, his pigsney is put up; and therefore
now I'll let him take the air, and follow Stellio's daughter
with all his learning, if he mean to be my heir. The
boy hath wit *sans* measure, more than needs; cats' meat

---

22. SD.] *Bracketed material / Bond.*　26. too] *Q2, Bl;* to *Q1.*　his²] *Q1;
not in Q2, Bl.*　29. sans] *Dilke;* sance *Q1, 2, Bl.*

---

21. *stand on thorns*] proverbial for being in a state of restless anxiety or
impatience (Tilley, T239).

23. *be as...banning*] Though the phrase is proverbial (Tilley, B65), no
agreement exists over its meaning in this context. Dilke proposes, 'I do not
curse my son when I discard him' (p. 227n.), while Bond (iii, p. 542) dismisses this interpretation as too literal, maintaining the phrase to be 'a
proverb with folk who think affairs are going well and call for no extraordinary effort'. Tydeman (p. 414), while broadly supporting Bond's position,
offers 'it's no curse [ban] to let things happen as they will' (cf. Daniel,
'Leaving things as they are isn't a bad idea': p. 378). Comparable instances
cited by Tilley suggest, however, that the meaning may be 'curse as we may,
things will be as they are'.

24. *charmed*] exerted my authority over. Compare Ceres' promise to
Cupid to 'charm my nymphs' following the intransigent behaviour of her
followers in *Love's Metamorphosis* (5.4.178).

24–6. *A hungry...logic too*] short rations, worn-out clothing, and a
beating have driven both love and learning from his mind.

26. *pigsney*] Tydeman notes: 'literally "pig's eye", a term of affection
much employed in the sixteenth century with the meaning "precious little
eye"' (p. 386). The term (which refers here to Livia) was primarily used in
relation to young women or girls. Compare *Roister Doister*: 'Then ist mine
owne pygsnie, and blessing on [her] heart' (Tydeman, ed., line 460).

*put up*] confined. Compare Prisius' declaration in the previous speech that
he has 'tied up the loving worm, my daughter' (lines 16–17).

27. *follow Stellio's daughter*] pursue (in the amatory sense) Silena.

29. sans] without.

29–30. *cats'...enough*] sufficient to have bits left over for scraps. Compare
Nashe, *Have with You to Saffron-Walden* (1596): 'and if my Booke bee *cats-
meate and dogs-meate*, his is much worse, since on hys mine hath his whole
foundation and dependence, and I doo but paraphrase vpon his text...*we
haue cats-meate & dogs-meate inough for these mungrels*' (Mckerrow, ed.,
*Nashe*, iii, p. 123).

and dogs' meat enough for the vantage. Well, without        30
Halfpenny all my wit is not worth a dodkin. That mite is
miching in this grove, for as long as his name is Halfpenny,
he will be banqueting for th'other halfpenny.

*Exit* [*into the tavern*].

Act[us] 2, Sce[na] 3

*Enter* CANDIUS.

*Candius.* He must needs go that the devil drives! A father? A
fiend, that seeks to place affection by appointment, and
to force love by compulsion! I have sworn to woo Silena,
but it shall be so coldly that she shall take as small delight

---

33. th'other] *Q2* (thother*); thether *Q1;* the other *Bl.*   33.1.] *Bracketed
material / Bond.*

0.1.] *Dilke; Candius. Silena. / Q1, 2, Bl (subst.).*   4. shall²] *Q1; not in Q2,
Bl.*

---

30. *for the vantage*] as well. Compare *Ham.*: "'Tis meet that some more
audience than a mother, /...should o'erhear / The speech of vantage'
(3.3.31-3).

31. *a dodkin*] literally, a doit (a Dutch coin of low value), but used figuratively for any small coin. The term sustains the word-play on Halfpenny's
name, in that, paradoxically, without his diminutive servant, Sperantus' own
wit is worthless. The expression 'Not worth a dodkin' is proverbial (Tilley,
D430).

*mite*] little fellow.

32. *miching*] playing truant (cf. *micher* at 1.3.215). Compare *England*:
'What made the gods so often to truant from heaven and miche here on
earth but beauty?' (p. 206).

*grove*] tavern (with reference to the ivy bush over the door).

33. *banqueting...other halfpenny*] obscure. Bond argues that though it is
possible that 'banqueting' might mean 'taking a nip', the 'context seems to
require "gambling"', and that the derivation of the word (from Italian
*banchetto*, little table), supports this interpretation (iii, p. 543). Tydeman, by
contrast, suggests that the phrase as a whole turns on Halfpenny's size, and
that 'by feasting and drinking [he] is trying to develop into a full penny' (p.
415). It is possible, however, that 'banqueting' may mean 'carousing' here
(cf. *OED*, Banquet, *sb.*¹ 4), and that Sperantus is maintaining that, as long
as his boy is called Halfpenny, he will spend his time drinking to the value
of his own name and as much besides. *OED* cites Holland, *Plutarch's Mor.*
612: 'A banket, where they shall be put to quaffe and carouse'.

1. *He must...drives*] proverbial (Tilley, D278) for one who is obliged to
pursue a course contrary to his own wishes.

2. *place...appointment*] direct love by command.

in my words as I do contentment in his commandment.     5
I'll teach him one school-trick in love. But behold, who
is that that cometh out of Stellio's house? It should seem
to be Silena by her attire.

*Enter* SILENA [*from Stellio's house*].

By her face I am sure it is she. Oh, fair face! Oh, lovely
countenance! How now, Candius, if thou begin to slip at     10
beauty on a sudden, thou wilt surfeit with carousing it at
the last. Remember that Livia is faithful; ay, and let thine
eyes witness Silena is amiable. Here shall I please my
father and myself. I will learn to be obedient, and come
what will, I'll make a way. If she seem coy, I'll practise     15
all the art of love; if I her cunning, all the pleasures of
love.

*Silena.* [*To the world at large*] My name is Silena, I care not
who know it, so I do not. My father keeps me close, so

<hr>

8.1.] *Bracketed material this ed.*   12. ay] *Andreadis;* I *Q1, 2, Bl.*   15. a
way] *Dilke;* away *Q1, 2, Bl.*   18. SD.] *This ed.*

6. *teach him...love*] show my father how scholars can deceive in amatory
matters.
8.1. from Stellio's house] See Silena's announcement that she has 'stolen
out' of her father's house (line 20 below) for textual support for the direction
supplied here.
9–17. *By her face...love*] The rapidity with which Candius abandons
his love for Livia at the sight of Silena's beauty forges a further link
with *Love's Metamorphosis* in which Petulius instantly forgets his love for
Protea in the face of the Siren's physical allure (though an abrupt shift
of affection is not exclusive, of course, to these plays: cf. *TGV* and
*MND*). For other possible links between *Love's Metamorphosis* and *Mother
Bombie*) see 1.3.40n., 52–7n., and 89–91n.
10–11. *slip at...sudden*] instantly shed all restraint at the sight of beauty
(metaphor drawn from hunting with dogs).
11–12. *surfeit with...last*] be sickened by your immoderation in the end.
13. *amiable*] lovely. Compare 1.2.1 above.
*Here*] By placing my affections here.
15. *coy*] unyielding.
16. if I her cunning] if I find her to be wise (elliptical). Both Bond's
emendation, 'if I <finde> her cunning', and Tydeman's (following a note
by Dilke), 'if I [find] her [coming]' (see Appendix), afford neat syntactic
parallels with 'If she seem coy' in the previous line, but are unnecessary, and
without textual support.
19. *so I do not*] no I don't. A childish assertion of independence.
*close*] shut away.

he does; and now I have stolen out, so I have, to go to        20
old Mother Bombie to know my fortune, so I will. For I
have as fair a face as ever trod on shoe sole, and as free
a foot as ever looked with two eyes.

*Candius.* [*Aside*] What? I think she is lunatic, or foolish! Thou
art a fool, Candius; so fair a face cannot be the scabbard     25
of a foolish mind! Mad she may be, for commonly in
beauty so rare there falls passions extreme. Love and
beauty disdain a mean, not therefore because beauty is
no virtue, but because it is happiness; and we scholars
know that virtue is not to be praised, but honoured. I will   30
put on my best grace. [*To Silena*] Sweet wench, thy face
is lovely, thy body comely, and all that the eyes can see
enchanting. You see how, unacquainted, I am bold to
board you.

*Silena.* My father boards me already; therefore I care not if   35
your name were Geoffrey.

---

21. Mother] *Q1; not in Q2, Bl.*   24. SD.] *Bond.*   31. SD.] *Bond.*

21-3. *For I have…two eyes*] an unintentionally humorous transposition
of the terms of two proverbial comparisons, 'As good a man as ever trod on
shoe leather' (Tilley, M66), and 'As fair a face as ever looked with two eyes'
(Dent, Fo.11), initiating Silena's mode of discourse through half-understood
sayings (see Candius' comment at lines 78–82 below). The confusion
between of the function of the parts of the body anticipates Bottom's similar
transpositions in *MND*. Compare: 'The eye of man hath not heard, the ear
of man hath not seen, man's hand is not able to taste, his tongue to conceive,
nor his heart to report, what my dream was' (4.1.209–12).

25-6. *so fair…mind*] The assertion depends upon the neoplatonic notion
that the face is the mirror of the soul, and that beauty of mind and body
should therefore coincide.

26-7. *commonly…extreme*] exceptional beauty is frequently subject to
extremes of emotion.

27-9. *Love and…happiness*] Bond comments: 'Lyly is thinking of the
Aristotelian doctrine of virtue as a mean between two vicious extremes, while
happiness, the end of virtue, sought for itself, is not to be measured by the
same standard of comparison' (iii, p. 543).

32. *comely*] pleasing to the eye.

33. *unacquainted*] though not known to you.

34, 35. *board…boards*] court (the meaning Candius intends)…provides
food and lodging (the sense in which Silena understands him).

35-6. *if your…Geoffrey*] The response turns on the misapplication of
the proverbial parting shot, 'Farewell gentle Geoffrey' (Tilley, G81), used
in dismissing someone unwelcome. Silena appears to take it to mean,
'whoever you are'.

*Candius.* [*Aside*] She raves, or overreaches. [*To Silena*] I am
one, sweet soul, that loves you, brought hether by
report of your beauty, and here languisheth with your
rareness.                                                                    40
*Silena.* I thank you that you would call.
*Candius.* I will always call on such a saint, that hath power to
release my sorrows. Yield, fair creature, to love!
*Silena.* I am none of that sect.
*Candius.* The loving sect is an ancient sect and an honour-        45
able, and therefore should be in a person so perfect.
*Silena.* Much!
*Candius.* I love thee much. Give me one word of comfort.
*Silena.* I'faith, sir, no! And so tell your master.
*Candius.* I have no master, but come to make choice of a          50
mistress.
*Silena.* Aha! Are you there with your bears?

---

37. SD. *Aside*] *Andreadis.    To Silena*] *This ed.; Aloud. / Andreadis.*   45. The]
*Q1;* Thy *Q2, Bl.*

---

37. *overreaches*] is seeking to trick.
38. *hether*] used consistently for 'hither' through *Q1* and preserved in this
edition as a possible indicator of the distinctive idiom of a provincial play
world (cf. 'hundreth' (1.1.95), 'thether' (5.3.48), 'hetherto' (5.3.309)).
40. *rareness*] rare loveliness.
41, 42. *call...call on*] visit (the meaning Silena intends)...invoke
(Candius' deft transposition of the term to the realms of courtly love.
See following note).
42. *saint*] term of address derived from the language of courtly love, in
which the lover's devotion to his lady is constructed in terms of a worship-
per's devotion to a sanctified being.
44. *that sect*] possibly an allusion to the 'Family of Love', a radical religious sect founded in Holland, which had gained a foothold in England by the
last quarter of the sixteenth century. The beliefs of the sect supply the back-
cloth for the amatory intrigue of Middleton's *The Family of Love* (pub. 1608).
45–6. *The loving...honourable*] The response refers to lovers in general
rather than the notorious 'Family of Love'.
47, 48. *Much...much*] a derisive expression of disbelief (the meaning
Silena intends)...a great deal (Candius' deliberate misconstruction).
49. *And so... master*] possibly intended literally as an imperious dismissal
(and thus an index of Silena's inability to determine class), but the injunction
may be another 'pert colloquialism', as Tydeman suggests (p. 415).
52. *Are...bears*] Are you on that topic again. The expression is attributed
by *OED* to a man 'who, not liking a sermon he heard on Elisha and the
bears [see 2 Kings, ii, xxiii–iv], went next Sunday to another church, only
to find the same preacher and the same discourse' (Bear, *sb.*¹ I. 1b).

*Candius.* [*Aside*] Doubtless she is an idiot of the newest cut.
I'll once more try her. [*To Silena*] I have loved thee long,
Silena.                                                           55
*Silena.* In your tother hose!
*Candius.* [*Aside*] Too simple to be natural; too senseless to be
artificial. [*To Silena*] You said you went to know your
fortune. I am a scholar, and am cunning in palmistry.
*Silena.* The better for you, sir. Here's my hand. What's      60
o'clock?
*Candius.* [*Seeming to read her palm*] The line of life is good;
Venus' mount very perfect. You shall have a scholar to
your first husband.
*Silena.* You are well seen in cranes' dirt. Your father was a   65
poulter. Ha, ha, ha!
*Candius.* Why laugh you?
*Silena.* Because you should see my teeth.

53. SD.] *Dilke (following* try her, *line 54 this ed.).* 54. SD.] *This ed; Aloud.
/ Andreadis.* 57. SD.] *Dilke (following* artificial, *line 58 this ed.).*
58. SD.] *This ed.; Aloud. / Andreadis.* 61. o'clock] *Daniel;* a clocke *Q1, 2,
Bl.* 62. SD.] *This ed.* 65. cranes'] *Q2 (*cranes*), Bl (*Cranes*); carnes Q1.*

53. *cut*] fashion.
56.] A colloquial response, described by Tilley as 'A mocking or evasive
answer, sometimes equivalent to "Not if I know it"' (H723).
57–8. *Too simple…artificial*] Too empty of meaning to be unaffected;
too lacking in sense to be a product of design. The comment may be a
reflection upon Silena's entire demeanour, not merely the vacuity of her
response.
59. *cunning*] knowledgeable.
60–1. *What's o'clock*] a proverbially absurd question (Tilley, O9a).
62, 63. *line of life…Venus' mount*] both features of the hand, significant
in palmistry. The line of life (the crease extending upwards across the palm
from the foot of the thumb) is held to denote length of life, while the mount
of Venus (the fleshy base of the thumb) affords information on amatory
matters. The latter term carries a double meaning in that it commonly
denoted part of the female genital region.
65. *well seen in cranes' dirt*] proverbial expression (Tilley, C806) belonging
to a group of insults objecting to the proximity of someone because of their
smell (*well seen in* = knowledgeable about).
66. *poulter*] officer in a large household responsible for the purchase of
poultry.
68.] proverbial for a type of vanity (Tilley, T428). Compare *LLL*: 'This
is the flower that smiles on everyone, / To show his teeth as white as whale's
bone' (5.2.331–2).
*Because*] So that.

*Candius.* [*Aside*] Alas, poor wench, I see now also thy folly.
A fair fool is like a fresh weed, pleasing leaves and          70
sour juice. I will not yet leave her; she may dissemble.
[*To Silena*] I cannot choose but love thee.
*Silena.* I had thought to ask you.
*Candius.* Nay then, farewell; either too proud to accept, or
too simple to understand.                                      75
*Silena.* You need not be so crusty; you are not so hard
baked!
*Candius.* [*Aside*] Now I perceive thy folly, who hath raked
together all the odd blind phrases that help them that
know not how to discourse, but when they cannot               80
answer wisely, either with jibing cover their rudeness, or
by some new-coined by-word bewray their peevishness.
I am glad of this. Now shall I have colour to refuse the
match, and my father reason to accept of Livia. I will
home, and repeat to my father our wise encounter; and        85
he shall perceive there is nothing so fulsome as a she
fool.                           *Exit* [*into Sperantus' house*].
*Silena.* Good God! I think gentlemen had never less wit in a
year! We maids are mad wenches. We gird them, and

---

69. SD.] *Dilke (following* dissemble, *line 71 this ed.).*    wench] *Q1;* wretch
*Q2, Bl.*    72. SD.] *This ed.; Aloud. / Bond.*    74. too] *Q2, Bl;* to *Q1.*
77. baked] *Dilke;* backt *Q1, 2, Bl.*    78. SD.] *This ed.*    raked] *Dilke;* rakt
*Q1;* rackt *Q2, Bl.*    81. jibing] *This ed;* gybing *Q1, 2, Bl.*    82. by-word] *Bl;*
buy worde *Q1, 2 (word).*    87. SD.] *Bracketed material this ed.*    88. SP.]
*Dilke (Sil.); Liu / Q1, 2, Bl.*

---

73.] proverbial expression, defined by Tilley as 'A mocking retort' (T225).
Compare Luce's derisive response to Antipholus of Ephesus' demand to be
admitted to his own house in *Err.* (3.1.55).
    75. *simple*] weak-witted.
    76–7.] proverbial metaphor drawn from the baking of bread (see Bond,
iii, p. 543).
    76. *crusty*] short-tempered.
    80. *discourse*] converse.
    81. *rudeness*] lack of sophistication.
    82. *bewray their peevishness*] betray their folly.
    83. *colour*] justification, excuse.
    85. *wise*] a sardonic reflection on Silena's vacuity.
    86. *fulsome*] nauseating. Compare *Anatomy*: 'Cherries be fulsome when
they be through ripe because they be plenty' (p. 30). The expression, 'A fool
is fulsome' is proverbial (Tilley, F463).
    88–91. *Good God...see it.*] Silena's belief that she has confounded
Candius by her wit confirms her father's comment in 1.2 that 'in this

flout them out of all scotch and notch, and they cannot          90
see it! I will know of the old woman whether I be a maid
or no, and then, if I be not, I must needs be a man.

[*She crosses to Mother Bombie's house, and calls.*]
God be here!

[*The door of the house opens to disclose*]
MOTHER BOMBIE [*sitting on a stool*].

*Mother Bombie.* Who's there?
*Silena.* One that would be a maid.                               95
*Mother Bombie.* If thou be not, it is impossible thou shouldst
    be; and a shame thou art not.
*Silena.* They say you are a witch.

---

92.1.] *This ed.; Knocks at* MOTHER BOMBIE'S *door.* / *Bond.*    93.1–2.] *This*
*ed.; Enter Mother Bombie.* / *Q1, 2, Bl.*

consisteth her simplicity, that she thinketh herself subtle…that she imag-
ines she is courtly…[and] over-weeneth of herself' (lines 22–5). The possibility that her responses did indeed constitute a witty device to frustrate
her suitor is obviated by her use here of another garbled proverb (Tilley,
F535: 'Fools had never less wit in a year') and her naive conclusion at lines
91–2 that if she is not a maid she must be a man.  *gird* = mock.

    90. *flout*] taunt.
    *out of…notch*] beyond all bounds (*OED* Scotch, *sb.*[1] 3).
    91–2. *I will know…or no*] Belief in potions (or other pseudo-scientific
means) for determining whether a woman had lost her virginity was current
in the early modern period, and virginity tests are alluded to in a number
of plays (see N. W. Bawcutt, ed., *The Changeling*, 1958, 4.1.25n.). The
context makes clear, however, that Silena has no understanding of the
difference between the two possible meanings of the word 'maid' ((*a*)
virgin; (*b*) unmarried young woman), and that her reasons for visiting
Mother Bombie are not related to any sexual experience.
    93.1–2.] Though *Q1, 2, Bl* simply indicate that Mother Bombie enters
when called (see collation note), a number of indicators in this and
subsequent scenes support the stage direction supplied here. The boys
knock loudly on her door, for example, prior to her appearance in 3.4,
confirming that she occupies some species of 'house', while Serena's angry
hope in 3.1 that she will 'sit on that stool till he and I marry by law'
(line 55), implies that in that scene, at least, she is sitting on a stool.
The fact that she is unable to see Silena's palm at lines 101.1–2 below,
when her visitor holds up her hand to be read, lends weight to the
proposition that she is seated, and thus disclosed on her stool at the
outset of the exchange, rather than entering on foot. For a fuller discussion of the staging of scenes involving Mother Bombie, see Introduction,
pp. 37ff.

*Mother Bombie.* They lie. I am a cunning woman.

*Silena.* Then tell me something.　　　　　　　　100

*Mother Bombie.* Hold up thy hand.

　　　　[*Silena holds up her hand too high for Mother Bombie
　　　　　　　　　　　　　　　　　　　　to inspect.*]

　　　Not so high!

　　　　[*Studying Silena's palm*] Thy father knows thee not;

　　　Thy mother bare thee not;

　　　Falsely bred, truly begot.　　　　　　　　　105

　　　Choice of two husbands, but never tied in bands,

　　　Because of love and natural bonds.

*Silena.* [*Imitating Mother Bombie*] I thank you for nothing,

　　　Because I understand nothing.

　　　Though you be as old as you are,　　　　　110

　　　Yet am I as young as I am;

　　　And because that I am so fair,

　　　Therefore are you so foul. —

　　　And so farewell, frost;

---

101.1–2.] *This ed.;* SILENA *holds it above her head.* / *Tydeman.* 103–7.]
*Lineation as Bond; continuous prose in Q1, 2, Bl.* 103. SD.] *This ed.* 108–
15.] *Lineation this ed.; continuous prose in Q1, 2, Bl.* 108. SD.] *This ed.*

---

99. *cunning woman*] person credited with exceptional percipience, consulted on a variety of matters in sixteenth-century England (see Introduction,
pp. 11–13 above), and deemed to be capable of interpreting dreams and
foretelling the future. For the distinction between a *cunning woman*, widely
regarded as a benevolent figure, and a *witch* (see line 98), thought to be aided
by demonic powers, see Introduction, pp. 11–13 and 30–1 above.

103–7.] Though *Q1, 2, Bl* print Mother Bombie's prophecies here and
elsewhere as prose (see collation note), the rhymes and ragged rhythms
support Dilke's assumption (endorsed by all subsequent editors, with the
exception of Andreadis) that the prophecies are intended as doggerel verse.

104. *bare thee not*] did not give birth to you.

105. *Falsely bred*] Not brought up by your real parents.

106. *tied in bands*] married.

107. *natural bonds*] the ties of kinship.

108–15.] All previous editors print Silena's response as continuous prose,
but the use of repetition, the see-saw rhythms, and closing couplet suggest
a childish attempt to imitate the old woman, in keeping with Silena's
belief in her own wit.

108.] proverbial (Tilley, N277).

114. *farewell, frost*] proverbial (Tilley, F769: glossed among the citations
as 'Spoken when they go off, whom we are glad to part with'). The
couplet at lines 114–15 may constitute a garbled version of 'Farewel frost,

My fortune naught me cost.                    *Exit.*   115
*Mother Bombie.* Farewell, fair fool. Little dost thou know thy
hard fortune. But in the end, thou shalt; and that must
bewray what none can discover. In the mean season, I
will profess cunning for all comers.
                    *Exit.* [*Mother Bombie's door closes.*]

Act[us] 2, Sce[na] 4

[*Enter from the tavern*] DROMIO, RISIO, HALFPENNY,
                    [*and*] LUCIO.

*Dromio.* We were all taken tardy.
*Risio.* Our masters will be overtaken if they tarry.
*Halfpenny.* Now must everyone by wit make an excuse, and
every excuse must be cozenage.
*Lucio.* Let us remember our complot.                    5
*Dromio.* We will all plod on that. Oh, the wine hath turned
my wit to vinegar!
*Risio.* You mean 'tis sharp.
*Halfpenny.* Sharp? I'll warrant 'twill serve for as good sauce
to knavery as –                    10
*Lucio.* As what?

119.1.] *Bracketed material this ed.*

1. were] *Q1;* are *Q2, Bl.*

nothing got nor nothing lost', a proverb noted in 1670 by Ray (cited
by Tilley under F769).
    115.] The first of four instances in which Mother Bombie is consulted and
receives nothing for her advice (cf. 3.1.47ff., 3.4.192–4, 5.2.1–27). Compare
her declaration at 3.4.194 that 'I take no money, but good words'.
    117. *hard*] adverse.
    118. *bewray*] reveal.
    *season*] time.
    119. *profess cunning*] dispense wisdom.

    1. *taken tardy*] caught unawares (i.e. taken by surprise by the unexpected
arrival of their masters in the tavern).
    2. *overtaken*] overcome by drink (with a pun on *taken* in the previous
line).
    *tarry*] linger (also at line 19 below).
    4. *cozenage*] trickery.
    5. *complot*] joint plan.
    6. *plod*] labour (with a pun on *complot* in the previous line).

*Halfpenny.* As thy knavery meat for his wit.

*Dromio.* We must all give a reckoning for our day's travail.

*Risio.* Tush, I am glad we 'scaped the reckoning for our
liquor. If you be examined how we met, swear by chance;        15
for so they met, and therefore will believe it. If how much
we drunk, let them answer themselves. They know best
because they paid it.

*Halfpenny.* We must not tarry. *Abeundum est mihi*: I must go
and cast this matter in a corner.                              20

*Dromio.* *I prae, sequar*; a bowl, and I'll come after with a
broom. Everyone remember his cue.

*Risio.* Ay, and his K, or else we shall thrive ill.

*Halfpenny.* When shall we meet?

*Risio.* Tomorrow, fresh and fasting.                          25

---

13. travail] *Daniel;* trauell *Q1, 2, Bl.*   21. SP.] *Dilke (Drom.); not in Q1, 2,
Bl.   I prae...and] *Bond (*bowle*); I presequar, a bowle, and Q1; Ipresequam,
a bowle, and Q2, Bl.*   22. cue] *Dilke;* que *Q1, 2, Bl.*   23. Ay] *Dilke (*Aye*);
I Q1, 2, Bl.*

12. *meat*] food (i.e. subject matter).

*his*] Dromio's.

13. *reckoning...travail*] account of our day's work.

14–15. *'scaped...liquor*] avoided the bill for our drink (presumably by
referring the tapster to their masters for payment, and slipping away before
being caught).

16. *they*] our masters.

19. Abeundum est mihi] I must remove myself.

19–20. *I must...corner*] (a) I must go away and privately reflect on
this issue; (b) I need to be sick in some out-of the-way place. Compare
*H5*: 'their villainy goes against my weak stomach, and therefore I must
cast it up' (3.2.53–4).

21. I prae, sequar] You go first, I'll follow. The quotation derives from
Terence (*Andria*, 1.1: TLN, 171), and is used by Lyly in *Endymion* both in
Latin at the close of 3.3, and in English at the end of 1.4, and 3.4.

21–2. *a bowl...broom*] get a bowl (to be sick in) and I'll follow you with
a broom (to clean up any mess).

22–3. *Everyone remember...ill*] quip turning on the proverbial saying, 'To
remember one's P's and Q's' (Tilley, P1), and depending on a series of puns
on the letters of the alphabet. *Cue, ay,* and *ill* are puns on Q, I, and L, while
*K* (pronounced 'key' until circa 1700) is more obscure, but may be designed
to imply 'how to pitch his part'.

25. *fresh and fasting*] early (i.e. before breakfast).

*Dromio.* Fast eating our meat; for we have drunk for
tomorrow, and tomorrow we must eat for today.
*Halfpenny.* Away, away! If our masters take us here, the
matter is marred.
*Lucio.* Let us everyone to his task!        *Exeunt,*        30

Act[us] 2, Sce[na] 5

[*Enter from the tavern*] MEMPHIO, STELLIO, PRISIUS,
[*and*] SPERANTUS [*tipsy*].

*Memphio.* How luckily we met on a sudden in a tavern, that
drunk not together almost these thirty years!
*Stellio.* A tavern is the rendezvous, the exchange, the staple
for good fellows. I have heard my great-grandfather tell
how his great-grandfather should say that it was an old        5
proverb when his great-grandfather was a child, that it
was a good wind that blew a man to the wine.
*Prisius.* The old time was a good time. Ale was an ancient
drink, and accounted of our ancestors authentical.
Gascon wine was liquor for a lord, sack a medicine for        10

---

0.1. *from the tavern*] *Tydeman.*   0.2. *tipsy*] *This ed.*   1. luckily] *Q1;* quickly
*Q2, Bl.*

26. *Fast eating*] Eating quickly (with a pun on *fasting* in the previous
line).
26–7. *for we…today*] because we've drunk enough today for both today
and tomorrow, and must eat enough tomorrow for both tomorrow and today.
0.2. tipsy] Stellio's laborious ascription of a pedestrian remark to a
distant forebear (lines 4–7) and Prisius' enthusiastic response (lines 8–12)
are indicative that the four men are 'overtaken' by wine, as Risio predicted
in the previous scene.
3. *exchange*] mercantile centre for the circulation of commercial news and
the transaction of business.
*staple*] authorized place of trade (for merchants).
6–7. *it was…wine*] cited by Tilley as proverbial (W420), but with no
supporting examples. The numerous variations on Tilley W421, 'It is an ill
(evil) wind that blows no man good (to good)' may suggest, however, either
that the phrase was current or that the 'proverb' is a further (in this case
drunken) example of Lyly's use of the corruption of familiar sayings as an
index of folly (cf. Silena's language in 2.3).
9. *accounted…authentical*] highly regarded by our ancestors.
10. *Gascon wine*] wine from south-west France.
*sack*] a class of white wine imported from Spain and the Canaries, widely
drunk by all classes in the sixteenth century. Compare *2H6*: 'Here, neigh-

the sick; and I may tell you, he that had a cup of red wine
to his oysters was hoisted in the Queen's subsidy book.

*Sperantus.* Ay, but now you see to what looseness this age is
grown. Our boys carouse sack like double beer, and
sayeth that which doth an old man good can do a young          15
man no harm. Old men, say they, eat pap; why should
not children drink sack? Their white heads have cozened
time out of mind our young years.

*Memphio.* Well, the world is wanton since I knew it first. Our
boys put as much now in their bellies in an hour as would     20
clothe their whole bodies in a year. We have paid for their
tippling eight shillings, and, as I have heard, it was as
much as bought Rufus, sometime king of this land, a pair
of hose.

*Prisius.* Is't possible?                                     25

---

13. Ay] *Andreadis;* I *Q1, 2, Bl.*    17. children] *Q1;* yong men *Q2,*
*Bl.*   cozened] *Q1 (*cosned); counted *Q2, Bl.*    20. now] *Q1;* wine *Q2,*
*Bl.*   21–2. We have…shillings] *Q1; not in Q2, Bl.*

---

bour Horner, I drink to you in a cup of sack; and fear not neighbour, you
shall do well enough' (2.3.59–61).

12. *oysters*] eaten by all social classes in the sixteenth century, rather than
a luxury food as today.

*hoisted…book*] promoted into the Queen's list of those deemed wealthy
enough to pay additional taxes when occasion required.

14. *double beer*] a beer of more than usual strength. The drink is among
those offered by his neighbours to Horner in *2H6* in order to strengthen his
resolution in his fight with Peter. Compare: 'And here's a pot of good double
beer, neighbour: drink and fear not your man' (2.3.64–5).

15. *sayeth*] say (agreeing with the plural *Our boys* in the previous line).

16. *pap*] baby food.

17–18. *Their white…years*] Old men [the boys say] have always cheated
young people like themselves.

19. *is wanton*] has become degenerate.

21–2. *We have…shillings*] The comment testifies to the boys' success in
referring the cost of their drinking bout to their masters. See 2.4.14–15n.

23. *Rufus*] William II (reigned 1087–1100), known as William Rufus
because of his red hair. Andreadis (p. 130) cites 'an apparently well-known
verse' about him included in William Camden's *Remaines of A greater Worke,
Concerning Britaine* (1605) in which the king rejects a pair of hose brought
to him by his chamberlain because they were too cheap to be worn by a
king, but accepts an inferior pair when told that they cost more.

*sometime*] once, formerly.

24. *hose*] probably stockings or leggings, rather than breeches (as in the
sixteenth century), in view of the early date from which versions of the story
are recorded.

*Stellio.* Nay, 'tis true. They say ale is out of request. 'Tis hogs'
   porridge, broth for beggars, a caudle for constables,
   watchman's mouth-glue; the better it is, the more like
   bird-lime it is, and never makes one stayed but in the
   stocks.                                                        30
*Memphio.* I'll teach my wag-halter to know grapes from
   barley!
*Prisius.* And I mine to discern a spigot from a faucet!
*Sperantus.* And I mine to judge the difference between a black
   bowl and a silver goblet!                                     35
*Stellio.* And mine shall learn the odds between a stand and a
   hogshead. Yet I cannot choose but laugh to see how my

---

26. *They say…request*] Made from fermented barley malt (as opposed to
beer, which was made from hops), ale was drunk in the sixteenth century
by the poorest sections of society. The boys' contempt for a drink appropriate to their class and preference for an imported wine (see lines 14–16 above)
reflects the challenge posed to the social hierarchy by the heightened social
mobility of Tudor England. (*They* = The boys.)
   *out of request*] unfashionable.
26–7. *hogs' porridge*] pig slop.
27. *caudle*] warm drink given to those in ill-health, consisting of a thin
gruel (oatmeal boiled in milk or water) blended with ale or wine and sweetened with sugar and spice.
28. *mouth-glue*] literally a type of glue, originally made from isinglass,
activated by moistening with the tongue. Hence, in this context, that which
seals a watchman's lips (i.e. making him too inebriated or sleepy to be alert
to the activities of malefactors).
29. *bird-lime*] glutinous substance smeared on twigs in order to catch
birds.
   *stayed*] (*a*) still; (*b*) sober (through prolonged enforced restraint).
31–2.] I'll make (with the implication of physical force) my gallows-bird
(*wag-halter*) understand that ale (*barley*) not wine (*grapes*) is the appropriate
drink for one of his class.
33. *spigot…faucet*] small plug used to stop the vent hole in a cask…the
tap on a barrel. The two are frequently found in conjunction (cf. the plumb-
ing term, a spigot and faucet joint), or employed interchangeably, but are
here used in opposition to denote wine (*spigot*) and ale (*faucet*).
34–5. *black bowl*] pitcher made of black leather, used to serve beer
or ale.
35. *silver goblet*] silver drinking vessel appropriate for wine.
36. *odds*] difference. Compare *Love's Metamorphosis*: 'This is the odds: we
miserable, and men; they immortal, and gods' (3.2.15–17).
   *stand*] large barrel holding thirteen gallons, traditionally used for ale or
beer.
37. *hogshead*] here a vessel containing sixty-three old wine gallons (equal
to 52.5 imperial gallons). A hogshead varied in capacity according to the
liquor it contained, and was not used exclusively for wine.

wag answered me, when I struck him for drinking
sack.

*Prisius.* Why, what said he?

*Stellio.* 'Master, it is the sovereignest drink in the world, and          40
the safest for all times and weathers. If it thunder, though
all the ale and beer in the town turn, it will be constant; if
it lighten, and that any fire come to it, it is the aptest wine
to burn, and the most wholesomest when it is burnt. So          45
much for summer. If it freeze, why it is so hot in operation that no ice can congeal it; if it rain, why then, he that
cannot abide the heat of it may put in water. So much for
winter.' And so ran his way; but I'll overtake him.

*Sperantus.* Who would think that my hop-on-my-thumb,          50
Halfpenny, scarce so high as a pint pot, would reason the
matter? But he learned his lear of my son, his young
master, whom I have brought up at Oxford, and I think
must learn here in Kent, at Ashford.

---

38. struck] *Andreadis;* stroke *Q1;* strooke *Q2, Bl.*     41–9.] *Quotation marks
/ Fairholt.*     41. sovereignest] *Dilke;* soueraigntest *Q1, 2, Bl.*     42. weathers…thunder, though] *Punctuation as Andreadis;* weathers, if it thunder,
though *Q1, 2* (thogh), *Bl.*     52. lear] *This ed.;* leere *Q1, 2, Bl.*     54. at] *Q1;*
of *Q2, Bl.*

---

38. *wag*] mischievous boy.

41. *sovereignest*] supreme in respect of both excellence and efficacy.

43. *turn*] go sour. The allusion is to the long-standing belief that ale and
beer are adversely affected by thunder.

*constant* ] retain its freshness.

43–4. *if it lighten*] if there is a flash of lightning.

45. *most wholesomest…burnt*] Burnt sack, generally understood as heated
or mulled wine, but possibly wine from Spain or the Canaries sweetened
with burnt sugar (see *MWW,* H. J. Oliver (ed.), Arden Shakespeare,
1971, 2.1.203–4n.), was a highly rated drink in the late sixteenth and
early seventeenth centuries.

48. *heat of it*] its alcoholic strength.

49. *ran his way*] ran off.

*overtake*] (*a*) catch; (*b*) be even with.

50. *hop-on-my-thumb*] term applied to a person so diminutive s/he might
be told hyperbolically to hop on one's thumb.

51. *reason*] argue. Compare *KL:* 'O, reason not the need' (2.2.456).

52. *lear of*] lesson from.

54. *must learn*] must now continue his education. The remark is designed
to emphasize that Candius' academic training is now at an end, and that he
must now turn his mind to matters closer to home.

*Kent, at Ashford*] one of a series of allusions locating the action of the play
in Kent (cf. the reference to Tonbridge knives at 2.1.121–2). Subsequent

*Memphio.* Why, what said he?                                            55

*Sperantus.* He boldly rapped it out; '*Sine Cerere & Baccho
friget Venus*': without wine and sugar his veins would wax
cold.

*Memphio.* They were all in a pleasant vein! But I must be
gone and take account of my boy's business. Farewell,      60
neighbours; God knows when we shall meet again.
[*Aside*] Yet I have discovered nothing; my wine hath
been my wit's friend. I long to hear what Dromio hath
done.                                                       *Exit.*

*Stellio.* I cannot stay, but this goodfellowship shall cost me   65
the setting on at our next meeting. [*Aside*] I am glad I
blabbed nothing of the marriage; now I hope to compass
it. I know my boy hath been bungling about it.     *Exit.*

*Prisius.* Let us all go, for I must to my clothes that hang on
the tenters. [*Aside*] My boy shall hang with them if he      70

---

56–7. '*Sine...Venus*'] Quotation marks / Andreadis.   56. Cerere] Dilke; Cere
/ Q1, 2, Bl.   62, 66, 70. SD. Aside] Dilke (positioned following done, about
it, day's work, lines 64, 68, 71, this ed.).

references (e.g. at 4.2.209 and 5.2.1–2) establish, however, that the play is
set not in Ashford but approximately thirty miles away in Rochester, and no
satisfactory explanation has been propounded for the reference to the former.
It may be that Lyly is simply punning on the names Oxford/Ashford to
denote Candius' removal from a scholarly to a provincial community.

56–7. Sine Cerere...Venus] Without Ceres and Bacchus Venus grows
cold (translated more colloquially in lines 57–8). The saying ultimately
derives from Terence (*Eunuchus*, 4.5.6, TLN 732: '*sine Cerere et Libero
friget Venus*'), but was proverbial by the sixteenth century. Tilley (C211)
cites numerous examples of the use of the proverb, including two (in
addition to *Mother Bombie*) from Lyly's work (*England*, p. 226 and
*Love's Metamorphosis*, 5.1.53).

59. *pleasant*] jocular. Compare Bianca's conciliatory words to her
neglected tutor in *Shrew*: 'Good master, take it not unkindly, pray, / That I
have been thus pleasant with you both' (3.1.55–6).

62. *discovered*] revealed.

62–3. *my wine...friend*] alcohol has not caused me to betray my
designs.

65–6. *shall...setting on*] will be at my expense.

67. *blabbed*] blurted out.

67–8. *compass it*] bring it about.

68. *bungling*] clumsily busy.

70. *tenters*] wooden frames on which cloth was suspended to allow it to
dry evenly and without shrinking after being fulled (i.e. cleaned with fuller's
earth or soap). Bond (iii, p. 544) takes the allusion to mean that Prisius 'is

answer me not his day's work.                           *Exit.*

*Sperantus.* If all be gone, I'll not stay. Halfpenny, I am sure,
hath done me a pennyworth of good, else I'll spend his
body in buying a rod.                                   *Exit.*

---

probably proprietor of some fulling-mills', citing his later threat to grind
Lucio to powder in his mill (cf. 5.3.159–60). The word 'tenters' survives in
the phrase 'to be on tenterhooks' (i.e. in a state of suspense).

   71. *answer me not*] doesn't give me a satisfactory account of.

   73–4. *spend his body*] lay out a halfpenny (a further play on the boy's
name).

   74. *rod*] cane (with which to beat Halfpenny for his undutiful behaviour).

# Act 3

[*Enter*] MAESTIUS [*and*] SERENA.

*Maestius.* Sweet sister, I know not how it cometh to pass, but
I find in myself passions more than brotherly.

*Serena.* And I, dear brother, find my thoughts entangled
with affections beyond nature, which so flame into my
distempered head that I can neither without danger          5
smother the fire, nor without modesty disclose my fury.

*Maestius.* Our parents are poor, our love unnatural. What can
then happen to make us happy?

*Serena.* Only to be content with our father's mean estate, to
combat against our own intemperate desires, and yield          10
to the success of Fortune, who, though she hath framed
us miserable, cannot make us monstrous.

*Maestius.* It is good counsel, fair sister, if the necessity of love
could be relieved by counsel. Yet this is our comfort, that
these unnatural heats have stretched themselves no          15
further than thoughts. Unhappy me that they should
stretch so!

---

9. father's] *Daniel;* fathers *Q1, 2, Bl.*

4. *beyond nature*] outside those sanctioned by the natural order.

5. *distempered*] disordered, out of proper balance.

6. *modesty*] shame. Tydeman notes (p. 417) that this is the only example
of the word bearing this meaning cited by *OED* (2d.), but as Bond
suggests (iii, p. 544) there may be a parallel usage in *Ham.*: 'There is
a kind of confession in your looks, which your modesties have not craft
enough to colour' (2.2.281–2).

8. *happy*] fortunate.

9. *father's*] Dilke's 'fathers" (see Appendix), followed by Andreadis, is
clearly misguided, in that Maestius and Serena still believe themselves to be
brother and sister at this point.

11. *success*] outcome.
*framed*] made.

15. *stretched*] extended.

17. *stretch so*] reach so far.

*Serena.* That which Nature warranteth, laws forbid. Strange
    it seemeth in sense that because thou art mine, therefore
    thou must not be mine.                                              20
*Maestius.* So it is, Serena. The nearer we are in blood, the
    further we must be from love; and the greater the kindred
    is, the less the kindness must be. So that, between broth-
    ers and sisters, superstition hath made affection cold;
    between strangers, custom hath bred love exquisite.                 25
*Serena.* They say there is, hard by, an old cunning woman,
    who can tell fortunes, expound dreams, tell of things that
    be lost, and divine of accidents to come. She is called the
    good woman, who yet never did hurt.
*Maestius.* Nor any good, I think, Serena. Yet, to satisfy thy          30
    mind, we will see what she can say.
*Serena.* Good brother, let us.
                    [*They approach Mother Bombie's house.*]
*Maestius.* [*Loudly*] Who is within?

            [*The door opens to disclose*] MOTHER BOMBIE
                        [*sitting on a stool*].

---

18–20.] *Q1; not in Q2, Bl.*  32.1.] *Andreadis (subst).*  33. SD.] *This
ed.*  33.1–2.] *Bracketed material this ed.; Enter Mother Bombie. / Q1, 2, Bl.*

---

18. *That which…forbid*] Whereas Maestius stresses from the outset that
the love between brother and sister is unnatural (cf. lines 7 and 15), Serena
argues that it is legal institutions, rather than Nature, that prohibit their love.
    *warranteth*] permits, justifies.
    19. *mine*] my brother.
    20. *mine*] my love.
    22–3. *the greater…must be*] proverbial (Tilley, K38). Compare *Ham.*: 'A
little more than kin and less than kind' (1.2.65).
    23. *kindness*] affection, love.
    24. *superstition*] irrational belief. The use of the word appears to mark a
shift in Maestius' view of the nature of the forces opposed to love between
siblings.
    26. *hard by*] close at hand.
    *cunning woman*] See 2.3.99n. and pp. 11–13 above for the construction of
the figure of the cunning woman here and elsewhere in Lyly's work (*cunning*
= wise).
    28. *divine of accidents*] foretell eventualities.
    33. 1–2.] See 2.3.93.1–2.n. for a justification of the stage directions gov-
erning the entrances of Mother Bombie in this edition.

*Mother Bombie.* The dame of the house.

*Maestius.* [*Aside*] She might have said the 'beldame', for her      35
   face, and years, and attire.

*Serena.* Good mother, tell us, if by your cunning you can,
   what shall become of my brother and me?

*Mother Bombie.* Let me see your hands, and look on me
   steadfastly with your eyes.                    [*They obey.*]      40
   You shall be married tomorrow, hand in hand,
   By the laws of God, Nature, and the land.
   Your parents shall be glad, and give you their land.
   You shall each of you displace a fool,
   And both together must relieve a fool.                            45
   If this be not true, call me old fool.

*Maestius.* [*Imitating her*] This is my sister; marry we cannot.
   Our parents are poor, and have no land to give us.
   Each of us is a fool,
   To come for counsel to such an old fool.                         50

---

35. SD.] *Tydeman.*   40. SD.] *This ed.*   41–6.] *Lineation as Dilke; continu-*
*ous prose in Q1, 2, Bl.*   41–2. hand, By] *Q1 (by),* 2; hand, and by
*Bl.*   42. God, Nature] *Q2, Bl;* good   nature *Q1.*   46. true, call] *Q1*
*(without comma);* true, then call *Q2, Bl.*   47–50.] *Lineation this ed.; continu-*
*ous prose in Q1, 2, Bl.*   47. SD.] *This ed.*

34. *dame*] mistress.

35. *'beldame'*] hag, witch.

35–6. *for her…attire*] by her looks, age, and clothes.

41–6.] The prophecy, here as elsewhere, is printed in all early editions as
prose, and is first set out as doggerel verse by Dilke (see 2.3.103–7n.).

42.] Canon law (i.e. church law, or the law of God), and common law
(i.e. the law of the land) varied at some points during this period in the definition of what constituted a valid marriage. Mother Bombie asserts that the
marriage between Maestius and Serena will be in conformity with all religious, biological, and social codes.

47–50.] As at 2.3.108–15, the response to the prophecy is printed in all
previous editions as prose rather than doggerel verse. Once again, however,
the rhymes and ragged rhythms echo the patterns of Mother Bombie's
speech, reinforcing the unexpected link forged between the seemingly
rational Maestius and the foolish Silena by the stance they adopt towards
the prophecies they receive.

*Serena.* These doggerel rhymes and obscure words, coming
out of the mouth of such a weather-beaten witch, are
thought divinations of some holy spirit, being but dreams
of decayed brains. For mine own part, I would thou
mightest sit on that stool till he and I marry by law.                    55
*Mother Bombie.* I say Mother Bombie never speaks but once,
and yet never spoke untruth once.
                              [*Mother Bombie's door closes.*]
*Serena.* Come, brother, let us to our poor home. This is our
comfort: to bewray our passions, since we cannot enjoy
our love.                                                                  60
*Maestius.* Content, sweet sister; and learn of me hereafter that
these old saws of such old hags are but false fires, to lead
one out of a plain path into a deep pit.          *Exeunt.*

---

57.1.] *This ed.*    59–60. enjoy our love] *Q1;* enioy them *Q2, Bl.*

51. *doggerel rhymes*] The term justifies the printing of Mother Bombie's
prophecies as verse in modern editions.
53–4. *dreams…brains*] the idle fantasies of a deteriorating mind.
55. *sit on that stool*] taken in this edition as an indication that Mother
Bombie is disclosed seated on her stool at line 33.1–2 (see 2.3.93.1–2n.), but
interpreted by previous editors in a variety of ways. Tydeman notes that the
stool 'presumably…remained on stage outside Mother Bombie's door
throughout the action' (p. 417), while Andreadis suggests that 'There is
perhaps an allusion here to the kind of tripod, or three-legged pot or caul-
dron, on which the priestess seated herself to deliver oracles at the shrine of
Apollo at Delphi' (p. 139). No allusion to Delphi may be intended, however,
a stool being the usual form of seating in a sixteenth-century household for
all but those of the highest rank. Compare *England*: 'Then the old
man…grace being said, called for stools, and sitting all by the fire, uttered
the whole discourse of his love' (p. 197).
59. *bewray*] reveal, lament.
*enjoy*] possess. Compare *John*: 'King o'er him and all that he enjoys'
(2.1.240). Lyly uses the word in the context of a disrupted amatory relationship in *Love's Metamorphosis*: 'And now, father, give me leave to enjoy my
Petulius, that on this unfortunate shore still seeks me, sorrowing' (4.2.19–
21). See also 5.3.352, 372, and 373 below.
62–3. *these old…deep pit*] The possibility that Mother Bombie's prophecies may be designed to delude and possibly damn (cf. the riddling utterances of the witches in *Macbeth*) runs counter to the title figure's reputation
as a 'good woman, who yet never did hurt' (3.1.29), bearing witness to the
uncertainty surrounding the status of those who were thought to possess
occult powers (see Introduction, pp. 12ff.).
62. *saws*] sayings, proverbial utterances.

Act[us] 3, Sce[na] 2

[*Enter*] DROMIO [*and*] RISIO [*from different directions*].

*Dromio.* [*To himself*] *Ingenium quondam fuerat pretiosius auro*:
the time was wherein wit would work like wax, and crock
up gold like honey.

*Risio.* [*Hearing him*] *At nunc barbarie est grandis, habere nihil*:
but now wit and honesty buy nothing in the market.          5

*Dromio.* What, Risio! How spedst thou after thy potting?

*Risio.* Nay, my master wrung all in the tavern, and thrust all
out in the house. But how spedst thou?

---

0.] *Q1* (*subst.*); Act. 3. Sce. 3: *Q2*; Actus tertius. Scaena tertia. *Bl.*
0.1. DROMIO [*and*] RISIO] Dilke; Dromio. Risio. Halfepenie. Luceo. / *Q1, 2,
Bl* (*subst.*); *from different directions* / *Tydeman.* 1. SD.] *This ed.*
4. SD.] *This ed.* 7. wrung all] *This ed;* rong all *Q1;* roong al *Q2;* rung all
*Bl.*

---

3.2.0. *Sce[na] 2*] For the misnumbering of scenes (see collation note),
here and at 1.2 and 5.1, see Introduction p. 1n. 5.

0.1.] Though the opening lines of the scene might seem to suggest that
the speakers enter in conversation, Dromio's salutation, *What, Risio!* at line
6, together with the question that follows, indicate that the boys enter from
different directions and that Domio is initially talking to himself.

1. Ingenium...auro] Time was when genius was more precious than
gold. The quotation, translated more colloquially by Dromio in the rest of
the speech, is from Ovid (*Am.*, iii.viii, 3).

2. *work like wax*] proverbial (Tilley, W138) for something easily manipulated or readily effected. Compare Lorenzo's comment on the success of his
schemes in Kyd's *The Spanish Tragedy*: 'This works like wax, yet once more
try thy wits' (3.4.60).

2-3. *crock up gold*] store up money in an earthenware pot. Fairholt notes
that 'The old money-pot for savings was made of coarse earthenware, and
broken when filled and the money was wanted' (ii, p. 274).

4. At nunc...nihil] But now to have nothing is monstrous barbarism.
The words, translated more colloquially by Risio in the second half of the
speech, complete Dromio's quotation from Ovid at the start of the scene.
The Loeb edition reads '*barbaria*' for '*barbarie*'.

6. *How spedst...potting?*] How did you fare after your tippling?

7-8. *wrung...house*] possibly, hurt every part (by squeezing) in the
tavern and expelled all the wine (by beating) at home, but the meaning
of the two halves of the sentence is disputed. The view that *Q1* 'rong'
(see collation note) represents modern English 'wrung', is supported by
Bond (iii, p. 545), but glossed by him as 'rated' or 'abused', while Andreadis
reiterates Bond's 'abused', but puzzlingly modernizes 'rong' to 'rung'.
Tydeman emends to 'rong all [out]', heightening the balance between the
two halves of the sentence, and proposing that the phrase means 'elicited

*Dromio.* I? It were a day's work to discourse it! He spake
nothing but sentences, but they were vengeable long     10
ones, for when one word was out, he made pause of a
quarter long till he spake another.

*Risio.* Why, what did he in all that time?

*Dromio.* Break interjections like wind, as *eho, ho, io!*

*Risio.* And what thou?                                   15

*Dromio.* Answer him in his own language, as *evax, vah, hui!*

*Risio.* These were conjunctions, rather than interjections. But
what of the plot?

*Dromio.* As we concluded. I told him that I understood that
Silena was very wise, and could sing exceedingly; that my   20
device was, seeing Accius his son a proper youth, and
could also sing sweetly, that he should come in the nick
when she was singing, and answer her.

---

14. *io*] *Andreadis;* to *Q1, 2, Bl.*   19. I²] *Q1;* we *Q2, Bl.*

---

what he wanted to know' (p. 417), but neither the context nor the ensuing
action suggest that Risio made any kind of confession to his master. Daniel
prints 'rung' for 'rong' and offers 'paid for the liquor' for the first phrase
and 'threw it all up' for the second (p. 379), shifting the focus of the
response from Risio to Stellio, but offers no justification for either gloss.
The reading proposed here is supported by a comparable usage of the
verb to wring to suggest the infliction of pain or injury in *A Whip for an
Ape* (cf. 'And *Martins* mate *Iacke Strawe* would alwaies ring / The Clergies
faults' (Bond, iii, p. 420, line 90)), and Dromio's account of the comparable reproof (verbal or physical) he suffered at home (cf. lines 9–16 below).

9. *were a day's…it*] would take all day to tell it.

10. *sentences*] (*a*) moral precepts; (*b*) complete grammatical expressions
of a single idea.

*vengeable*] terribly.

11–12. *a quarter*] a quarter of an hour.

13–17.] The exchange draws on the passage on interjections in William
Lily's *A Shorte Introduction of Grammar* (1577 ed.): 'An interiection is a parte
of speache which betokeneth a sodayne passion of the minde…Some are
of myrth: as Euax, vah. Sorow: as Heu, hei…Disdayning as: Hem, vah…
Skorning: as Hui…Calling: as Eho, oh, io' (Ciiir). Lyly alludes to the same
passage in *Endymion* (3.3.3–6).

17. *conjunctions*] possibly a pun, as Tydeman suggests (p. 417) on the
grammatical term for a connective and a number of linked exclamations
occurring in sequence.

19. *concluded*] agreed.

20. *exceedingly*] beyond comparison.

21. *seeing…youth*] his son Accius being a handsome young man.

22. *in the nick*] at exactly the right moment.

*Risio.* Excellent.

*Dromio.* Then he asked how it should be devised that she might        25
come abroad. I told that was cast already by my means.
Then, the song being ended, and they seeing one another,
noting the apparel, and marking the personages, he should
call in his son, for fear he should overreach his speech.

*Risio.* Very good.                                                    30

*Dromio.* Then, that I had gotten a young gentleman that
resembled his son in years and favour, that having Accius'
apparel should court Silena; whom she finding wise,
would after that by small entreaty be won without mo
words. And so the marriage clapped up by this cozenage,                35
and his son never speak word for himself.

*Risio.* Thou boy! So have I done in every point – for the song,
the calling her in, and the hoping that another shall woo
Accius, and his daughter wed him. I told him this wooing
should be tonight, and they early married in the morning,              40
without any words, saving to say after the priest.

*Dromio.* All this fodges well. Now, if Halfpenny and Lucio
have played their parts, we shall have excellent sport! And
here they come! — How wrought the wine, my lads?

---

28. marking] *Q1;* thanking *Q2, Bl.*    34. mo] *Q1;* my *Q2, Bl.*

26. *abroad*] out of the house.
*that was cast*] that matter was already devised.
27–8. *seeing one…personages*] Bond (iii, p. 545) assumes some confusion
in the details of the plot both here and at lines 31–5 below in that no substitute
courtship ultimately takes place. It is made clear in 4.2, however, that Lucio
and Halfpenny mishandle their part of the intrigue, while the information
supplied to the masters may not accord with the real intentions of the boys.
28. *personages*] personal appearances.
29. *overreach his speech*] betray himself by saying too much.
31. *that*] I told Memphio that.
32. *years and favour*] age and appearance.
32–3. *having Accius' apparel*] dressed as Accius.
34. *mo*] more.
35. *clapped up*] would be quickly agreed to.
37. *Thou boy*] an exclamation of approval (as here) or wondering disap-
probation (as at 5.3.419).
39. *wed him…him*] marry Accius. I told Stellio.
41. *saving to say*] except those they are required to pronounce.
42. *fodges*] works out.
44. *How wrought the wine?*] What effect did the wine have? For the play
on *wrought*, see line 46n. below. The salutation heralds the entrance of

*Enter* HALFPENNY [*and*] LUCIO.

*Halfpenny.* How? Like wine! For my body being the rundlet,      45
   and my mouth the vent, it wrought two days over, till I
   had thought the hoops of my head would have flown
   asunder.
*Lucio.* The best was, our masters were as well whittled as we,
   for yet they lie by it.                                       50
*Risio.* The better for us! We did but a little parboil our livers;
   they have sod theirs in sack these forty years.
*Halfpenny.* That makes them spit white broth as they do. But
   to the purpose. Candius and Livia will send their attires;
   you must send the apparel of Accius and Silena. They          55
   wonder wherefore, but commit the matter to our quadripartite wit.
*Lucio.* If you keep promise to marry them by your device, and
   their parents' consent, you shall have ten pounds apiece
   for your pains.                                               60

---

59. their] *Q1;* your *Q2, Bl.*

Halfpenny and Lucio, implying that they are already visible to the audience
prior to the point at which their entrance is signalled in the text.
   45–8. *For my body…asunder*] The image depends upon the notion of
the body as a small barrel (*rundlet*) in danger of splitting apart from
the force of the fermented liquor spilling from the bung hole (i.e. the
speaker's mouth).
   46. *wrought two days over*] Tydeman (p. 418) notes that the pun depends
on the working of yeast, and cites a comparable usage in Barnaby Googe's
translation of Heresbach's *Foure bookes of husbandry* (1577): 'The hony…is
suffered to stand uncovered a fewe dayes tyll it have wrought, and cast up
a lofte all his drags' (iv, 183b). *wrought* = fermented.
   49. *well whittled*] thoroughly intoxicated.
   50. *yet they lie by it*] (*a*) can still attest to it; (*b*) are still laid low by it.
   51, 52. *parboil…sod*] half-cook…steeped (both terms drawn from the
preparation of food).
   53. *white broth*] spittle associated with heavy drinking. Compare *2H4*: 'If
it be a hot day, and I brandish anything but a bottle, I would I might never
spit white again' (1.2.210–12).
   55. *They*] Candius and Livia.
   56–7. *our quadripartite wit*] the joint intelligence of the four of us.
   59. *their parents' consent*] with the consent of their parents.

*Dromio.* If we do it not, we are undone, for we have broached
a cozenage already, and my master hath the tap in his
hand, that it must needs run out. Let them be ruled and
bring hither their apparel, and we will determine. The
rest commit to our intricate considerations. Depart!          65
                        *Exeunt* HALFPENNY [*and*] LUCIO.

            *Enter* ACCIUS [*from Memphio's house*] *and* SILENA
                        [*from Stellio's house*].

*Dromio.* Here comes Accius tuning his pipes. I perceive my
master keeps touch.
*Risio.* And here comes Silena with her wit of proof. Marry, it
will scarce hold out question shot. Let us in to instruct
our masters in the cue.                                        70
*Dromio.* Come, let us be jogging. But were't not a world to
hear them woo one another?
*Risio.* That shall be hereafter, to make us sport. But our
masters shall never know it.
        *Exeunt* [*severally Dromio and Risio, into their masters' houses.*
                        ACCIUS *and* SILENA *remain*].


65.2–3.] *Bracketed material this ed.; Enter Accius and Silena* / *Q1, 2,
Bl.* 67. master] *Q1;* Maister *Q2;* Masters *Bl.* 70. cue] *Dilke;* que *Q1, 2;*
Q   *Bl.* 72. woo] *Bl;* woe   *Q1, 2.* 74.1. *severally...houses*] / *this
ed.* 74.2.] *Daniel (positioned following* Act[us] *3,* Sce[na] *3 this ed.).*

61–2. *broached   a   cozenge*] initiated   a   piece   of   deception   (image
drawn from the tapping of a wine or beer barrel, developed in the following
line).
62–3. *hath...hand*] i.e. is already in process of setting it in motion.
63. *must needs run out*] will inevitably take its course.
64. *determine*] govern the outcome.
66. *tuning his pipes*] preparing to sing.
67. *keeps touch*] is true to his agreement.
68. *wit of proof*] impregnable wit (metaphor relating to the impenetrabil-
ity of armour).
69. *hold out question shot*] withstand questions as slight as gun shot
pellets.
71. *jogging*] going.
*were't not a world*] wouldn't it be wonderful (proverbial: Tilley, W878).
Compare *Anatomy*: 'It is a world to see how commonly we are blinded with
the collusions of women' (p. 95).
74.1. *into...houses*] See the implied direction (*Let us in to instruct our
masters in the cue*) at lines 69–70 above.

## Act[us] 3, Sce[na] 3

[ACCIUS] *and* [SILENA *come forward*] *singing.*

### SONG

*Accius.*     O Cupid! Monarch over kings,
          Wherefore hast thou feet and wings?
          It is to show how swift thou art,
          When thou woundst a tender heart.
          Thy wings being clipped and feet held still,    5
          Thy bow so many could not kill.

*Silena.*     It is all one in Venus' wanton school,
          Who highest sits, the wise man or the fool.

---

0.] *Q1 (subst., following 3.3.01 this ed.), 2 (subst.);* Actus tertius, Scaena tertia *Bl (following 3.3.14 this ed.). Positioning here as Bond.* 0.1.] *Andreadis (following 3.2.74.1 this ed.); Memphio and Stellio singing.* / *Q1, 2, Bl. (following* / *Exeunt.* / *3.2.74.1 this ed.);* ACCIUS *and* SILENA *singing.* / *Bond (positioning as this ed.).* 0.2–14.] *Bl (following SD. at 3.2.74.1 this ed.); not in Q1, 2. Positioning here as Bond.* 1. SP.] *Daniel;* Memp. *Bl (Memphio); Sil.* / *Bond (Silena).* 5. held] *Dilke;* hel'd *Bl.* 7. SP.] *Daniel;* Stel. *Bl (Stellio); Acc.* / *Bond (Accius).* 8. wise man] *Fairholt;* wiseman / *Bl.*

---

3.3.0. *Act[us] 3, Sce[na] 3]* Bond's repositioning of the break between scenes 2 and 3 is adopted here (see collation note), since the simpletons' song clearly heralds the start of a new scene, while the later positioning of the scene break in *Q1, 2, Bl* may well be a product of the omission of the song from the quartos.

0.1. All three early editions indicate that it is Memphio and Stellio, rather than Accius and Silena, who sing here (see collation note), but Bond's emendation is clearly in accordance with the plot in that it is the simpletons, rather than their fathers, who are to encounter one another through a song.

1–14.] The song (like those at 2.1.164ff., 3.4.42ff., and 5.3.65ff.) does not appear in the quartos, but is derived from the edition of 1632. Blount assigns the lines to Memphio and Stellio, however, rather than to Accius and Silena (see collation note), and the order in which the simpletons sing is consequently a matter of dispute. Since the previous scene establishes that it is Accius who enters first, and the opening verse concerns Cupid, the first stanza is assigned in this edition to him, while the second, which concerns Venus and the difficulty of lovers understanding the female sex, is assigned to Silena. Tydeman's suggestion that the concluding couplet is sung by both, 'as a kind of symbolic coda' (p. 418), rather than by the singer of the preceding verse, is adopted here in that it suggests the success of the strategy to bring the two young people together.

5. *Thy wings being*] If your wings were.

7. *all one*] of no importance.

8.] The line alludes to the practice, common in schools in England until the second half of the twentieth century, of ordering the seating of children

       Fools in love's college
       Have far more knowledge             10
       To read a woman over
       Than a neat, prating lover.

*Together.*      Nay 'tis confessed,
       That fools please women best.

     [*Enter*] MEMPHIO [*from his* house] *and* STELLIO
               [*from his house*].

*Memphio.* Accius, come in, and that quickly! What, walking   15
   without leave?
*Stellio.*  Silena, I pray you, look homeward. It is a cold air, and
   you want your muffler.
                   *Exeunt* ACCIUS [*into his house*] *and*
                       SILENA [*into her house*].
*Memphio.* [*Aside*] This is pat. If the rest proceed, Stellio is like
   to marry his daughter to a fool. But a bargain is a bargain!   20
*Stellio.* [*Aside*] This frames to my wish. Memphio is like to
   marry a fool to his son. Accius' tongue shall tie all
   Memphio's land to Silena's dowry. Let his father's teeth
   undo them if he can. [*He sees Memphio.*] But here I
   see Memphio. I must seem kind, for in kindness lies   25
   cozenage.

---

13. SP.] *Tydeman; lines assigned to previous singer in other eds.* 14.1–
2.] *Bracketed material this ed.* 18. your] *Q1;* a *Q2, Bl.* 18.1–2.] *Bracketed
material this. ed.; Exeunt / Q2, Bl; Exunt / Q1.* 19, 21. SD.] *Bond.* 24. SD.]
*This ed.*

in a classroom according to ability. Hence *Who sits highest* is the pupil in the
most prestigious position (usually at the front).
   10–11. *knowledge…over*] ability to understand a woman.
   12. *neat, prating*] trim, eloquent.
   13. *confessed*] universally admitted.
   18. *want*] lack.
   19. *is pat*] falls out perfectly.
   *like*] likely (also at line 21).
   21. *frames to*] is shaping itself in accordance with.
   22–4. *Accius' tongue…he can*] an adaptation of a proverbial expression
regarding the indissolubility of marriage (Tilley, K167: 'He has tied a knot
with his tongue that he can't untie with all his teeth'). Lyly uses the same
saying in the context of Surius' marriage to Camilla in *England*: 'This was the
cause that we all meet here, that before this good company we might knit that
knot with our tongues that we shall never undo with our teeth' (p. 347).
   25. *kind*] friendly.

*Memphio.* [*Aside*] Well, here is Stellio. I'll talk of other
matters, and fly from the mark I shoot at, lapwing-like
flying far from the place where I nestle. [*More loudly*]
Stellio! What make you abroad? I heard you were sick          30
since our last drinking.
*Stellio.* You see reports are no truths. I heard the like of you,
and we are both well. I perceive sober men tell most lies,
for *in vino veritas*. If they had drunk wine, they would
have told the truth.                                         35
*Memphio.* Our boys will be sure, then, never to lie, for they
are ever swilling of wine. But, Stellio, I must strain
courtesy with you. I have business I cannot stay.
*Stellio.* In good time, Memphio, for I was about to crave your
patience to depart; it stands me upon. [*Aside*] Perhaps     40
move his patience ere it be long.

---

27. SD.] *Bond.*    29. SD.] *Bond (subst.)*.    33. lies] *Q1, Bl;* likes *Q2*
*(Boston and Huntington library copies only)*.    38. courtesy] *Daniel;* cursie *Q1,*
*2, Bl.*    40. SD.] *Dilke.*    41. be long] *Q2, Bl;* belong *Q1.*

28. *fly...shoot at*] aim wide of my true target (metaphor drawn from
archery).
28–9. *lapwing-like...nestle*] proverbial analogy, used by Lyly on a number
of occasions, drawn from the lapwing's strategy of feigning an injury to draw
potential predators away from its nest (Tilley, L68). Compare Hephestion's
accusation in *Campaspe* that, in denying his love for Timoclea rather than
for Campaspe, Alexander resembles 'the lapwing, who crieth most where
her nest is not' (2.2.11–12).
30. *What make you abroad?*] What are you doing out of doors?
34. *in vino veritas*] in wine there is truth (proverbial: Tilley, W465). John
Baret, *An Aluearie or Quadruple Dictionarie* (1580), notes of the saying: 'A
Proverbe vsed, when as a man being overseene with wine, doth euen vtter
the secretes of his minde' (I, entry 264).
37–8. *strain courtesy*] be less than mannerly. Lyly uses the same phrase in
*England,* where it appears to carry the opposite sense: 'At the last, though
long time straining courtesy who should go over the stile when we had both
haste, I...began first to unfold the extremities of my passions' (p. 347).
38. *I have...stay*] The introduction of a mark of punctuation following
'business' in all modern editions (see Appendix) obscures the probable sense
of the passage as represented by *Q1, 2, Bl.* Rather than apologizing for being
unable to remain ('I have business. I cannot stay here'), Memphio is feigning
sorrow that his business is too pressing to allow him to stop ('I have business
that I cannot defer').
39. *In good time*] That's fortunate.
40. *it stands me upon*] it's incumbent upon me. Compare *R2:* 'It stands
your grace upon to do him right' (2.3.137).

*Memphio.* [*Aside*] Good silly Stellio! We must buckle shortly.

*Exeunt.*

### Act[us] 3, Sce[na] 4

[*Enter*] LUCIO [*and*] RIXULA [*with clothes belonging to Livia, and*]
HALFPENNY [*with clothes belonging to Candius*].

*Lucio.* Come, Rixula, we have made thee privy to the whole
pack; there lay down the pack.
*Rixula.* I believe, unless it be better handled, we shall out of
doors.
*Halfpenny.* I care not. *Omnem solum forti patria*: I can live in          5
Christendom as well as in Kent.
*Lucio.* And I'll sing *Patria ubicunque bene*: every house is my
home where I may stanch hunger.

42. SD.] *Dilke.*

0.1–2.] *Bond (subst.); Halfepenie. Luceo. Rixula. Dromio. Risio. / Q1, 2
(Lucio), Bl.*    1. the whole] *Q1;* our whole *Q2, Bl.*

___

42. *silly*] simple.
*buckle*] clash.

01–2.] Though Lucio and Rixula enter with Livia's clothes, and Halfpenny
with Candius' clothes, inviting the supposition that they emerge separately
from the houses of their masters, the ensuing dialogue appears to suggest
that they are already in conversation at the start of the scene, and that they
therefore enter together along the street.
    2. *pack...pack*] plot (cf. *MWW*, 4.2.112–13: 'there's a knot, a gin, a pack,
a conspiracy against me')...bundle.
    3–4. *out of doors*] be turned out (i.e. dismissed).
    5. Omnem solum forti patria] Every land is to the brave his own country
(Ovid, *Fa.*, i, 493).
    5–6. *I can...Kent*] a variant of the proverbial expression, 'Neither in Kent
nor Christendom' (Tilley, K16). The phrase occurs in the September
eclogue of Spenser's *The Shepherd's Calendar* (1579) where it is accompanied
by the note: 'This saying seemeth to be strange and unreasonable; but indeed
it was wont to be an old proverb and common phrase. The original whereof
was, for that most part of England in the reign of King Ethelbert was chris-
tened, Kent only excepted, which remained long after in misbelief and
unchristened: So that Kent was counted no part of Christendom' (quoted
from Henderson, p. 78). *Christendom* = any part of the Christian world.
    7. Patria ubicunque bene] One's country is wherever one does well. The
phrase has its origins in Pacuvius' *Teucer* (see LCL, *Remains of Old Latin*, ii,
p. 302), but is used by Cicero, as Bond notes (iii, p. 546), in his *Tusculanarum
Disputationum* (v, 37). The LCL edition of Cicero reads, '*patria est ubi-
cumque est bene*'.
    8. *stanch*] staunch, assuage.

*Rixula.* Nay, if you set all on hazard, though I be a poor
   wench I am as hardy as you both. I cannot speak Latin,    10
   but in plain English, if anything fall out cross, I'll run
   away.

*Halfpenny.* He loves thee well that would run after.

*Rixula.* Why, Halfpenny, there's no goose so grey in the lake
   that cannot find a gander for her make.    15

*Lucio.* I love a nut-brown lass. 'Tis good to recreate.

*Halfpenny.* Thou meanest a brown nut is good to crack.

*Lucio.* Why, would it not do thee good to crack such a nut?

*Halfpenny.* I fear she is worm-eaten within, she is so moth-
   eaten without.    20

*Rixula.* [*Offended*] If you take your pleasure of me, I'll in and
   tell your practices against your masters.

*Halfpenny.* In faith, sour heart, he that takes his pleasure on
   thee is very pleasurable.

---

21. SD.] *This ed.*

---

9. *set all on hazard*] are prepared to risk everything.

10. *hardy*] brave.

11. *cross*] adversely.

13. *run after*] pursue you.

14–15. *there's no…make*] there's no woman, however seemingly unattractive, that cannot find a partner (proverbial: Tilley G362). Tydeman (p.
419) cites Chaucer's 'The Wife of Bath's Tale': 'Ne noon so grey goos gooth
ther in the lake / As…wol been withoute make' (Robinson, III (D), 269–70).
For a comparable use of the term *make* (= mate), cf. *Anatomy*: 'The wolf
chooseth him for her make that hath or doth endure most travail for her
sake' (p. 82).

16. *nut-brown lass*] dark-complexioned girl. Andreadis (p. 152) cites
Randle Cotgrave's *A Dictionarie of the French and English Tongues* (1611),
which notes under 'Fille': 'Fille brunette est de nature gaye, & nette: Prov.
*The nut-browne lasse for mirth and neatnesse doth surpasse*'.

*recreate*] enjoy yourself (with sexual implications, as Halfpenny suggests
in the following line).

17. *a brown…crack*] (*a*) dark nuts are worth the trouble of breaking open;
(*b*) dark-complexioned girls are well worth seducing.

18. *would it…nut?*] (*a*) wouldn't you enjoy eating such a nut?; (*b*)
wouldn't it lift your spirits to make love to a girl like that?

19–20.] She's so ravaged externally, I'm afraid she may be inwardly
diseased.

21. *take your pleasure of*] (*a*) make fun of (the meaning Rixula intends);
(*b*) enjoy yourself sexually with (the unintended implication exploited by
Halfpenny at line 23–4 below).

22. *practices*] plots.

23. *sour heart*] a parodic endearment (cf. sweet heart).

24. *very pleasurable*] easily pleased.

*Rixula.* You mean knavishly; and yet, I hope, foul water will    25
    quench hot fire as soon as fair.

*Halfpenny.* [*Placating her*] Well then, let fair words cool that
    choler which foul speeches hath kindled. And because we
    are all in this case, and hope all to have good fortune,
    sing a roundelay, and we'll help, such as thou wast wont    30
    when thou beatest hemp.

*Lucio.* It was crabs she stamped, and stole away one to make
    her a face!

*Rixula.* I agree, in hope that the hemp shall come to your
    wearing. A halfpenny halter may hang you both; that is,    35
    Halfpenny and you may hang in a halter.

*Halfpenny.* Well brought about.

*Rixula.* 'Twill, when 'tis about your neck.

*Lucio.* Nay, now she's in, she will never out.

---

27. SD.] *This ed.*    28. speeches] *Q1;* words *Q2, Bl.*

---

25. *knavishly*] to be mischievously malicious.

25–6. *foul water…fair*] i.e. a plain woman will satisfy the sexual appetite
as much as a beautiful one (proverbial: Tilley, W92). Compare *England*:
'Hot fire is not only quenched by the clear fountain, nor love only satisfied
by the fair face' (p. 293).

28. *choler*] anger.

30. *roundelay*] song with a recurring refrain.
*wast wont*] were acustomed to do.

31. *when…hemp*] a further slight upon Rixula in that, as Dilke notes
(p. 245), 'Persons confined for small offences in the house of correction
[were] employed in beating hemp' (a preliminary process in the manu-
facture of rope). The imputation carries a bawdy double meaning (sustained in the song that follows), in that, as Lancashire indicates, 'It is
almost impossible to avoid the conclusion that "beating hemp" meant
sexual intercourse to Elizabethans' (p. 240).

32. *crabs*] crab apples. The fruit was pressed by treading (hence *she
stamped*) and used for the production of verjuice (a sour juice employed for
a variety of culinary purposes).

32–3. *make her a face*] turn her face sour.

34–5. *that the…wearing*] that you will eventually wear the hemp yourself
(i.e. be hung by the rope made from its fibres).

36. *halter*] noose.

37. *Well brought about*] (*a*) a clever twist or riposte (Halfpenny's meaning);
(*b*) a good turn of the rope (the sense upon which Rixula's response depends
in the next line).

39. *she's in…out*] she's got started, she will never leave matters alone.

*Rixula.* Nor when your heads are in, as it is likely, they should　　40
　　　not come out. But hearken to my song.

　　　　　　　　　　　　　　　　　　　　　　*Cantant.*

　　　　　　　　　　　SONG

*Rixula.*　　Full hard I did sweat,
　　　　　　When hemp I did beat,
　　　　　　Then thought I of nothing but hanging.
　　　　　　The hemp being spun,　　　　　　　　　45
　　　　　　My beating was done;
　　　　　　Then I wished for a noise
　　　　　　Of crack-halter boys
　　　　　　On those hempen strings to be twanging.
　　　　　　Long looked I about,　　　　　　　　　50
　　　　　　The city throughout –
*Boys.*　　　And found no such fiddling varlets.

---

41.1.] *Q1, 2, Bl. Not distinguished as SD. from previous speech in Q1, 2 (*song,
*Cantant.).*　41.2–61.] *Bl. Not in Q1, 2.*　52, 55, 60. SP.] *This ed.; 4.* Pag.
*(i.e.* Pages) / *Bl (*4. Pa. *at line 60).*

　　40. *in*] in the noose.
　　41.1. Cantant.] They sing.
　　41.2–61.] omitted from the quartos, in common with the rest of the
songs in the play. The text is derived here from the edition of 1632, but
emends the speech prefixes at lines 52, 55, and 60 in view of the inap-
propriateness of the term 'Page' (see collation note) to the world of the
play. Blount's assignment of these lines to all four youths is clearly erroneous in that Dromio and Risio enter severally after the song is over, and
their opening lines establish that they are not party to the previous exchange
(see lines 62–3 below). Daniel's repositioning of their entrance to allow
for their participation in the song (see Appendix) is untenable in that it
runs counter to the tenor of their opening comments.
　　42–3.] See line 31n. for the bawdy innuendo here.
　　44.] attributable to the fact that the hemp will be used for the making of
rope, but also capable, according to Lancashire (p. 239), of referring to
'sexual play'. For similar word-play on the sexual connotations of hanging,
see 5.3.38–40 below and *Midas,* 1.2.39ff.
　　47. *noise*] band of musicians. Compare *2H4*: 'see if thou canst find out
Sneak's noise. Mistress Tearsheet would fain hear some music' (2.4.9–11).
　　48. *crack-halter boys*] boys destined for the gallows.
　　49.] (*a*) to be strumming on those cords (with a possible sexual innuendo); (*b*) to be making those hangman's ropes twang with their weight.
　　52. *fiddling varlets*] string-playing rogues (with a possible sexual innuendo: *fiddling* = engaging in sexual intercourse).

*[handwritten note:]* This play is basically a musical – not just songs but dialogue in song

| *Rixula.* | Yes, at last, coming hither, |
| | I saw four together – |
| *Boys.* | May thy hemp choke such singing harlots! |   55
| *Rixula.* | 'Tu-whit, tu-whoo', the owl does cry, |
| | 'Phip, phip', the sparrows as they fly; |
| | The goose does hiss, the duck cries, 'Quack', |
| | 'A rope', the parrot that holds tack. |
| *Boys.* | The parrot and the rope be thine. |   60
| *Rixula.* | The hanging yours, but the hemp mine! |

*Enter* DROMIO *[from Memphio's house with Accius' clothes,
and]* RISIO *[from Stellio's house with Silena's].*

*Dromio.* Yonder stands the wags. I am come in good time.
*Risio.* All here before me? You make haste.
*Rixula.* I believe, to hanging; for I think you have all robbed
your masters. Here's every man his baggage.          65

56–9.] *Quotation marks* / *Tydeman.*  61.1–2.] *from Memphio's house...from
Stellio's house* / *this ed.; other bracketed material* / *Tydeman (subst.); Enter
Dromio, Risio.* / Q1, 2 (subst.), Bl.

55. *singing harlots*] vocal whores (in both a literal and a sexual sense).
56–9.] All the birds and their cries have some association with sexual
activity, sustaining the multiple meanings of the previous lines. Williams
(1997) notes that, 'As a night bird [the owl] is associated with deeds
of darkness, including whoring and adultery' (p. 223), while its cry of
*Tu-whit, tu-whoo* is an exhortation to mate (cf. *Endymion*, 3.3.141–6);
the *sparrow* is traditionally associated with lechery; *goose* and *duck* were
colloquial terms for prostitute (see Williams, 1994); while *rope* was a
slang term for penis, frequently taught to parrots. For a full discussion
of Lyly's sexual word-play both here and in the context of jokes turning
upon the cry of the parrot, see Lancashire, *passim*, and Bevington, in
Hunter and Bevington, eds, *Galatea: Midas*, 1.2.45–6 LN).
59. '*A rope'*] prophetic cry of the parrot warning the boys of their inevi-
table fate.
*holds tack*] keeps unswervingly to one position (metaphor drawn from
sailing), i.e. the single cry it has been taught. Compare *Err.*: 'respect your
end, or rather, to prophesy like the parrot, beware the rope's end'
(4.4.43–5).
60.] May you have both the parrot and the noose.
61.] You may have the hanging but I will have the rope (i.e. the sexual
pleasure).
62–3.] The lines indicate that Dromio and Risio arrive separately rather
than together (cf. the entrance of Lucio, Rixula and Halfpenny at 0.1–2
above), while Rixula's comment at lines 64–5 suggests that they emerge, as
indicated here, from their masters' houses with the borrowed clothes.
65. *Here's...baggage*] Every man has a bundle.

*Halfpenny.* That is, we are all with thee; for thou art a very
　　baggage.

*Rixula.* Hold thy peace, or of mine honesty, I'll buy a
　　halfpenny purse with thee.

*Dromio.* Indeed, that's big enough to put thy honesty in. But　　70
　　come, shall we go about the matter?

*Lucio.* Now it is come to the pinch, my heart pants.

*Halfpenny.* I, for my part, am resolute. *In utrumque paratus:*
　　ready to die or to run away.

*Lucio.* But hear me. I was troubled with a vile dream, and　　75
　　therefore it is little time spent to let Mother Bombie
　　expound it. She is cunning in all things.

*Dromio.* Then will I know my fortune.

*Rixula.* And I'll ask for a silver spoon which was lost last day,
　　which I must pay for.　　　　　　　　　　　　　　　　　　80

*Risio.* And I'll know what will become of our devices.

*Halfpenny.* And I.

*Dromio.* Then let us all go quickly. We must not sleep in this
　　business, our masters are so watchful about it.

　　　　　[*They cross to Mother Bombie's house and knock.*]

　　　　[*The door opens to disclose* MOTHER BOMBIE
　　　　　　　　*seated on her stool.*]

*Mother Bombie.* Why do you rap so hard at the door?　　　　85

*Dromio.* Because we would come in.

*Mother Bombie.* Nay, my house is no inn.

*Halfpenny.* [*Aside*] Cross yourselves; look how she looks!

---

73. *utrumque*] *Dilke; untranque* / *Q1; utramque* / *Q2, Bl.*　84.1–3.] *This ed.;*
*no entry marked in Q1, 2, Bl. They knock at Bombie's door.* / *Dilke; Bond sup-*
*plies* / *Enter* MOTHER BOMBIE. / *following Dilke's direction.*　88. SD.]
*Tydeman.*

---

67. *baggage*] strumpet.
68. *of mine honesty*] female (lower-class) equivalent of 'on my honour'.
70. *honesty*] chastity.
73. In utrumque paratus] Prepared to go in either direction.
79. *last day*] yesterday.
81. *become*] be the outcome.
84.1–3] See 2.3.93.1–2n. for a discussion of the stage directions relating
to encounters with Mother Bombie in this edition.
88. *Cross yourselves*] Make the sign of the cross (as a defence against the
evil implied by her looks).

*Dromio.* [*Aside*] Mark her not; she'll turn us all to apes!

*Mother Bombie.* What would you with me?       90

*Risio.* They say you are cunning, and are called the good
     woman of Rochester.

*Mother Bombie.* If never to do harm be to do good, I dare say
     I am not ill. But what's the matter?

*Lucio.* I had an ill dream, and desire to know the    95
     signification.

*Mother Bombie.* Dreams, my son, have their weight. Though
     they be of a troubled mind, yet are they signs of fortune.
     Say on.

*Lucio.* In the dawning of the day, for about that time by my    100
     starting out of my sleep I found it to be, methought I saw
     a stately piece of beef, with a cape cloak of cabbage,
     embroidered with pepper, having two honourable pages
     with hats of mustard on their heads, himself in great
     pomp, sitting upon a cushion of white brewish, lined with    105
     brown bread. Methought, being powdered, he was much

89. SP.] *Q1 (Dro.); not in Q2, Bl.* SD.] *Tydeman.* 95. an] *Q2, Bl;* a
*Q1.* 106. powdered] *Dilke;* poudred *Q1;* powdred *Q2, Bl.*

89. *Mark her not*] Don't look at her.
*she'll turn...apes*] The exclamation betrays Dromio's fear that Mother
Bombie has diabolic powers, and is capable of robbing those who approach
her of their souls. Andreadis notes that Robert Burton in *The Anatomy
of Melancholy* (1676 ed.) claims that 'Sorcerers, Witches, Inchanters,
Charmers...can...alter and turn themselves and others into several forms, at
their pleasures' (quoted from Andreadis, p. 157). Compare the transformation
of Dick into an ape by Mephostophilis in scene x of Marlowe's *Doctor Faustus*.
     94. *ill*] bad (also at line 95 below).
     100. *In the. . . day*] The timing of the dream is significant in that dreams
in the early hours of the morning were proverbial for their truth (Tilley,
D591). Tilley cites, among other examples, Palsgrave's *Acolastus*: 'After
mydnyght men saye, that dreames be true'.
     102. *cape cloak*] cloak with a short, integrated cape over the shoulders for
extra protection against the weather, used here as a metaphor for the cabbage
leaves encasing the beef. Compare *Pappe with an Hatchet*: 'He shall not bee
brought in as whilom he was...but in a cap'de cloake, and all the best apparell he ware the highest day in the yeare' (Bond, iii, p. 408). The following
lines sustain the image of the beef as a powerful nobleman sitting in state.
     104. *himself* ] the beef.
     105. *pomp*] state.
     *brewish*] bread soaked in broth.
     106. *powdered*] salted (referring to the powder used by those of high rank).

troubled with the salt rheum, and therefore there stood
by him two great flagons of sack and beer, the one to dry
up his rheum, the other to quench his choler. I, as one
envying his ambition, hungering and thirsting after his    110
honour, began to pull his cushion from under him,
hoping by that means to give him a fall; and with putting
out my hand awaked, and found nothing in all this dream
about me but the salt rheum.

*Dromio.* A dream for a butcher!                            115

*Lucio.* Soft, let me end it. Then I slumbered again, and
methought there came in a leg of mutton.

*Dromio.* What, all gross meat? A rack had been dainty.

*Lucio.* Thou fool! How could it come in, unless it had been
a leg? Methought his hose were cut, and drawn out with    120
parsley. I thrust my hand into my pocket for a knife,
thinking to hox him, and so awaked.

*Mother Bombie.* Belike thou wentst supperless to bed.

---

107. troubled] *Bl;* trobled *Q1;* troubed *Q2.*    108. sack] *Q1;* wine *Q2,*
*Bl.*    113. hand awaked] *Q1* (awakt)*;* hand I awakt *Q2, Bl.*    119–20. in,
unless...leg?] *Punctuation as Q2 (ten extant copies, see Introduction, n. 20),*
*Bl;* in, vnlesse it had bin a leg, *Q1;* in? vnlesse it had bin a leg, *Q2 (Boston*
*and Huntington copies only).*

---

107. *rheum*] watery matter secreted from the mucous glands, specifically
from the eyes or nasal organs. Compare *Err.*, 3.2.128, 'the salt rheum that
ran between France and [England]', as a metaphor for streaming eyes and
a runny nose. The image refers to the juices running from the joint.

108–9. *the one... rheum*] the sack to dehydrate him (and thus dry up the
mucous matter emanating from him).

109. *the other...choler*] the beer to cool him down. (Choler, one of the
four humours, was associated with excessive heat.)

110. *ambition*] pride of state.

112. *give him a fall*] bring him down.

114. *salt rheum*] watery matter (see line 107n. above), in this case tears.

116. *Soft*] Wait a moment.

118. *gross meat*] large joints, lacking in delicacy.

*rack*] neck or ribs (usually of mutton) served in broth or as one or more
chops.

120–1. *his hose...parsley*] an allusion to the slashed hose fashionable in
the late sixteenth century which allowed material of a complementary colour
or texture to show through. The image refers to the parsley dressing the joint.

122. *hox him*] cut his hamstrings.

123.] Dreaming of food when hungry is cited by Bateman as an example
of the soul seeing 'suche Images and lykenesse of things, as it assayeth

*Lucio.* So I do every night but Sundays. Prisius hath a weak
    stomach, and therefore we must starve.                    125
*Mother Bombie.* Well, take this for answer, though the dream
    be fantastical:
        They that in the morning sleep dream of eating
        Are in danger of sickness, or of beating,
        Or shall hear of a wedding fresh a-beating.                130
*Lucio.* This may be true.
*Halfpenny.* Nay then, let me come in with a dream, short
    but sweet, that my mouth waters ever since I waked.
    Methought there sat upon a shelf three damask prunes
    in velvet caps and pressed satin gowns, like judges; and   135
    that there were a whole handful of currants to be arraigned
    of a riot, because they clunged together in such clusters.
    Twelve raisins of the sun were empanelled in a jury, and
    as a leaf of whole mace, which was bailiff, was carrying

---

128–30.] *Lineation as Dilke; continuous prose in Q1, 2, Bl.*    137. of a riot] *Q1;*
of riot *Q2, Bl.*    138. raisins] *Andreadis;* raisons *Q1, 2, Bl.*

---

sometime waking'. Compare: 'he that is an hungred dreameth of meate, and
a dronken man that is thirstie, dreameth of drinke' (*Batman vppon Bartholome,
his booke De proprietatibus Rerum*, 1582, vi, 27: Pvr, Pvv). *Belike* = I presume.
    128–30.] printed as prose in *Q1, 2, Bl*, in common with Mother Bombie's
prophecies throughout. The lineation here, as at lines 155–7, 161–3, 174–6,
and 189–91 below, follows Dilke (see collation note).
    130. *fresh a-beating*] being newly hammered out (i.e. in the making).
    132–3. *short but sweet*] proverbial (Tilley, S396). Compare *R2*: 'The word
[pardon] is short, but not so short as sweet' (5.3.115).
    134. *damask prunes*] damsons (with a bawdy implication, in that 'stewed
prune' was a colloquial term for prostitute).
    135. *pressed satin*] type of satin fabric produced by the application of
heat (*OED*, Pressed, *ppl.a.*[1]. Fairholt (ii, p. 275) glosses *pressed* as 'glazed'
but supplies no supporting evidence that the word was capable of bearing
this meaning.
    136–7. *arraigned of*] brought to trial accused of.
    137. *because they clunged…clusters*] an allusion to the continuing fear of
civic authorities of large gatherings of people (defined in the reign of George
I as twelve or more). The sticky character of currents causes them to adhere
to one anther, forming gatherings comparable to clusters of people engaged
in a public disturbance. *clunged* = clung.
    138. *raisins of the sun*] Bond notes: '"sun-raisins" are raisins dried on the
vine, the leaves being removed, and the cluster-stem sometimes half-severed'
(iii, p. 547).
    139. *mace*] the outer covering of the nutmeg, used as a spice. The choice
of spice is appropriate to the figure it represents in that a bailiff carried a

the quest to consult, methought there came an angry　140
cook, and gelded the jury of their stones, and swept both
judges, jurors, rebels, and bailiff into a porridge pot.
Whereat I, being melancholy, fetched a deep sigh that
waked myself and my bedfellow.

*Dromio.* This was devised, not dreamed, and the more　145
foolish, being no dream, for that dreams excuse the
fantasticalness.

*Halfpenny.* Then ask my bedfellow – you know him – who
dreamed that night that the King of Diamonds was
sick.　　　　　　　　　　　　　　　　　　　　150

*Mother Bombie.* But thy years and humours, pretty child, are
subject to such fancies, which, the more unsensible they
seem, the more fantastical they are. And therefore this
dream is easy:

　To children this is given from the gods,　　　155
　To dream of milk, fruit, babies, and rods.
　They betoken nothing, but that wantons must
　　have rods.

*Dromio.* Ten to one thy dream is true. Thou wilt be swinged.

---

152. unsensible] *Q1;* vincible *Q2, Bl.*　155–7.] *Lineation as Dilke; continuous prose in Q1, 2, Bl. (Also at lines 161–3 below.)*

mace (i.e. a staff of office) as a symbol of his authority. Compare the word-play surrounding the Sergeant's mace at 5.3.436–42.

139–40. *carrying the quest*] leading away the jury (*quest* = inquest).

141. *stones*] (*a*) grape pips; (*b*) testicles.

146. *for that*] because.

148–50. *who dreamed...sick*] The response bears out Mother Bombie's contention at lines 155–7 below that children dream of things pertinent to their own concerns. The boys dream of food, the process of the law, and playing cards.

151. *humours*] capricious disposition (a product of the relationship between the four elements making up the human body).

152–3. *unsensible they seem*] removed they appear to be from the world apprehended through the senses.

153. *fantastical they are*] they spring from the imagination.

155–7.] See 128–30n. above.

156. *babies*] dolls.

157. *betoken...rods*] signify nothing except that naughty children must be beaten.

158. *swinged*] thrashed.

*Rixula.* Nay, gammer, I pray you tell me, who stole my spoon
    out of the buttery?                                                          160
*Mother Bombie.* Thy spoon is not stolen, but mislaid;
    Thou art an ill housewife, though a good maid;
    Look for thy spoon where thou hadst like to be no
      maid.
*Rixula.* Body of me! Let me fetch the spoon. I remember the
    place!                                          [*She makes to leave.*]   165
*Lucio.* [*Detaining her*] Soft, swift! The place, if it be there now,
    it will be there tomorrow.
*Rixula.* Ay, but perchance the spoon will not.
*Halfpenny.* Wert thou once put to it?
*Rixula.* No, sir boy, it was put to me.                                       170
*Lucio.* How was it missed?
*Dromio.* I'll warrant for want of a mist. But what's my fortune,
    mother?                                          [*He shows her his hand.*]

---

159. gammer] *Q1, 2;* Grammer *Bl.*   165. SD.] *This ed.*   166. SD.] *This
ed.*   167. it will] *Q1;* will *Q2, Bl.*   168. Ay] *Andreadis;* I *Q1, 2, Bl.*
171. missed] *Daniel;* mist *Q1, 2, Bl.*   173. SD.] *This ed.*

159. *gammer*] contraction of 'grandmother', used in rural communities as
a title, or form of address to an elderly woman (cf. the title-figure of *Gammer
Gurton's Needle*).
   160. *buttery*] room for the storage of provisions, specifically ale, bread,
and butter (from Old French *boterie* = *bouteillerie*).
   161-3.] See 128-30n. above.
   162. *ill housewife*] poor housekeeper.
   *good maid*] well-intentioned young woman.
   163. *where thou...maid*] where you were in danger of losing your
virginity.
   *maid*] virgin.
   164. *Body of me*] exclamation denoting surprise or distress.
   166. *Soft, swift*] variant of the proverb 'Soft and fair goes far' (Tilley,
S601), implying that haste is not necessarily productive of speed. Compare
'Make haste slowly' (Tilley, H192), and 'The more haste the less speed'
(Tilley, H198).
   168. *perchance*] perhaps.
   169. *put to it*] obliged to defend your virginity.
   170. *it was put to me*] I was the object of a sexual advance.
   171.] How did the attempt fail?
   172. *I'll warrant...mist*] Tydeman takes the jibe (which depends on a play
on the homophones *missed* and *mist*) to mean that 'there was nothing to
conceal the fact that it [Rixula's virginity] had gone' (p. 420), but it seems
more likely that the comment is a further reflection on the girl's lack of beauty
(i.e. there was nothing to hide her plainness from her would-be seducer).

*Mother Bombie.* Thy father doth live because he doth dye,
    Thou hast spent all thy thrift with a die,                    175
    And so like a beggar thou shalt die.
*Risio.* I would have liked well if all the gerunds had been
    there: *di*, *do*, and *dum*. But all in die, that's too deadly.
*Dromio.* My father indeed is a dyer, and I have been a dicer;
    but to die a beggar, give me leave not to believe, Mother    180
    Bombie. And yet it may be. I have nothing to live by but
    knavery, and if the world grow honest, welcome beggary!
    But what hast thou to say, Risio?
*Risio.* Nothing, till I see whether all this be true that she hath
    said.                                                         185
*Halfpenny.* [*To Dromio*] Ay, Risio would fain see thee beg.
*Risio.* Nay, mother, tell us this: what is all our fortunes? We
    are about a matter of legerdemain; how will it fodge?

---

174–6] *Lineation as Dilke; continuous prose in Q1, 2, Bl.*    174. dye] *Dilke;*
die *Q1, 2, Bl.*    179. and] *Dilke;* but *Q1, 2, Bl.*    180. believe, Mother] *punctuation as Bond;* belccue Mother / *Q1, 2 (*mother*), Bl.*    186. SD.] *Tydeman.*
Ay] *Andreadis; I Q1, 2, Bl.*

174–6.] See 128–30n. above.
174. *he doth dye*] he earns his living by dyeing cloth (initiating the punning on 'die' in the following lines).
175.] You have squandered all your resources gambling at dice.
*die*] singular of dice.
177. SP.] The differentiation between *Ri.* = Risio and *Rix.* = Rixula in the speech prefixes in this scene in all early editions supports Dilke's assumption that it is Risio who is the speaker here, rather than Rixula, as indicated by Andreadis (see Appendix). The fact that Rixula announces her ignorance of Latin at the start of the scene (see line 10 above) also works against the proposition that a joke turning on the niceties of Latin grammar should be assigned to her.
177–8.] As Tydeman notes, 'all Latin verbs have a gerund form, which compares roughly to the English verbal noun ending in "-ing". Its case-endings are *-dum*, *-di*, *-do*' (p. 420). Risio jokes that Mother Bombie's prophecy, with its insistent *die* endings, has a much more ominous ring than would have been the case had she employed more gerunds.
182. *if the…beggary*] should cheating cease to be a natural condition of the world, then I am happy to be a beggar (i.e. it's very unlikely that there will never be a place for someone like me).
186. *fain*] gladly.
187. *mother*] polite term of address used towards an old woman.
*what…fortunes*] what will be the outcome of our joint enterprise.
188. *about…legerdemain*] engaged in a piece of sleight of hand.
*fodge*] work out, succeed.

*Mother Bombie.* You shall all thrive like cozeners,
  That is, to be cozened by cozeners;     190
  All shall end well, and you be found cozeners.
*Dromio.* Gramercy, Mother Bombie! We are all pleased, if
  you were for your pains.
*Mother Bombie.* I take no money, but good words. Rail not if
  I tell true; if I do not, revenge. Farewell.    195
         [*Mother Bombie's door closes.*]
*Dromio.* Now have we nothing to do but to go about this
  business. [*To Halfpenny*] Accius' apparel let Candius put
  on, and I will array Accius with Candius' clothes.
*Risio.* Here is Silena's attire. – Lucio, put it upon Livia, and
  give me Livia's for Silena. This done, let Candius and  200
  Livia come forth; and let Dromio and me alone for the rest.
*Halfpenny.* What shall become of Accius and Silena?
*Dromio.* Tush, their turn shall be next. All must be done
  orderly. Let's to it, for now it works!    *Exeunt.*

---

189–91.] *Lineation as Dilke; continuous prose in Q1, 2, Bl.* 192. Gramercy.
..We] *Punctuation as Tydeman;* Gramercie mother *Bombie,* we *Q1, 2
(Mother), Bl.* 195.1.] *This ed.; Exit Bom.* / *Q1, 2, Bl.* 197. SD.] *This ed.*

189–91.] See 128–30n. above. *cozeners* = tricksters.
192. *Gramercy*] Many thanks (French '*grand merci*').
192–3. *We are all…pains*] No agreement exists among editors over the
meaning of Dromio's response, or the stage business involved. Bond (iii, p.
547) supposes *if you were* to be an abbreviated form of '[if you were] found
cozener, or cozened', implying that Dromio believes that Mother Bombie is
a fraudster, and that they will be pleased if she is cozened in turn. Tydeman,
by contrast, interpolates a stage direction, '*Offers her money*', following *pains,*
and notes that Bond's gloss 'hardly accords with [Dromio's] thanks or offer
of money', paraphrasing the response as, 'If you were happy to tell our
fortunes, we are thankful for the trouble you took' (p. 420). In fact, there is
no textual indication that Dromio offers money, and a readiness to pay
accords with neither the indigence of the boys nor their impudent indifference to financial obligations (compare their evasion of payment for their
wine in 2.3, and treatment of the Hackneyman in 4.2 and 5.3). It seems
more probable that Dromio's response means that everyone will be pleased,
including Mother Bombie, if she took pleasure in the trouble she took in
telling their fortunes, as that will be all the reward she will get.
194. *I take…words*] taken by Tydeman as a repudiation of the payment
offered by Dromio (see previous note), but more likely to be an assertion of
indifference to his refusal to pay, in that no money was expected (see p. 12
above), and that civility (or a favourable report) is all that Mother Bombie
looks for in those that who seek her aid.
 *Rail not*] Don't blame me.
201. *let Dromio…rest*] leave the rest to Dromio and me.

# Act 4

Act[us] 4, Sce[na] 1

[*Enter*] LIVIA [*and*] CANDIUS [*dressed as Silena and Accius*].

*Livia.* This attire is very fit; but how if this make me a fool,
and Silena wise? You will then woo me, and wed her.

*Candius.* Thou knowest that Accius is also a fool, and his
raiment fits me; so that if apparel be infectious, I am
also like to be a fool, and he wise. What would be the      5
conclusion, I marvel.

*Enter* DROMIO [*and*] RISIO.

*Livia.* Here comes our counsellors.

*Dromio.* Well said. I perceive turtles fly in couples.

*Risio.* Else how should they couple?

*Livia.* So do knaves go double, else how should they be so     10
cunning in doubling?

*Candius. Bona verba*, Livia.

*Dromio.* I understand Latin. That is 'Livia is a good word'.

*Candius.* No, I bid her use good words.

*Risio.* And what deeds?                                         15

*Candius.* None but a deed of gift.

*Risio.* What gift?

*Candius.* Her heart.

0.1.] *This ed.; Candius, Liuia, Dromio, Risio, Sperantus, Prisius. / Q1, 2
(subst.), Bl; Enter* CANDIUS *and* LIVIA, *in the clothes of* ACCIUS *and* SILENA,
*respectively. / Bond (following listing of characters' names as in early eds).*   5. fool,
and he wise. What] *Punctuation as Daniel;* foole, and hee wist what *Q1, 2
(*he*), Bl.* wise] *Dilke;* wist *Q1, 2, Bl.*   13. 'Livia...word'] *Quotation
marks / Daniel.*

1. *fit*] (*a*) well-fitting (cf. *TGV*, 4.4.159–60: 'Which served me as fit, by
all men's judgements, / As if the garment had been made for me'; (*b*) becom-
ing (in being of better quality than the clothes to which Livia is
accustomed).

8. *turtles*] turtle doves (see 1.3.133–4n.).

*in couples*] in pairs.

9. *couple*] mate.

10. *double*] in twos.

11. *doubling*] trickery.

*Dromio.* Give me leave to pose you, though you be a graduate;
  for I tell you, we in Rochester spur so many hackneys  20
  that we must needs spur scholars, for we take them for
  hackneys.
*Livia.* Why so, sir boy?
*Dromio.* Because I knew two hired for ten groats apiece to say
  service on Sunday, and that's no more than a post-horse  25
  from hence to Canterbury.
*Risio.* He knows what he says, for he once served the
  post-master.
*Candius.* Indeed, I think he served some post to his master.
  But come, Dromio, post me.  30
*Dromio.* You say you would have her heart for a deed?
*Candius.* Well.
*Dromio.* If you take her heart for *cor*, that heart in her body,
  then know this: *Molle eius levibus, cor enim inviolabile telis,*

33. heart¹] *Q2, Bl;* hart *Q1.*

___

19. *pose you*] put a question to you.
 *though you be a graduate*] even though you are a learned man (whereas
Dromio is merely a servant).
 20–1. *spur so many hackneys...spur scholars*] urge on (by applying the
sharp instruments on our boots to) so many hired horses...ply the learned
with pointed questions. Bond notes in relation to the pun on *spur* here:
'simply the term of horsemanship applied, by established metaphor, to
scholastic disputation' (iii, p. 547).
 21–2. *we take...hackneys*] we regard them in the same way that we regard
hired horses. The comment depends on the fact, as Dromio explains in the
following lines, that scholars and post-horses could be hired for the same
price.
 24. *ten groats*] forty pence in pre-decimalization English currency. The
small size of the sum is a satiric reflection on the low value placed upon
scholarship during the period.
 26. *hence*] this place (i.e. Rochester). The distance from Rochester to
Canterbury is approximately 26 miles.
 28. *post-master*] person charged with the hiring out of horses at staging
posts on major routes, for both travellers and the dispatch of mail.
 29. *post to*] unapprehending fool for. Compare *AYL*, 4.1.8–9: 'JACQUES.
Why, 'tis good to be sad and say nothing. / ROSALIND. Why then, 'tis good
to be a post'.
 30. *post me*] chase after me with your wit (with a pun on *post* in the previous line).
 31. *her heart for a deed*] Livia's heart pledged to you.
 32. *Well*] (*a*) Yes; (*b*) What of it?
 33. cor] heart (Latin).
 34. *Molle...telis*] The line is taken from Ovid's *Heroides* (xv, 79) and
reads '*molle meum levibusque cor est violabile telis*' in the LCL edition ('Tender

a woman's heart is thrust through with a feather. If you          35
mean she should give a hart named *cervus*, then are you
worse, for *cornua cervus habet*, that is, to have one's hart
grow out at his head, which will make one ache at the
heart in their body.

*Enter* PRISIUS [*and*] SPERANTUS.

*Livia.* I beshrew your hearts. – I hear one coming; I know it     40
is my father by his coming.
*Candius.* What must we do?
*Dromio.* Why, as I told you; and let me alone with the old
men. Fall you to your bridal.
*Prisius.* Come, neighbour, I perceive the love of our children    45
waxeth key cold.
*Sperantus.* I think it was never but lukewarm.

---

36, 37. hart] *This ed.;* heart *Q1, 2, Bl.*    46. key] *Q1; not in Q2, Bl.*

is my heart, and easily pierced by the light shaft'). The errors in the quotation in the first quarto are preserved here in that they may be an index of
the uncertainty of Dromio's latinity, rather than a printing error as assumed
by Bond (iii, p. 547). Lyly uses the line in *Love's Metamorphosis* at 5.2.10–11,
again with the omission of *que* from *levibusque*, suggesting his immediate
source is William Lily's Latin grammar. For the process underlying the successive stages of the corruption of the passage in *Q1, 2, Bl* (see Appendix),
see Bond, iii, pp. 547–8.
    36. cervus] hart (Latin), i.e. male deer after its fifth year.
    37. cornua cervus habet] a hart has horns.
    37–8. have one's...head] have horns spring from one's forehead (a refer-
ence to the horns traditionally associated with cuckoldry).
    40. *I beshrew your hearts*] (a) A plague on your hearts (variation of the
commonplace expression, 'Beshrew your heart'); (b) A plague on your inces-
sant punning on *hearts/harts*.
    41. coming] gait. Dilke's emendation to 'coughing' (see Appendix) avoids
the repetition of 'coming' in the previous line, and is supported by references
to Prisius' cough elsewhere in the text (e.g. at 1.3.70–1). *Coming* is retained
here, however, as the emendation is without textual support, and the word
makes sense in the context.
    43–4. *let me...men*] leave the old men to me.
    44. *Fall...bridal*] You get on with your marriage. The injunction looks
forward to the exchange of vows between Candius and Livia at lines 51ff.
below.
    46. *key cold*] proverbial for a state of extreme coldness (Tilley, K23).
Compare *Luc.*: 'And then in key-cold Lucrece' bleeding stream / He falls'
(1774–5).

*Prisius.* Bavins will have their flashes, and youth their fancies;
the one as soon quenched as the other burnt. [*He sees the
disguised lovers.*] But who be these?                                    50
*Candius.* [*To Livia*] Here I do plight my faith, taking thee for
the staff of my age, and of my youth my solace.
*Livia.* [*To Candius*] And I vow to thee affection which nothing
can dissolve, neither the length of time, nor malice of
fortune, nor distance of place.                                          55
*Candius.* [*To Livia*] But when shall we be married?
*Livia.* [*To Candius*] A good question, for that one delay in
wedding brings an hundred dangers in the church. We
will not be asked, and a licence is too chargeable, and to
tarry till tomorrow too tedious.                                         60
*Dromio.* [*To Prisius and Sperantus*] There's a girl stands on
pricks till she be married!
*Candius.* [*To Livia*] To avoid danger, charge, and tedious-
ness, let us now conclude it in the next church.

---

49–50. SD.] *Andreadis (subst.)*.   51, 53, 56, 57. SD.] *This ed.*   59. too] *Q2,
Bl;* to *Q1.*   61. SD.] *This ed.; aside / Tydeman.*   63. SD.] *This ed.*

48. *Bavins*] bundles of brushwood, proverbial for the brightness and
speed with which they burn (Tilley, B107). Compare *Anatomy*: 'the bavin,
though it burn bright, is but a blaze' (p. 64).
51–6.] The exchange of marital vows between lovers constituted a legal
betrothal, or marriage *per verba de praesenti tempore*, in Elizabethan law (see
1.3.171–2n. above). While being legally binding in common law terms,
however, the ecclesiastical authorities required *per verba de praesenti* marriages to be solemnized in the presence of a priest. Hence Candius' question
at line 56.
58. *dangers in the church*] probably 'problems with the ecclesiastical
authorities' rather than 'risks attendant on the asking of the banns' as suggested by Bond (iii, p. 548).
59. *be asked*] have the banns called (formal announcements of a forth-
coming marriage, made in three successive weeks prior to a wedding in
Christian practice).
*licence*] permission to marry without the usual delays occasioned by the
calling of banns (see previous note).
*chargeable*] expensive.
61–2. *stands on pricks*] can't be still (i.e. is very eager), with a bawdy pun
on *pricks*.
63. *charge*] expense.
63–4.] Having conducted a private betrothal ceremony, the couple now
merely require the blessing of a priest to validate their marriage rather than
observing the usual formalities.
64. *next*] nearest.

*Livia.* [*To Candius*] Agreed.                                                65
*Prisius.* [*To Dromio*] What be these that hasten so to marry?
*Dromio.* Marry, sir, Accius, son to Memphio, and Silena,
    Stellio's daughter.
*Sperantus.* [*To Prisius*] I am sorry, neighbour, for our pur-
    poses are disappointed.                                                    70
*Prisius.* [*To Sperantus*] You see, marriage is destiny; made in
    heaven, though consummated on earth.
*Risio.* [*To Prisius and Sperantus*] How like you them? Be they
    not a pretty couple?
*Prisius.* Yes, God give them joy, seeing in spite of our hearts              75
    they must join.
*Dromio.* I am sure you are not angry, seeing things past
    cannot be recalled; and being witnesses to their contract,
    will be also well-willers to the match.
*Sperantus.* For my part, I wish them well.                                    80
*Prisius.* And I. And since there is no remedy, that I am glad
    of it.
*Risio.* But will you never hereafter take it in dudgeon, but
    use them as well as though yourselves had made the
    marriage?                                                                  85
*Prisius.* Not I.
*Sperantus.* Nor I.
*Dromio.* [*Approaching Candius and Livia*] Sir, here's two old
    men are glad that your loves, so long continued, is so
    happily concluded.                                                         90

---

65, 66, 69, 71, 73, SD.] *This ed.*   86. Not I] *Q2, Bl;* Not, I *Q1.*   88. SD.]
*This ed.; to* CANDIUS / *Tydeman.*

70. *disappointed*] frustrated.
71-2. *marriage...earth*] proverbial (Dent, M688). Compare Euphues'
comment regarding the unexpected marriages of Surius and Philautus in
*England*: 'marriages are made in heaven though consummated in earth' (p. 349).
75. *hearts*] desires.
78-87. *being witnesses...Nor I*] By enlisting the consent of Prisius and
Sperantus to the lovers' precontract, Dromio seeks to make them the unwitting accessories to a binding legal agreement (see lines 51-6n. above and
5.3.189-96 below).
83. *take it in dudgeon*] become angry about it.
84. *use*] treat.
86. *Not I*] No, I will not (be angry). Also *Nor I* at line 87.
89-90. *loves, so long...concluded*] The use of a plural subject in conjunction with a single verb is not uncommon in Elizabethan English when the
subject might be regarded as a composite entity. Compare 5.3.210-11 below.

*Candius.* We thank them; and if they will come to Memphio's
house they shall take part of a bad dinner. [*Aside*] This
cottons, and works like wax in a sow's ear.

                    *Exeunt* CANDIUS [*and*] LIVIA.

*Prisius.* [*To Sperantus*] Well, seeing our purposes are prevented, we must lay other plots; for Livia shall not have        95
Candius.

*Sperantus.* Fear not, for I have sworn that Candius shall not
have Livia. But let not us fall out because our children
fall in.

*Prisius.* Wilt thou go soon to Memphio's house?        100

*Sperantus.* Ay, and if you will, let us, that we may see how
the young couple bride it, and so we may teach our own.

                                        *Exeunt.*


                    Act[us] 4, Sce[na] 2

              *Enter* LUCIO [*and*] HALFPENNY.

*Lucio.* By this time I am sure the wags have played their parts.
There rests nothing now for us but to match Accius and
Silena.

---

92. bad] *Q1;* hard *Q2, Bl.*   SD.] *Bond.*   94. SD.] *This ed.*   95. other]
*Q1; not in Q2, Bl.*   101. Ay] *Dilke (*Aye*);* I *Q1, 2, Bl.*   will, let] *Bond;* will
let *Q1, 2, Bl.*

0.1.] *Dilke (subst.); Accius, Silena, Linceo, Halfepenie. / Q1, 2 (*Halfpenie*), Bl
(*Lincio, Halfpenie*).*

---

91–2. *Memphio's house*] In inviting Prisius and Sperantus to Memphio's
house, Candius is sustaining the pretence that he is Accius (preparing, in
terms of the structuring of the action, for the mounting confusion, and final
clarification, in Act 5).

92. *bad dinner*] probably intended not literally but as the conventional
show of modesty when extending an invitation. Compare the wealthy
Capulet's reference to 'my poor house' when inviting Paris to his 'old
accustom'd feast' (*R&J*, 1.2.24 and 20).

93. *cottons*] is all working according to plan.

*works...ear*] proverbial (Tilley, S599 and W138) for something accomplished with ease. See 3.2.2n. above.

98. *fall out*] quarrel.

99. *fall in*] have come together.

102. *bride it*] play the part of bride and groom (i.e. conduct themselves
at their wedding). Compare *Shrew*: 'Shall sweet Bianca practise how to bride
it?' (3.2.250).

2. *rests*] remains.

*Halfpenny.* It was too good to be true; for we should laugh
    heartily, and without laughing my spleen would split. But        5
    whist, here comes the man –

    *Enter* ACCIUS [*from Memphio's house, in Candius' clothes*].

    and yonder the maid. Let us stand aside.
                                          [*They stand aside.*]
    *Enter* SILENA [*from Stellio's house, in Livia's* clothes].

*Accius.* [*To himself*] What means my father to thrust me forth
    in another boy's coat? I'll warrant 'tis to as much purpose
    as a hem in the forehead.                                        10
*Halfpenny.* [*Aside to Lucio*] There was an ancient proverb
    knocked in the head!
*Accius.* [*To himself*] I am almost come into mine nonage, and
    yet I never was so far as the proverbs of this city.
*Lucio.* [*Aside to Halfpenny*] There's a quip for the suburbs of  15
    Rochester.
*Halfpenny.* [*Aside to Lucio*] Excellently applied.

---

6.1.] *from Memphio's house* / *this ed.; other bracketed material* / *Bond.*    7.1.] *This*
*ed.*    7.2.] *from Stellio's house* / *this ed.; other bracketed material* /
*Bond.*    8. SD.] *This ed.*    9. another boy's] *Dilke;* anothers boyes *Q1;* an
other boies *Q2, Bl.*    11. SD.] *This ed.; aside* / *Tydeman.*    13. SD.] *This ed.*
15, 17. SD.] *This ed; aside* / *Tydeman.*

---

4. *It was...true*] It would be too good to be true (if we accomplished the
meeting between the two fools).
    6. *whist*] hush.
    6.1, 7.1.] Though there are no stage directions in the three early editions
indicating that the simpletons enter from the houses of Memphio and Stellio
respectively, those supplied here are supported by Accius' resentment at
being *thrust...forth in another boy's coat* (lines 8–9) and the fact that Stellio
habitually keeps his daughter locked away.
    9–10. *as much...forehead*] probably a garbled version of 'As fat as a hen
in the forehead', proverbial for thinness rather than futility (Tilley, H416).
    13. *nonage*] minority (rather than majority, as Accius appears to
suppose).
    14. *yet...city*] The comment (depending upon a confusion between
'proverbs' and 'suburbs' as Lucio sardonically makes clear in the following
line) is unwittingly accurate, in that Accius consistently displays his lack of
mastery of proverbial sayings. The intended meaning appears to be that he
has never been beyond the city walls (see following note).
    15. *suburbs*] residential areas lying immediately outside or adjacent to
the city walls.

*Silena.* [*To herself*] Well, though this furniture make me a
sullen dame, yet I hope in mine own I am no saint.

*Halfpenny.* [*Aside to Lucio*] A brave fight is like to be between     20
a cock with a long comb and a hen with a long leg.

*Lucio.* [*Aside to Halfpenny*] Nay, her wits are shorter than her
legs.

*Halfpenny.* [*Aside to Lucio*] And his comb longer than his wit.

*Accius.* [*Seeing Silena*] I have yonder uncovered a fair girl. I'll     25
be so bold as spur her. [*To Silena*] What might a body
call her name?

*Silena.* I cannot help you at this time. I pray you, come again
tomorrow.

*Halfpenny.* [*Derisively aside*] Ay, marry, sir!                     30

*Accius.* You need not be so lusty. You are not so honest!

*Silena.* I cry you mercy, I took you for a joint stool.

*Lucio.* [*Aside to Halfpenny*] Here's courting for a conduit, or
a bake house!

*Silena.* But what are you for a man? Methinks you look as     35
pleaseth God.

18. SD.] *This ed.*   20, 22, 24. SD.]   *This ed.; aside / Tydeman.*   25. SD.] *This
ed.*   26. SD.] *Tydeman.*   30. SD.] *This   ed.;   aside   /   Tydeman.*   Ay]
*Andreadis;* I *Q1, 2, Bl.*   32. joint] *Bl (*ioynt*);* ioynd *Q1, 2.*   33, 38. SD.] *This
ed.; aside / Tydeman.*

18. *furniture*] apparel.
19. *sullen*] dull.
*in my own*] in my own clothes.
21. *cock with a long comb*] coxcomb (i.e. a fool).
*hen with a long leg*] bird able to move quickly away (i.e. to start from the
point). Though a number of proverbs turn on the behaviour of farmyard
fowl, no comparable example of the image has been traced.
25. *uncovered*] driven from cover (with an unintended bawdy innuendo).
The term derives from the hunting of game.
26. *spur her*] ply her with questions (see 4.1.20–1n.).
30. *Ay, marry, sir*] So much for you, sir.
31. You need not be so pert. You are not as chaste as all that.
32.] a proverbial apology (Tilley, M897) for failing to acknowledge that
someone is present (cf. *King Lear*, 3.6.51). A joint stool was one fitted together
from separate parts by a joiner, rather than roughly cut from a block.
33–4. *courting...bake house*] love-making at a water fountain or a bakery
(both places where the lowest classes gathered, and thus representative of a
simplistic style of conversation at odds with the speakers' social position).
35. *what are you for a man*] what kind of man are you.
35–6. *Methinks...God*] possibly a confused recollection of the proverb,
'God makes and apparel shapes but money makes the man' (Tilley, G206),
given that Accius is dressed in a poor man's clothes.

*Accius.* What? Do you give me the boots?

*Halfpenny.* [*Aside to Lucio*] Whether will they? Here be right
cobblers' cuts.

*Accius.* I am taken with a fit of love. Have you any mind of    40
marriage?

*Silena.* I had thought to have asked you.

*Accius.* Upon what acquaintance?

*Silena.* Who would have thought it?

*Accius.* Much in my gaskins, more in my round hose. All my    45
father's are as white as daisies, as an egg full of meat.

*Silena.* And all my father's plate is made of crimson velvet.

*Accius.* That's brave with bread.

---

45. gaskins] *Andreadis;* gascoins *Q1, 2;* gascoines *Bl.*   46. father's] *Fairholt;*
fathers *Q1, 2, Bl.*   47. crimson] *Q2, Bl;* Crimosin *Q1.*   48. That's] *Q2,
Bl (*thats*);* That *Q1.*

---

37. *Do you...boots*] Are you making fun of me (proverbial: Tilley, B537).
Compare *TGV*: 'VALENTINE. You are over boots in love.../ PROTEUS.
Over the boots? Nay, give me not the boots' (1.1.25-7).

38. *Whether will they?*] Where will they go to (in terms of their conversation) next? (*Whether* = whither.)

39. *cobblers' cuts*] unrelated bits and pieces (metaphor drawn from shoemaking, suggested by *boots* in the preceding speech).

42-4.] polite social exchanges devoid here of relevance or sense.

45. *Much in my...hose*] The phrase is explained by Andreadis by reference to a passage from Linthicum, pp. 208-9: 'Galligaskins [variant of
gaskins] were usually loose slops [wide breeches], but some followed the
bombast style [in which material was used to puff out the breeches]...this
bombasting, standing for pride, explains the expression..."Much in my
gascoins...more in my round hose"...for the round hose were padded
more than were the galligaskins...Taken literally it meant that more material was needed for round hose than for galligaskins...Thus a person
seemed great or fine in bombasted clothes, but was small without such
bombast' (quotation and explanatory glosses, Andreadis, p. 178). The
saying has no relevance here, other than as an index of the speaker's
vacuity.

46. *father's*] presumably 'father's gaskins', though the lack of an apostro-
phe in *Q1, 2, Bl* (see collation note) leaves the meaning open to doubt.

*an egg...meat*] Compare Halfpenny's use of the contents of an egg as a
measure of fullness at 2.1.81-2. The seemingly irrelevant image may have
been prompted here by the word *white* in the preceding comparison.
*meat* = edible matter.

47. *plate*] gold or silver tableware.

48. *brave*] excellent.

*Halfpenny.* [*Aside to Lucio*] These two had wise men to their
    fathers.                                                                50
*Lucio.* [*Aside to Halfpenny*] Why?
*Halfpenny.* [*Aside to Lucio*] Because when their bodies were
    at work about household stuff, their minds were busied
    about commonwealth matters.
*Accius.* [*Gesturing to some part of her costume*] This is pure      55
    lawn. What call you this? A preface to your hair?
*Silena.* Wisely you have picked a raisin out of a frail of figs.
*Accius.* Take it as you list; you are in your own clothes.
*Silena.* Saving a reverence, that's a lie. My clothes are better.
    My father borrowed these.                                          60
*Accius.* Long may he so do. I could tell that these are not
    mine, if I would blab it like a woman.
*Silena.* I had as lief you should tell them it snowed.

---

49. SD.] *This ed.; aside* / *Tydeman.*   two] *Dilke;* three *Q1, 2, Bl.*   51,
52. SD.] *This ed.; aside* / *Tydeman.*   55. SD.] *This ed.*   56. preface] *Q1;*
pretie face *Q2, Bl* (prettie).

49–54.] The comment depends upon the belief that the mental condition
of marital partners at the moment of conception affects the nature of the
child (cf. the discussion between Dromio and Memphio at 1.1.21–35 over
how Accius came to be a fool). Halfpenny attributes the blame here to the
inattention of Memphio and Stellio, in that their minds were on state business (*commonwealth matters*) rather than connubial affairs (*household stuff*).
    56. *lawn*] fine linen.
    *A preface…hair*] obscure. The *Q1* reading is retained here, as the alterna-
tive offered by *Q2, Bl* ('pretie face') and Dilke's emendation to 'heir' (see
Appendix) are equally difficult to interpret. Accius may simply be groping
for a term lost now beyond recovery.
    57.] The response has the ring of a proverbial expression, but no compa-
rable example has been traced.
    *frail*] rush basket.
    58. *list*] wish.
    *you are…clothes*] possibly another proverbial expression, but no compa-
rable example has been traced.
    59. *Saving a reverence*] polite apologetic formula (corruption of *salva rev-
erentia*), often prefacing a contradiction or objection. *a* = your.
    61. *Long may he so do*] gracious expression of approval, wholly inappropri-
ate in the context.
    62. *blab it*] blurt it out.
    63. *had as lief*] would be as glad (usually implying neither alternative to
be desirable). Compare *TN*: 'I would as lief be a Brownist as a politician'
(3.2.30–1).

*Lucio.* [*Aside to Halfpenny*] Come, let us take them off, for we
    have had the cream of them.                                   65
*Halfpenny.* [*Aside to Lucio*] I'll warrant if this be the cream,
    the milk is very flat. Let us join issue with them.
                [*They approach Accius and Silena.*]
*Lucio.* [*Aside to Halfpenny*] To have such issues of our bodies
    is worse than have an issue in the body. [*To Silena*] God
    save you, pretty mouse.                                          70
*Silena.* You may command and go without.
*Halfpenny.* [*Aside to Lucio*] There's a gleek for you! Let me
    have my gird. [*To Silena*] On thy conscience, tell me what
    'tis a clock.
*Silena.* I cry you mercy, I have killed your cushion.               75
*Halfpenny.* I am paid, and struck dead in the nest! I am sure
    this soft youth, who is not half so wise as you are fair,

---

64, 66. SD.] *This ed.; aside / Tydeman.*   67.1.] *This ed.*   68. SD.] *This ed.;
aside / Tydeman.*   69. SD.] *Bond.*   72. SD.] *Tydeman (subst.).*   a] *Q1; not
in Q2, Bl.*   73. SD.] *Bond.*   76. struck] *Dilke;* stroke *Q1;* strooke *Q2, Bl.*

---

64. *take them off* ] part them (term drawn from blood sports). Compare
*Mac.*: 'much drink may be said to be an equivocator with lechery…it sets
him on, and it takes him off' (2.3.31–3). The metaphor sustains the analogy
with cock fighting initiated at the start of the encounter (see lines 20–1
above).
    64–5. *we…them*] we have had the best of their conversation.
    67. *join issue*] enter into debate.
    68. *such issues*] children of this kind.
    69. *an issue*] a suppurating ulcer.
    70. *pretty mouse*] term of endearment employed towards a young woman.
Compare Feste's request to Olivia for a reply to his 'catechism' in *TN*: 'Good
my mouse of virtue, answer me' (1.5.59–60).
    71.] possibly a garbled variant of the proverb, 'Ask and have' (Tilley,
A343).
    72. *gleek*] taunting jest.
    73. *gird*] jibe.
    73–4. *what 'tis a clock*] what time it is.
    75. *cry you mercy*] beg your pardon.
    *I have…cushion*] possibly a confused recollection of 'to miss the cushion',
a proverbial expression for a failed endeavour (Tilley, C928), but as Tydeman
notes (p. 422), 'I kry you mercy, I kylled your cussheyn' appears under
'Crye' in John Palsgrave's *Lesclarcissement de la langue francoyse* (1530), sig.
CCCii, though no explanation is offered for the phrase.
    76. *paid*] mortally wounded with a counter-thrust.
    *dead…nest*] insensible (proverbial: Tilley, N123).
    77. *soft*] probably 'foolish' here rather than 'gentle', though *OED* does

nor you altogether so fair as he is foolish, will not be so
captious.

*Accius.* Your eloquence passes my recognizance.                    80

    *Enter [severally]* MEMPHIO *[and]* STELLIO *[unseen by
    one another, and initially by the servants].*

*Lucio.* I never heard that before. But shall we two make a
match between you?

*Silena.* I'll know first who was his father.

*Accius.* My father? What need you to care? I hope he was
none of yours.                                                      85

*Halfpenny.* [*Aside to Lucio*] A hard question, for it is odds but
one begat them both. He that cut out the upper leather
cut out the inner, and so with one awl stitched two soles
together.

*Stellio.* [*Aside to Lucio, having attracted his notice*] What is she?    90

*Lucio.* [*Aside to Stellio*] 'Tis Prisius' daughter.

---

80. passes] *Bl;* passe *Q1, 2.*     recognizance] *Dilke;* recognoscence *Q1, 2, Bl.*
80.1–2.] *This ed.; Enter Memphio, Stellio.* / *Q1, 2, Bl; Enter* MEMPHIO,
STELLIO *<severally behind>.* / *Bond.*    86. SD.] *Tydeman (subst.)*    90. SP.]
*Bond (correcting this and the five subsequent speech prefixes of all early eds); Mem.
/ Q1, 2; Memp.* / *Bl.*    SD.] *This ed.; aside to* LUC. / *Bond.*    91. SP.] *Bond;
Half.* / *Q1, 2, Bl.*    SD.] *This ed.; aside* / *Tydeman.*

---

not record the term being used in this sense before 1621.

  79. *captious*] ready to cavil.

  80. *passes my recognizance*] surpasses my understanding.

  86. *odds but*] a good bet that.

  87–9. *He that cut…together*] The person that created the one made its
parallel, inseparably uniting the two. The image sustains the shoemaking
metaphor initiated at line 39 with *cobblers' cuts*, enabling the concluding pun
on *soles*/souls.

  90, 91, 92, 93, 95, 96. SP.] The speech prefixes here follow Bond, rather
than *Q1, 2, Bl* (see collation notes) which appear to look back to a corrupt,
or misguidedly 'corrected' text. Though at first sight each father might be
expected to enquire (as in the three early editions) with whom his child is
conversing, in fact, as Bond points out, 'Each parent expects to find, not his
own child, but some one [im]personating his child; and each, being behind
his child's back, asks who the [im]personator is, and does not recognize that
only the clothes are changed, until the children speak or turn round' (iii,
p. 549). The series of questions and answers at lines 149–53 below confirms
the order of speakers adopted here.

*Stellio.* [*To himself*] In good time; it fodges.

*Memphio.* [*Aside to Halfpenny, having attracted his notice*] What
    is he?

*Halfpenny.* [*Aside to Memphio*] Sperantus' son.                    95

*Memphio.* [*To himself*] So, 'twill cotton.

*Accius.* [*To Silena*] Damsel, I pray you, how old are you?

*Memphio.* [*Aside, in alarm*] My son would scarce have asked
    such a foolish question!

*Silena.* I shall be eighteen next bear-baiting.                    100

*Stellio.* [*Aside, in alarm*] My daughter would have made a
    wiser answer!

*Halfpenny.* [*Aside to Lucio*] Oh, how fitly this comes off!

*Accius.* My father is a scold. What's yours?

*Memphio.* [*Aside*] My heart throbs; I'll look him in the face.    105
    And yonder I espy Stellio!

*Stellio.* [*Aside*] My mind misgives me. But whist! Yonder is
    Memphio!

*Accius.* [*Seeing his father*] In faith, I perceive an old saw, and
    a rusty. No fool to the old fool. I pray you, wherefore was    110
    I thrust out like a scarecrow in this similitude?

92. SP.] *Bond; Mem.* / *Q1, 2; Memp.* / *Bl.*  SD.] *This ed.; aside* /
*Tydeman.*  93. SP.] *Bond; Stel.* / *Q1, Bl; Ste.* / *Q2.*  SD.] *This ed.; aside to*
HALF. / *Bond.*  95. SP.] *Bond; Lin.* / *Q1, 2; Liu.* / *Bl; Luc.* / *Dilke.*  SD.] *This*
*ed.; aside* / *Tydeman.*  96. SP.] *Bond; Stel.* / *Q1, 2, Bl.*  SD.] *This ed.; aside*
/ *Tydeman.*  97. SD.] *This ed.*  98. SD.] *Bond (subst.).*  101. SD.] *Bond*
*(subst.).*  103. SD.] *Bond (subst.).*  off] *Q2, Bl; of Q1.*  105. SD.] *This*
*ed.*  I'll look] *Bond (*looke*); I looke Q1, 2, Bl.*  107. SD.] *This*
*ed.*  109. SD.] *This ed.; to* MEMP. / *Bond.*

92. *it fodges*] the plan is working.

96. *'twill cotton*] the plan will succeed.

100. *bear-baiting*] sport involving the worrying of a chained bear by dogs.
The spectacle was an infrequent one outside London, depending on the
visits of travelling showmen, and thus a ludicrous means of determining
dates. Compare *MWW*: 'Be there bears i'the town?' (1.1.270).

104. *scold*] nag (i.e. one prone to chiding).

109-10. *I perceive…old fool*] Though the lines are assigned to Accius in
*Q1, 2, Bl*, Dilke and Bond suspect further corruption at this point, arguing
that the comment appears to be inappropriately astute (see Bond, iii, p. 549).
As Tydeman notes, however, to assign the lines to Stellio, as Bond suggests,
would 'destroy the symmetry of Memphio's and Stellio's parallel speeches'
(p. 422), while the fact that the expression *No fool to the old fool* is proverbial
(Tilley, F506) aligns the lines with the speech habits of the fools rather than
their fathers. As Tydeman again points out, moreover, the comment *I per-*
*ceive an old saw, and a rusty* possesses 'a kind of unwitting irony on the lips

*Memphio.* [*Aside*] My son! And I ashamed! Dromio shall die.

*Silena.* [*Seeing Stellio*] Father, are you sneaking behind? I pray
you, what must I do next?

*Stellio.* [*Aside*] My daughter! Risio, thou hast cozened me!          115

*Lucio.* [*Aside to Halfpenny*] Now begins the game!

*Memphio.* [*To Accius*] How came you hether?

*Accius.* Marry, by the way from your house hether.

*Memphio.* How chance in this attire?

*Accius.* How chance Dromio bid me?                                     120

*Memphio.* [*To himself*] Ah! Thy son will be begged for a
concealed fool!

*Accius.* [*Hearing him*] Will I? I'faith, sir, no!

*Stellio.* [*To Silena*] Wherefore came you hether, Silena,
without leave?                                                          125

*Silena.* Because I did. And I am here because I am.

*Stellio.* Poor wench, thy wit is improved to the uttermost.

*Halfpenny.* Ay, 'tis an hard matter to have a wit of the old
rent. Everyone  racks his commons so high.

112. SD.] *This ed.*    My...ashamed!] *Punctuation as Bond;* My sonne and
I ashamd, / *Q1, 2* (ashamde), *Bl* (asham'd).    113, 115. SD.] *This ed.*    116.
SD.] *Tydeman (subst.).*    117, 121. SD.] *This ed.*    123, 124. SD.] *This
ed.*    126. am²] *Q1;* came *Q2, Bl.*    128. Ay] *Andreadis;* I *Q1, 2, Bl.*

of Accius' (p. 422), cf. his remark at 4.2.14, *I never was so far as the proverbs
of this city.*

109. *saw*] (*a*) toothed tool for cutting; (*b*) proverbial saying.

110. *No fool...fool*] There's no fool comparable to an old fool for
folly.

111. *similitude*] likeness, guise.

115. *cozened*] tricked.

117, 118, 124. *hether*] See 2.3.38n.

118. *Marry*] exclamation denoting surprise at a question. Compare
modern English 'Why!'

119. How does it come about that you are wearing these clothes?

120. *bid me*] told me (to dress this way).

121–2.] See 1.1.41n. for the situation of those intellectually incapable of
governing their own affairs.

125. *leave*] permission.

128–9.] The response depends on a pun on the word *improved* in the
previous speech: (*a*) developed (the sense Stellio's intends in line 127);
(*b*) raised (Halfpenny's meaning, drawing on the contemporary application
of the term to the raising of rents). Compare Beaumont and Fletcher, *A
King and No King:* 'Arbaces. Do the wenches encroach upon thee?...Didst
thou sit at an old rate with 'em?...And do they improve themselves? /
*Mardonius.* Ay, ten shillings to me every new young fellow they come

*Memphio.* [*Aside*] Dromio told me that one should meet          130
    Stellio's daughter and court her in person of my son.
*Stellio.* [*Aside*] Risio told me one should meet Memphio's
    son, and plead in place of my daughter.
*Memphio.* [*Aside*] But, alas, I see that my son hath met with
    Silena himself, and bewrayed his folly.                      135
*Stellio.* [*Aside*] But I see my daughter hath prattled with
    Accius, and discovered her simplicity.
*Lucio.* [*To Halfpenny*] A brave cry, to hear the two old mules
    weep over the young fools.
*Memphio.* [*With renewed hope*] Accius, how likest thou Silena?   140
*Accius.* I take her to be pregnant.
*Silena.* [*To her father*] Truly, his talk is very personable.
*Stellio.* [*To Silena*] Come in, girl; this gear must be fetched
    about.
*Memphio.* [*To Accius*] Come, Accius, let us go in.               145
*Lucio.* [*Intervening*] Nay, sir, there is no harm done. They
    have neither bought nor sold. They may be twins for their
    wits and years!

---

130. SD.] *Bond.*   132. SP.] *Q1; not in Q2, Bl.*   SD.] *Bond.*   132–3. Risio
...son] *Q1; not in Q2, Bl (see following note).*   133. and plead...daugh-
ter] *Q1; assigned to Memphio as a continuation of the preceding speech in Q2,
Bl.*   134. SD.] *Bond.*   136. SD.] *Bond.*   138. SD.] *Tydeman.*   138–9.
mules weep] *Q1;* mules to weepe *Q2, Bl.*   140. SD.] *This ed.*   141. preg-
nant] *Q1;* repugnant *Q2 Bl.*   142, 143, 145. SD.] *This ed.*   146. SD.] *This
ed.; to* STELLIO / *Bond.*

---

acquainted with' (Robert K. Turner Jr, ed., Regents Renaissance Drama,
1964, 1.1.407–13). *racks his commons* = raises his charges.
   130. *one*] someone.
   133. *plead*] urge his suit.
   135. *bewrayed*] exposed.
   137. *discovered*] revealed.
   138. *brave cry*] splendid clamour (with a pun on *cry* = weep).
   141. *pregnant*] an unwitting pun, neither meaning possibly being intended:
(*a*) witty; (*b*) with child. Q2, Bl 'repugnant' (see collation note) is equally
probable, but may well represent an unwarranted attempt to make sense of
the response.
   142. *personable*] good-looking.
   143–4. *gear...about*] affair must be approached a different way (metaphor drawn from sailing). Compare *John*: 'Like a shifted wind unto a sail, /
It makes the course of thoughts to fetch about' (4.2.23–4).
   146–7. *They have...sold*] They haven't committed themselves to anything.

*Memphio.* [*To Halfpenny*] But why didst thou tell me it was
  Sperantus' son?                                          150
*Halfpenny.* Because I thought thee a fool to ask who thine
  own son was.
*Lucio.* [*To Stellio*] And so, sir, for your daughter. Education
  hath done much, otherwise they are by nature soft-witted
  enough.                                                  155
*Memphio.* Alas, their joints are not yet tied. They are not yet
  come to years and discretion.
*Accius.* Father, if my hands be tied, shall I grow wise?
*Halfpenny.* Ay, and Silena too, if you tie them fast to your
  tongues.                                                 160
*Silena.* You may take your pleasure of my tongue, for it is no
  man's wife.
*Memphio.* Come in, Accius.
*Stellio.* Come in, Silena. I will talk with Memphio's son. But
  as for Risio – !                                         165
*Memphio.* As for Dromio – !
  *Exeunt* MEMPHIO [*into his house with*] ACCIUS, [*and*]
        STELLIO [*into his house with*] SILENA.

---

149. SD.] *Bond.*   150. Sperantus'] *Bond;* Prisius *Q1, 2 Bl (Prisius).*
153. SD.] *Bond.*   And so…Education] *Punctuation as Andreadis;* And so
sir for your daughter, education *Q1, 2, Bl.*   159. Ay] *Dilke (*Aye*);* I *Q1, 2,
Bl.*   too] *Q2, Bl;* to *Q1.*   166.1–2.] *Bracketed material this ed.*

150. *Sperantus'*] Bond's emendation is adopted here in preference to the
'Prisius' of *Q1, 2, Bl* (see collation note) in that Prisius has a daughter rather
than a son. The confusion is a further instance of the corruption suffered by
the text in this scene, possibly arising from a mistaken intervention at some
point in the stage history of the play (cf. the error in the assignment of
speeches at lines 90–6 above).
156. *their…tied*] they are not yet fully mature (literally, their joints are
not yet firmly knit together).
156–7. *They…discretion*] They are still young and have yet to learn
judgement.
158. *tied*] tied up (a childish misunderstanding of Memphio's use of 'tied'
in line 158).
159–60. *if…tongues*] if you are prevented from using your tongues as well
(i.e. if you are unable to betray your folly through your speech).
161. *take your pleasure of*] (a) do what you wish with (the sense Silena
intends); (b) enjoy yourself sexually with (the unintended bawdy implication).
161–2. *no man's wife*] proverbial expression for independence of will
(Tilley, M460).

*Halfpenny.* Ass for you, all four!

*Enter* DROMIO [*and*] RISIO.

*Dromio.* How goes the world? Now we have made all sure.
Candius and Livia are married, their fathers consenting,
yet not knowing.                                                    170
*Lucio.* We have flat marred all. Accius and Silena courted one
another; their fathers took them napping; both are
ashamed, and you both shall be swinged.
*Risio.* Tush, let us alone. We will persuade them that all falls
out for the best. For if underhand this match had been     175
concluded, they both had been cozened; and now, seeing
they find both to be fools, they may be both better
advised. But why is Halfpenny so sad?

*Enter* SERGEANT [*and*] HACKNEYMAN.

*Halfpenny.* Because I am sure I shall never be a penny.
*Risio.* Rather pray there be no fall of money, for thou wilt     180
then go for a q.                    ———————  *devaluation*
*Dromio.* But did not the two fools currently court one another?
*Lucio.* Very good words, fitly applied, brought in in the nick.

---

168. world? Now we] *Punctuation this ed.;* worlde, now we *Q1, 2 (*world,
now wee*), Bl.*   175. if underhand this] *Q1;* if I understand this *Q2,
Bl.*   181. q.] *Dilke;* que *Q1, 2, Bl*   183. in in] *Q1; in Q2, Bl.*

---

167. *Ass for you*] Ass (i.e. fool) to you too (with a pun on *As* in the previous line).
168. *How...world?*] How are things?
171. *flat marred*] completely ruined.
172. *took them napping*] came upon them unawares.
173. *swinged*] beaten.
174. *let us alone*] leave it to us.
175. *underhand*] by clandestine means.
176. *cozened*] cheated.
177–8. *be both better advised*] both act more wisely.
178.1. HACKNEYMAN] one who keeps horses or hackney carriages for
hire.
180–1.] a further joke on the significance of Halfpenny's name. A devaluation in the currency would make him worth less than his current value,
reducing his worth from a half to a quarter of a penny (i.e. to a farthing
or *q*).
182. *currently...another*] make love fluently to each other (with a pun on
*currently*, looking back to the joke on coinage in the previous line).
183. *in the nick*] at precisely the right time.

*Sergeant.* [*Laying a hand on Dromio*] I arrest you.

*Dromio.* Me, sir? Why then didst not bring a stool with thee,     185
that I might sit down?

*Hackneyman.* He arrests you at my suit for a horse.

*Risio.* The more ass he. If he had arrested a mare instead of
an horse, it had been but a slight oversight; but to arrest
a man that hath no likeness of a horse is flat lunacy or     190
ale-acy.

*Hackneyman.* Tush, I hired him a horse.

*Dromio.* I swear then he was well ridden.

*Hackneyman.* I think in two days he was never baited.

*Halfpenny.* Why, was it a bear thou ridst on?     195

*Hackneyman.* I mean he never gave him bait.

*Lucio.* Why, he took him for no fish.

*Hackneyman.* I mistake none of you when I take you for fools.
I say thou never gavest my horse meat.

*Dromio.* Yes, in four-and-forty hours I am sure he had a bottle     200
of hay as big as his belly.

*Sergeant.* Nothing else? Thou shouldst have given him
provender.

*Dromio.* Why, he never asked for any.

---

184. SD.] *Bond (subst.).*     189. but¹] *Q1; not in Q2, Bl.*     191. ale-acy]
*Tydeman n. (subst.);* alecie *Q1, 2, Bl.*     204. SP.] *Fairholt; Ri.* / *Q1, 2,
Bl.* for] *Q1; not in Q2, Bl.*

---

185–6. *Why then…down*] The question depends on a pun on *arrest you*
in the previous line: (*a*) seize you by the authority of the law; (*b*) give you a
rest.

187. *for*] (*a*) over the matter of (the meaning the Hackneyman intends);
(*b*) as (the meaning Risio attributes to him in the following lines).

191. *ale-acy*] drunkenness (term coined by Risio to parallel *lunacy*).

194. *baited*] again susceptible, as Halfpenny exhibits in the following
line, of being understood in more than one way: (*a*) rested; (*b*) subjected to
worrying by hounds.

196. *bait*] (*a*) a halt for refreshment in a journey (the Hackneyman's
meaning); (*b*) morsel of food used by fishermen as a lure (the meaning Lucio
attributes to him in the following line).

199. *meat*] food.

200. *bottle*] bundle of feed judged adequate for a horse's needs by
sixteenth-century stablemen. Compare the translated Botttom's 'great desire
to a bottle of hay' in *MND* (4.1.32–3).

203. *provender*] dry, cereal-based horse feed. Compare *MND*: 'TITANIA.
Say, sweet love, what thou desir'st to eat? / BOTTOM. Truly a peck of provender; I could munch your good dry oats' (4.1.30–2).

*Hackneyman.* Why, dost thou think an horse can speak?          205
*Dromio.* No, for I spurred him till my heels ached, and he
said never a word.
*Hackneyman.* Well, thou shalt pay sweetly for spoiling him.
It was as lusty a nag as any in Rochester, and one that
would stand upon no ground.                                      210
*Dromio.* Then is he as good as ever he was, I'll warrant. He'll
do nothing but lie down.
*Hackneyman.* I lent him thee gently.
*Dromio.* And I restored him so gently that he neither would
cry 'wyhie' nor wag the tail.                                    215
*Hackneyman.* But why didst thou bore him thorough the ears?
*Lucio.* It may be he was set on the pillory, because he had not
a true pace.
*Halfpenny.* No, it was for tiring.
*Hackneyman.* He would never tire! It may be he would be so   220
weary he would go no further, or so.
*Dromio.* Yes, he was a notable horse for service; he would tire
and retire.

---

211. was, I'll warrant. He'll] *Punctuation as Andreadis;* was, Ile warrant,
heele *Q1;* was Ile warrant heele *Q2, Bl.*    215.] *Quotation marks / Tydeman.*

---

206. *spurred him*] (a) set my spurs to; (b) plied him with questions. See
4.1.20–1 and n. for the same pun.
210. *would stand…ground*] another potentially ambiguous claim, as exhibited by Dromio's response: (a) wouldn't stand still (the sense the Hackneyman
intends); (b) wouldn't stand up (Dromio's construction in the following lines).
213. *gently*] willingly, with good will (cf. Ariel's promise to Prospero in
*Temp.* to 'do my spriting gently': 1.2.298).
214. *so gently*] in such a quiet state.
214–15. *he neither would…tail*] proverbial for a broken-down mount
(Tilley, H671: 'It is an ill horse that can neither whinny nor wag his tail').
216. *bore…ears*] a method of indicating the ownership of livestock (suggesting that Dromio may have intended to sell the horse as his own). Lucio's
tongue-in-cheek explanation in the following speech turns on the fact that
boring in the ears was a contemporary punishment for malefactors.
217–8. *he had…pace*] he was irregular in his gait (with a pun on *true*:
honest/regular).
219. *tiring*] possibly intended in the sense of 'tugging' (cf. *Anatomy*,
p. 151: 'I tired at a dry breast three years'), but taken by the Hackneyman
to mean 'growing weary' (see his response in the following line).
222. *service*] (a) work; (b) military action (anticipating the pun on *retire*
in the following clause).

*Hackneyman.* Do you think I'll be jested out of my horse? –
Sergeant, wreak thy office on him!                        225
*Risio.* Nay, stay! Let him be bailed.
*Hackneyman.* So he shall, when I make him a bargain.
*Dromio.* It was a very good horse, I must needs confess; and
now hearken to his qualities – and have patience to hear
them, since I must pay for him. He would stumble three   230
hours in one mile. I had thought I had rode upon adzes
between this and Canterbury. If one gave him water,
why, he would lie down and bathe himself like a hawk.
If one ran him, he would simper and mump, as though
he had gone a-wooing to a malt mare at Rochester. He    235
trotted before and ambled behind, and was so obedient
that he would do duty every minute on his knees, as
though every stone had been his father.
*Hackneyman.* I am sure he had no diseases.
*Dromio.* A little rheum or pose. He lacked nothing but an   240
handkercher.
*Sergeant.* Come, what a tale of a horse have we here! I cannot
stay. Thou must with me to prison.
*Risio.* If thou be a good fellow, Hackneyman, take all our
four bonds for the payment. Thou knowest we are town-   245

---

226. stay] *Q1; not in Q2, Bl.*   229. to¹] *Q1; of Q2, Bl.*   231. adzes] *Daniel;*
addeces *Q1, 2;* addices *Bl.*   244. SP.] *Q1 (Ri.); Li. (i.e. Lucio) / Q2,*
*Bl.* fellow] *Q1; not in Q2, Bl.*   245. knowest] *Q1, 2, Bl²; not in Bl.*

225. *wreak*] execute.
227. *make…bargain*] come to a satisfactory agreement with him.
231. *adzes*] sharp-edged tools with the blades set at right angles to the
handles.
232. *this*] this place (i.e. Rochester). See 4.1.26n. for the distance involved.
234. *simper and mump*] look coy and mope.
235. *malt mare*] female dray horse.
236. *before…behind*] with his front legs…with his back legs.
237. *do duty…knees*] constantly go down on his knees, like a dutiful son.
240. *rheum or pose*] running of the eyes, or cold in the head. Compare
*Midas*: 'Belike if thou shouldst spit often, thou wouldst call it the rheum.
Motto, in men of reputation and credit it is the rheum; in such mechanical
mushrooms it is a catarrh, a pose, the water evil' (5.2.114–17).
241. *handkercher*] archaic variant of 'handkerchief'.
245–6. *town-born*] local. Compare *Anatomy*: 'Philautus being a town-born
child, both for his own countenance and the great countenance which his

born children, and will not shrink the city for a pelting
jade.
*Halfpenny.* I'll enter into a statute merchant to see it answered.
But if thou wilt have bonds, thou shalt have a bushelful!
*Hackneyman.* Alas, poor ant, thou bound in a statute mer-      250
chant? A brown thread will bind thee fast enough. But if
you will be content all four jointly to enter into a bond,
I will withdraw the action.
*Dromio.* Yes, I'll warrant they will. [*To his companions*] How
say you?                                                        255
*Halfpenny.* I yield.
*Risio.* And I.
*Lucio.* And I.
*Hackneyman.* Well, call the Scrivener.
*Sergeant.* Here's one hard by. I'll call him.                  260
                    [*He knocks at the Scrivener's door.*]
*Risio.* A Scrivener's shop hangs to a Sergeant's mace like a
burr to a frieze coat.

                    [*Enter* SCRIVENER.]

*Scrivener.* What's the matter?
*Hackneyman.* You must take a note of a bond.

---

254. SD.] *This ed.*   260.1.] *Dilke (subst.).*   261. to a Sergeant's] *Q2, Bl;*
to Sergeants *Q1.*   262.1.] *Andreadis; not in Q1, 2, Bl.*

---

father had while he lived, crept into credit with Don Ferardo, one of the
chief governors of the city' (p. 46).
   246. *shrink*] slip away from (*OED, v.* 6).
   246–7. *for...jade*] because of a paltry, broken-down horse. For a comparable use of *pelting* (= paltry) compare *Measure*: 'Could great men thunder
/ As Jove himself does, Jove would ne'er be quiet, / For every pelting petty
officer / Would use his heaven for thunder' (2.2.111–14).
   248. *statute merchant*] type of bond which permitted the creditor to seize
the debtor's goods in case of default.
   *see it answered*] guarantee its repayment.
   250. *ant*] a further allusion to Halfpenny's diminutive size.
   251. *brown thread*] piece of cheap string.
   259. *Scrivener*] one engaged to draw up, or copy, legal documents.
   261. *hangs....mace*] clings to a Sergeant's metal-headed staff of office
(used here to represent the office itself).
   262. *frieze*] coarse woollen cloth.
   264. *bond*] legal agreement.

*Dromio.* Nay, a pint of courtesy pulls on a pot of wine. In this     265
     tavern we'll dispatch.
*Hackneyman.* Agreed.     *Exeunt [into the tavern, all but Risio].*
*Risio.* Now, if our wits be not in the wane, our knavery shall
     be at the full. They will ride them worse than Dromio rid
     his horse; for if the wine master their wits, you shall see     270
     them bleed their follies.          *Exit [into the tavern].*

267. SD.] *Bracketed material / Tydeman (subst.); Exeunt. / Q1, 2, Bl.*
271. SD.] *Bracketed material / Tydeman.*

265. *a pint...wine*] generous dealing leads to good fellowship. As
Tydeman notes, the expression 'has a proverbial ring' (p. 423), but no
comparable example has been traced.
     *pot*] cup.
266. *dispatch*] conclude our business.
269–70. *They will...horse*] They (i.e. the boys) will manage them worse
(i.e. treat the Hackneyman, the Sergeant, and the Scrivener more badly)
than Dromio managed his horse. Lyly employs the same metaphor in
*Pappe*, but with the roles of horse and rider reversed: 'If he ride me, let
the foole sit fast, for my wit is verie kickish' (Bond, iii, p. 395).
271. *bleed their follies*] vent their stupidity and suffer for it (image drawn
from the spurring of a horse).

# Act 5

Act[us] 5, Sce[na] 1

[*Enter*] DROMIO, RISIO, LUCIO, [*and*] HALFPENNY
[*from the tavern*].

*Dromio.* Every fox to his hole, the hounds are at hand!

*Risio.* The Sergeant's mace lies at pawn for the reckoning,
and he under the board to cast it up!

*Lucio.* The Scrivener cannot keep his pen out of the pot!
Every goblet is an inkhorn!                                      5

*Halfpenny.* The Hackneyman, he whisks with his wand as if
the tavern were his stable and all the servants his horses!
– 'Jost there up, bay Richard!' – And white loaves are
horsebread in his eyes.

*Dromio.* It is well I have my acquittance, and he such a bond   10
as shall do him no more good than the bond of a faggot.

---

0.] *Q1 (subst.), Bl (subst.);* Act. 5. Sce. 8 *Q2.* 0.1–2.] *Tydeman (subst.);*
*Dro, Risio, Linceo, Halfpenie. / Q1, 2, Bl (subst.).* 8. 'Jost...Richard']
*Quotation marks / Dilke.* Jost] *Fairholt; Iost Q1, 2 (iost), Bl.* up,
bay] *Punctuation as Q2, Bl;* up bay *Q1.* 10. such a bond] *Q1;* such bonds
*Q2, Bl.*

---

1. *Every...hole*] Let everyone make his escape (metaphor drawn from fox
hunting).

2. *reckoning*] bill.

3. *he under the board*] the Sergeant under the table (overcome with
drink).

*cast it up*] (a) calculate the bill; (b) vomit what he has drunk. The boys
use versions of the same joke on two previous occasions (at 2.1.141–2, and
2.4.19–20 above).

4. *pen*] (a) quill; (b) nose.

5. *inkhorn*] ink-well.

8. *'Jost...Richard'*] probably a coachman's call of encouragement to a
horse, though Tydeman notes that a mounting block was known in Kent as a
'joss-block', implying that the cry may be an instruction to mount (p. 423).

8–9. *white loaves...eyes*] He mistakes fine bread for horse feed. Another
instance of the Hackneyman's drunken delusion that the tavern is his stable.

10–11. *I have...faggot*] I have a document releasing me from debt and
he [the Hackneyman] has a bond in exchange that is as valueless as the band
securing a bundle of firewood.

11. *faggot*] bundle of firewood, traditionally held together with a bond (or
band).

Our knaveries are now come to the push, and we must
cunningly dispatch all. [*To Risio*] We two will go see how
we may appease our masters. [*To Lucio and Halfpenny*]
You two, how you may conceal the late marriage. If all    15
fall out amiss, the worst is beating; if to the best, the worst
is liberty!

*Risio.* Then let's about it speedily; for so many irons in the
fire together require a diligent plumber.          *Exeunt.*

Act[us] 5, Sce[na] 2

[*Enter*] VICINIA.

*Vicinia.* My heart throbs, my ears tingle, my mind misgives
me, since I hear such muttering of marriages in Rochester.
My conscience, which these eighteen years hath been
frozen with congealed guiltiness, begins now to thaw in

---

13. SD.] *This ed.*    14. appease] *Q1;* appeale    *Q2, Bl.* SD.] *This
ed.*    15. the late] *Q1;* your late *Q2, Bl.*    19. fire] *Q2, Bl; not in Q1.*
0.1.] *Bond (following Q1 /* VICINIA. BOMBIE.*);* Vicina. Bombie. / *Q2,
Bl.*    2. such] *Q1;* some    *Q2, Bl.*    2–3. Rochester. My] *Punctuation as
Bond;* Rochester, my *Q1, 2, Bl.*    4. with congealed] *Q1 (*coniealed*); with
this coniealed Q2, Bl (*congealed*).*

---

12. *are...push*] have arrived at the point of execution.
16–17. *if...liberty*] if everything goes well, the least we can expect is our
freedom. The suggestion of slavery contributes to the play's conflation of
historical periods (cf. 1.1.73–6 above).
18–19. *so many irons in the fire*] proverbial (Tilley, I99) for having a
number of affairs in progress at once.
19. *plumber*] solderer or worker in metal. Andreadis suggests that the
metaphor is 'deliberately mixed' (p. 198), but the term 'plumber' was not
restricted in the sixteenth century to one skilled in the fitting or mending of
water pipes, cisterns, etc.

0.1. VICINIA] emended by Andreadis to 'Vicina', following *Q2, Bl* (see
Appendix) on the grounds that 'the Q1 [*sic*] compositor probably misread
the ms. at this point and made a minim error in setting the name, which is
so obviously representative of the character's function in the play' (Latin
*vicina* = neighbour). *Vicinia* is retained here, however, in that the name
consistently appears in that form in *Q1*, in both the dialogue and stage directions, and is equally suggestive of the character's role (cf. Latin *vicinia* =
neighbourhood), while *Q2 'Vicina'* may itself be a mistaken reading or
regularization.

open grief. But I will not accuse myself till I see more   5
danger. The good old woman, Mother Bombie, shall try
her cunning upon me, and if I perceive my case is desperate by her, then will I rather prevent, although with
shame, than report too late, and be inexcusable. [*She
knocks at Mother Bombie's door.*] God speed, good mother.   10

[*The door opens to reveal* MOTHER BOMBIE *sitting on her stool.*]

*Mother Bombie.* Welcome, sister.
*Vicinia.* I am troubled in the night with dreams, and in the
day with fears. Mine estate bare, which I cannot well
bear; but my practices devilish, which I cannot recall. If,
therefore, in these same years there be any deep skill, tell   15
what my fortune shall be, and what my fault is.
*Mother Bombie.* In studying to be over-natural,
Thou art like to be unnatural,
And all about a natural.
Thou shalt be eased of a charge,                               20
If thou thy conscience discharge;
And this I commit to thy charge.

9–10. SD.] *Bond (subst.).*   10.1.] *This ed. No entry indicated in Q1, 2, Bl.*
15–16. tell what] *Q1, 2;* tell me what *Bl.*   17–22.] *Lineation as Dilke; printed
as continuous prose in Q1, 2, Bl.*   19. a] *Q1; not in Q2, Bl.*

6. *try*] test.
7–8. *desperate*] hopeless.
8. *prevent*] i.e. come forward and confess.
10. *God speed*] May God prosper you.
10.1.] See 2.3.93.1–2n. for a justification of the stage directions governing
the entrances of Mother Bombie in this edition.
11. *sister*] polite term of address to another woman of similar age and
class.
14. *recall*] revoke.
15. *in...years*] in this your great age.
17–22.] printed as continuous prose in Q1, 2, Bl (see collation note), but
the use of rhyme again suggests doggerel verse (see 2.3.103–7n.). The lineation here follows Dilke.
17. *studying to be over-natural*] trying to be excessively maternal.
18. *unnatural*] an offender against the laws of nature.
19. *natural*] simpleton.
20. *eased of a charge*] (*a*) spared the burden of a cost; (*b*) relieved of a
responsibility.
21. *discharge*] relieve.

*Vicinia.* Thou hast touched me to the quick, mother. I understand thy meaning, and thou well knowest my practice.
I will follow thy counsel. But what will be the end?          25
*Mother Bombie.* Thou shalt know before this day end.
Farewell.                    [*Mother Bombie's door closes.*]
*Vicinia.* Now I perceive I must either bewray a mischief or
suffer a continual inconvenience. I must haste home-
wards, and resolve to make all whole. Better a little shame          30
than an infinite grief. The strangeness will abate the fault,
and the bewraying wipe it clean away.          *Exit.*

Act[us] 5, Sce[na] 3

[*Enter*] THREE FIDDLERS: SYNIS, NASUTUS,
[*and*] BEDUNENUS.

*Synis.* Come, fellows, 'tis almost day. Let us have a fit of
mirth at Sperantus' door, and give a song to the bride.
*Nasutus.* I believe they are asleep; it were pity to awake them.
*Bedunenus.* 'Twere a shame they should sleep the first night.
*Synis.* But who can tell at which house they lie? At Prisius' it          5
may be. We'll try both. [*They approach Sperantus' house.*]
*Nasutus.* Come, let's draw like men.
*Synis.* Now tune, tune, I say. [*In frustration as Bedunenus tunes
up*] That boy, I think, will never profit in his faculty. He

27. SD.] *This ed.; Exit Bom.* / *Q1, 2 (subst.); Exit. Bomb.* / *Bl.*
6. SD.] *This ed.*   8–9. SD.] *This ed.*

23. *touched...quick*] proverbial (Tilley, Q13) for making a comment particularly pertinent to the situation or feelings of another.
24. *practice*] device, deception.
28. *bewray*] reveal.
29. *suffer...inconvenience*] permit an enduring harm.
31. *abate*] lessen.
32. *bewraying*] revealing.

0.2. BEDUNENUS] See 'Characters', 23n.
1–2. *fit of mirth*] joyful strain of music.
7. *draw like men*] apply ourselves manfully to our fiddles (grandiloquent
use of a phrase usually applied to the unsheathing of swords prior to battle.
Compare *Where is my scabbard? Everyone sheath his science*, at line 107 below).
9. *profit...faculty*] do well in his art.

loses his rosin, that his fiddle goes 'cush, cush', like as      10
one should go wetshod; and his mouth so dry that he
hath not spittle for his pin as I have.

*Bedunenus.* [*Resentfully*] Marry, sir, you see I go wetshod
[*showing his worn shoes*], and dry-mouthed, for yet could
I never get new shoes or good drink. Rather than I'll lead      15
this life, I'll throw my fiddle into the leads for a hobbler.

*Synis.* [*Offended*] Boy, no more words. There's a time for all
things. Though I say it that should not, I have been a
minstrel these thirty years, and tickled more strings than
thou hast hairs, but yet was never so misused.                  20

*Nasutus.* Let us not brabble, but play. Tomorrow is a new
day.

*Bedunenus.* [*Contritely to Synis*] I am sorry I speak in your cast.
What shall we sing?

---

10. loses] *Dilke;* looses *Q1, 2, Bl.*    rosin] *Dilke;* rosen *Q1;* roson *Q2;* Rozen
*Bl.*    'cush, cush'] *Quotation marks / Tydeman.*    13. SD.] *This ed.*    14. SD.]
*This ed.*    16. I'll throw] *Q1 (*Ile*), Bl (subst.);* I throw *Q2.*    17. SD.] *This
ed.*    There's a time] *Q1 (*theres*);* there is time *Q2, Bl.*    23. SD.] *This ed.*

10. *rosin*] solid residue of distilled oil of turpentine, used on bow strings.
11. *should go wetshod*] would walk with wet feet.
11–12. *his mouth…I have*] The criticism turns on the fact that fiddlers
customarily used spittle to moisten the holes in which the pegs used for
tuning their instruments were set. Compare *Shrew*: 'HORTENSIO. Madam,
my instrument's in tune. / BIANCA. Let's hear. O fie! The treble jars. /
LUCENTIO. Spit in the hole, man, and tune again' (3.1.37–9).
16. *into…hobbler*] on to the roof, as if it were a spinning top that had begun
to wobble. Compare W. de Britaine (1686), *Hum. Prud.* xix, 85, cited under
*OED*, hobbler². 2: 'Like a Top, which hath been for a long time scourged,
and run well, yet at the last, to be lodged up for a Hobler'. The term was used
metaphorically for one of unstable or unreliable disposition. Compare George
Gascoigne, *The Glasse of Gouernement* (1575), 'Shall I be cast vp for a hobler
then? I am sure I was neuer yet vntrusty to any of you both' (1.5: Ciir).
17–18. *There's…things*] proverbial (Tilley, T314). Compare Ecclesiastes,
iii, 1: 'To every thing there is a season, and a time to every purpose under
the heaven'.
21. *brabble*] quarrel. Compare *TN*: 'In private brabble did we apprehend
him' (5.1.62).
21–2. *Tomorrow…day*] proverbial (Tilley, T380) for deferring a matter
to a more favourable time.
23. *speak…cast*] proverbial (Tilley, C118) for interrupting someone in
the course of a speech. Compare Iffida's intervention in Fidus' celebration
of wine in *England*: 'If I may speak in your cast, quoth Iffida…I think wine
is such a whetstone for wit…it will quickly grind all the steel out' (p. 202).

*Synis.* 'The Love Knot', for that's best for a bridal.        25
                                                  *Sing.*
Good morrow, fair bride, and send you joy of your
bridal.

                    SPERANTUS *looks out.*

*Sperantus.* What a mischief make the twanglers here? We have
no trenchers to scrape! It makes my teeth on edge to hear
such grating! Get you packing, or I'll make you wear        30
double stocks, and yet you shall be never the warmer.
*Synis.* We come for good will, to bid the bride and bridegroom God give them joy.
*Sperantus.* Here's no wedding.
*Synis.* Yes. Your son and Prisius' daughter were married,        35
though you seem strange. Yet they repent it not, I am
sure.

---

25. 'The Love Knot'] *Quotation marks / Andreadis.*  25.1.] *First differenti-
ated from text by Bond (following a note by Fairholt). Printed as part of
Synis' speech at lines 25–6 this ed. in Q1 (*bridall. Sing. God*), 2, Bl (*Bridall.
Sing. Good*). 26. Good] *Bl*; God *Q1, 2.*  28. twanglers] *Q1*; twangers
*Q2, Bl.*  32–3. bridegroom God] *Punctuation as Q2, Bl*; bridegroome,
God *Q1.*  34. Here's] *Bl*; hers *Q1*; heres *Q2.*  35–6. married...Yet]
*Punctuation this ed.;* maryed, though you seeme strange, yet *Q1, 2, Bl
(with spelling variants).*

25.1.] Though the word *Sing* is not distinguished from the dialogue in
*Q1, 2, Bl* (see collation note) all twentieth-century editions followed
Fairholt's proposal (ii, p. 277) that it should be regarded as a stage direction.
No text is supplied for the song, however, in either the quartos or Blount's
collected edition, and a number of reasons have been advanced for its omission. Fairholt suggests that the piece was a popular song, rather than one
written by Lyly himself, and that no text was consequently required, while
Tydeman argues (p. 424) that the most likely explanation is that lines 26–7
this ed. form the first line of the song, which is then cut short by Sperantus'
intervention, rather than (as here) a salutation to the bride. As Bond points
out, however, Blount fails to supply songs on a number of occasions where
they are clearly required in other plays, presumably because he was unable
to recover the text (iii, pp. 551 and 592–3). For a detailed discussion of the
problems surrounding the songs in Lyly's plays, see Hunter, pp. 367–72.
    28. *twanglers*] a depreciative term for fiddlers.
    29. *trenchers to scrape*] wooden platters to be picked over for scraps
(implying the fiddlers are looking for alms).
    30–1. *make...stocks*] (*a*) make you wear two sets of stockings; (*b*) have
both your feet put in the stocks (and hence grow colder rather than warmer).
    36. *seem strange*] pretend ignorance of the matter. Compare *Tim.*: 'I know
thee well; / But in thy fortunes am unlearn'd and strange' (4.3.56–7).

*Sperantus.* My son, villain! I had rather he were fairly
　　hanged!

*Nasutus.* So he is, sir; you have your wish.　　　　　　　40

　　　　*Enter* CANDIUS [*from his father's house*].

*Candius.* [*In a low voice, giving Synis money*] Here, fiddlers,
　　take this, and not a word. [*More loudly*] Here is no
　　wedding. It was at Memphio's house. Yet gramercy.
　　Your music, though it missed the house, hit the mind.
　　We were a-preparing our wedding gear.　　　　[*Exit.*]　　45

*Synis.* [*To Sperantus*] I cry you mercy, sir. I think it was
　　Memphio's son that was married.

*Sperantus.* Oho! The case is altered. Go thether, then, and be
　　haltered for me.　　　　　　　[*Sperantus withdraws.*]

*Nasutus.* What's the alms?　　　　　　　　　　　　　　50

*Synis.* An angel!

---

38. My son, villain!] *Punctuation as Dilke;* My sonne villaine, *Q1, 2 (*son*);*
My sonne villaine! *Bl.* 40.1.] *Bracketed material this ed.* 41. SD.] *This
ed.* 42. SD.] *This ed.* 45. SD.] *Andreadis; not in Q1, 2, Bl.* 48. SP.] *Q1,
Bl; not in Q2.* 49. SD.] *This ed.; Exit. | Andreadis.*

40.] The response depends upon a pun on the word *hanged* in the previous line: (*a*) executed on the gallows (Sperantus' meaning); (*b*) sexually
fulfilled (see 3.4.44 and n.).

44. *hit the mind*] was in accordance with our intentions.

45. *a-preparing…gear*] making our wedding preparations. The remark,
intended for Sperantus' ears, is designed to maintain the pretence that
Candius is still unmarried.

46. *cry you mercy*] beg your pardon.

46–7. *I think…married*] Andreadis (p. 205) assumes that Synis is
deliberately furthering Candius' deception, but the fact that he then
proceeds to Memphio's house in the expectation of reward indicates
that he is himself deceived and is an unwitting agent of the young
lovers' plot.

48. *The case is altered*] proverbial (Tilley, C111) for a fresh perspective on,
or sudden alteration in, a situation. The expression was adopted by Jonson
for the title of a comedy.

49. *haltered*] hung (with a pun on *altered* in the previous line).

50.] How much did we get?

51. *angel*] a gold coin, worth ten shillings in pre-decimalization English
currency. An angel was a considerable sum, substantially more than a skilled
craftsman could hope to earn in a week. Compare the 6–8 shillings paid to
hired actors by Henslowe.

*Bedunenus.* I'll warrant there's some work towards! Ten
    shillings is money in master Mayor's purse!
*Synis.* Let us to Memphio's and share equally. When we have
    done, thou shalt have new shoes.                            55
*Bedunenus.* Ay, such as they cry at the 'Sizes: 'A mark in
    issues' and 'Mark in issues', and yet I never saw so much
    leather as would piece one's shoes.
*Synis.* No more. [*He divides the payment.*] There's the money.
*Bedunenus.* A good handsel and, I think, the maidenhead of     60
    your liberality.              [*They cross to Memphio's house.*]
*Nasutus.* Come, here's the house. What shall we sing?
*Synis.* You know Memphio is very rich, and wise. And
    therefore let us strike the gentle stroke, and sing a catch.
                                                            *Sing.*

                            SONG

*All 3.*        The bride this night can catch no cold,          65
                No cold, the bridegroom's young, not old;

---

53. Mayor's] *Dilke;* Maiors *Q1, 2, Bl.*   56. Ay] *Andreadis;* I *Q1, 2,
Bl.*   56-7.] *Quotation marks* / *Andreadis.*   57. and] *Not in Bl.*   58. one's]
*Q1 (*ones*); my Q2, Bl.*   59. SD.] *This ed.*   61. SD.] *This ed.; They cross
the stage.* / *Tydeman.*   64.1.] *Q1; as text, following* catch, *line 64 this ed.* / *Q2,
Bl.*   64.2-84.] *Bl; not in Q1, 2.*

52. *some work towards*] some plot in hand.
53. *is money…purse*] is a substantial sum, even to a wealthy man.
54. *to*] go to.
56. *'Sizes*] Assizes (sessions held periodically in each county for the
administration of justice).
56-7. *mark in issues*] (*a*) fines (*issues*) of thirteen shillings and four pence
(*mark*); (*b*) flaw in his shoes. The joke turns on a pun on 'in issues' and 'in's
shoes'.
58. *piece*] patch.
60. *handsel*] earnest of more money to come.
60-1. *maidenhead…liberality*] first time you have been generous.
64. *catch*] strictly a composition for a number of voices in which each
singer takes up the tune in turn, the second beginning the first line as the
first goes on to the next, etc. As set out by Blount (see lines 65-84 below)
the song does not precisely accord with a traditional catch.
64.1-84.] Though the word *Sing,* unlike the direction at line 25.1 above,
is distinguished as a stage direction in *Q1* (though not in *Q2, Bl*), neither
the heading SONG nor the text of the catch appear in either of the quartos
(see collation note). In common with the rest of the songs in the play, the
text given here derives from *Bl.*

Like ivy he her fast does hold,

*1 Fid[dler].*     And clips her,

*2 [Fiddler].*     And lips her,

*3 [Fiddler].*     And flips her too.                                  70

*All 3.*     Then let them alone, they know what they do.

*1 [Fiddler].* At laugh and lie down, if they play,

*2 [Fiddler].* What ass against the sport can bray?

*3 [Fiddler].* Such tick-tack has held many a day.

*1 [Fiddler].*     And longer.                                          75

*2 [Fiddler].*     And stronger.

*3 [Fiddler].*     It still holds too.

*All 3.*     Then let them alone, they know what they do.

This night,

In delight,                                      80

Does thump away sorrow.

Of billing

Take your filling,

So good morrow, good morrow!

*Nasutus.*  God morrow, mistress bride, and send you a huddle!     85

---

68. SP.] *Bracketed material | Andreadis.*  69, 70, 72, 73, 74, 75, 76,
77. SP.] *Bracketed material | Dilke (subst.).*  85. God] *Q1, 2;* Good *Bl.*

---

68. *clips*] embraces.

69. *lips*] kisses. Compare *Oth.*: 'O, 'tis the spite of hell, the fiend's arch-mock, / To lip a wanton in a secure couch / And to suppose her chaste' (4.1.70–2).

70. *flips*] playfully smacks.

72. *laugh...down*] proverbial for a light-hearted expression of guilt (Tilley, L92), but used here for its sexual connotations. Compare *TNK*: 'EMILIA. I am wondrous merry-hearted: I could laugh now. / WOMAN. I could lie down, I am sure. / EMILIA. And take one with you?' (2.2.151–2).

74. *tick-tack*] literally a form of backgammon involving the insertion of pegs in holes, but used colloquially as a synonym for sexual intercourse. Compare Lucio's response in *Meas.* to the news that Claudio has been condemned to death for fornication: 'I would be sorry [if thy life] should be thus foolishly lost at a game of tick-tack' (1.2.186–8).

*held*] been in fashion.

81. *thump*] beat (with a sexual double meaning).

82. *billing*] kissing.

85. *a huddle*] an embrace.

[MEMPHIO *looks out, with* DROMIO *by him.*]

*Memphio.* What crowding knaves have we there? Case up
your fiddles, or the constable shall cage you up. What
bride talk you of?

*Synis.* Here's a wedding in Rochester, and 'twas told me first
that Sperantus' son had married Prisius' daughter. We          90
were there, and they sent us to your worship, saying your
son was matched with Stellio's daughter.

*Memphio.* Hath Sperantus, that churl, nothing to do but
mock his neighbours? I'll be even with him! And get you
gone, or I swear by the rood's body I'll lay you by the        95
heels.

*Nasutus.* [*Angrily*] Sing a catch! Here's a fair catch, indeed!
Sing till we catch cold on our feet, and be called knave
till our ears glow on our heads. Your worship is wise, sir!

*Memphio.* Dromio, shake off a whole kennel of officers to      100
punish these jarring rogues! I'll teach them to stretch
their dried sheep's guts at my door, and to mock one that
stands to be Mayor!

*Dromio.* I had thought they had been sticking of pigs, I heard
such a squeaking! I go, sir.                                     105
[*Memphio and Dromio withdraw from the window.*]

85.1.] *This ed.; not in Q1, 2, Bl; Memphio looks out. / Dilke.* 86. crowd-
ing] *Dilke;* crouding *Q1, 2, Bl.* 94. mock his] *Q1,* mock with his
*Q2, Bl.* 97. SD.] *This ed.* 101. rogues] *Q1;* tongues *Q2, Bl.* 105.1.]
*Tydeman (subst.).*

86. *crowding*] (*a*) fiddling (from Welsh *crwth*, an ancient Celtic stringed
instrument); (*b*) clustering.
91. *your worship*] honorific title used in addressing a social superior, rather
than a signifier of a particular rank.
95. *the rood's body*] the body of the crucified Christ.
95–6. *lay...heels*] have you arrested (specifically consigned to the
stocks).
97–8. *catch...catch...catch*] round...reward...contract.
99. *till our...heads*] proverbial (Tilley, E14) for a consciousness of being
talked of, but used here as an index of having been roundly abused.
*Your...sir*] an ironic rejoinder, implying Memphio is a fool.
100. *shake...officers*] unleash a pack of officers of the law (metaphor
drawn from hunting with hounds).
101. *jarring*] (*a*) discordant; (*b*) quarrelsome.
102. *dried sheep's guts*] fiddle strings (traditionally made from animal
intestines).
103. *stands to be*] has expectations of being made.
104. *sticking of* ] slaughtering (by thrusting a knife into the throat).

*Synis.* [*Anxiously, to his companions*] Let us be packing.
*Nasutus.* Where is my scabbard? Everyone sheathe his science.
*Bedunenus.* [*Struggling with his instrument*] A bots on the shoe-
   maker that made this boot for my fiddle. 'Tis too strait.
*Synis.* No more words. 'Twill be thought they were the four    110
   waits, and let them wring. As for the wags that set us on
   work, we'll talk with them.                          *Exeunt.*

[*Enter*] MEMPHIO [*and*] DROMIO [*from Memphio's house*].

*Dromio.* They be gone, sir.
*Memphio.* If they had stayed, the stocks should have stayed
   them. But, sirrah, what shall we now do?             115
*Dromio.* As I advised you. Make a match; for better one house
   be cumbered with two fools than two.
*Memphio.* 'Tis true. For it being bruited that each of us have
   a fool, who will tender marriage to any of them that is
   wise? Besides, fools are fortunate; fools are fair; fools are   120
   honest.

---

106. SD.] *This    ed.*    108. SD.] *This    ed.*    112.1.] *Substantive    bracketed*
*material this ed.*    116. advised] *Q1*; advise *Q2, Bl.*

---

106. *packing*] going.
107. *scabbard*] fiddle case.
*sheathe his science*] put his instrument back in its case. For the use of the
same metaphor, see 5.3.7 above.
108–9. *A bots…strait*] A plague on the leatherworker who made this case
for my instrument. It's too narrow.
110–11. *they…waits*] the offenders were the four musicians maintained
at public charge.
111. *wring*] suffer. Compare *MAdo*: ''tis all men's office to speak patience /
To those that wring under the load of sorrow' (5.1.27–8).
111–12. *that…work*] who instigated this. Compare Emilia's accusation
against Iago in *Oth.* that 'your reports have set the murder on' (5.2.185).
114. *stayed…stayed*] remained…arrested.
116–17. *better…two*] a variant of the proverb, 'Two fools in one house
are too many' (Tilley, F555). Compare *England*: 'I could not find it in my
heart to marry a fool…for two fools in one bed are too many' (p. 208).
117. *cumbered*] encumbered, burdened.
118. *bruited*] rumoured.
119. *tender*] make an offer of.
120. *fools…fair*] Compare the similar linking of folly, beauty, and good
fortune in *England*: 'Maidens be they never so foolish yet, being fair, they
are commonly fortunate' (p. 205). The notion that 'fools are fortunate' was
proverbial (Tilley, F536).
120–1. *fools are honest*] possibly a variant of the proverb, 'A fool cannot
speak unlike himself' (Tilley, F459).

*Dromio.* Ay, sir, and more than that, fools are not wise. A wise
  man is melancholy for moonshine in the water; careful,
  building castles in the air; and commonly hath a fool to
  his heir.                                                          125
*Memphio.* But what sayest thou to thy dame's chaffing?
*Dromio.* Nothing, but all her dishes are chafing-dishes.
*Memphio.* I would her tongue were in thy belly.
*Dromio.* I would as lief have a raw neat's tongue in my
  stomach.                                                           130
*Memphio.* Why?
*Dromio.* Marry, if the clapper hang within an inch of my heart
  that makes mine ears burn a quarter of a mile off, do you
  not think it would beat my heart black and blue?
*Memphio.* Well, patience is a virtue, but pinching is worse      135
  than any vice. – I will break this matter to Stellio, and if
  he be willing, this day shall be their wedding.

---

122. Ay] *Andreadis;* I *Q1, 2, Bl.*    133. off, do] *Punctuation as Dilke;* off. Do
*Q1, 2, Bl (Doe).*

123. *is melancholy...water*] longs for the impossible (proverbial: Tilley,
M1128).
  *careful*] full of care, anxious.
124. *building...air*] constructing impossible schemes (proverbial: Tilley,
C126).
126. *dame's chaffing*] mistress's fretting.
127. *chafing-dishes*] literally, vessels with hot charcoal in the base, used
for keeping food warm, but used metaphorically here for constant nagging
(with a pun on *chaffing* in the previous line).
128.] The wish (a variant of the proverbial 'I wish it were in your belly
for me': Tilley, B299) constitutes a means of resolving two of Memphio's
preoccupations: (*a*) silencing his wife; (*b*) satisfying Dromio's hunger and
thus staunching a drain on his purse.
129. *lief*] willingly.
  *neat's*] ox's.
132–4.] The response turns on an equation between the tongue of
Dromio's mistress and the clapper of a bell, audible over a distance of a
quarter of a mile, and thus so powerful in operation that were it inside him,
as Memphio wishes at line 128, it would discolour his (i.e. Dromio's) heart
with bruises. For *ears burn*, see line 99n. above.
135. *patience...virtue*] proverbial (Tilley, P109).
  *pinching*] fault-finding, cavilling (*OED, vbl. sb.* 3). The opposition between
*patience* and *pinching* constitutes a rueful summation of the stance that
Memphio is obliged to adopt on the one hand, and his wife's shrewish disposition on the other.
136. *break...to*] broach this subject with.

*Dromio.* Then this day shall be my liberty!

*Memphio.* Ay, if Stellio's daughter had been wise, and by thy
    means cozened of a fool.                                        140

*Dromio.* Then, sir, I'll revolt, and dash out the brains of your
    devices.

*Memphio.* Rather thou shalt be free.           *Exeunt.*

    [*Enter*] SPERANTUS [*with*] HALFPENNY [*from one direction,*
        *and*] PRISIUS [*with*] LUCIO [*from another*].

*Sperantus.* Boy, this smoke is a token of some fire. I like not
    the luck of it. Wherefore should these minstrels dream of   145
    a marriage?

*Halfpenny.* Alas, sir, they rustle into every place. Give credit
    to no such words.

*Sperantus.* I will to Prisius; I cannot be quiet. [*Seeing Prisius*]
    And in good time I meet him. – God morrow,   150
    neighbour.

*Prisius.* [*Angrily*] I cast the morrow in thy face, and bid good-
    night to all neighbourhood!

---

139. Ay] *Dilke (Aye); I Q1, 2, Bl.*   143.1–2.] *Bracketed material this ed.;*
*Sperantus, Halfepenie, Prisius, Linceo.* / *Q1, 2 (Lincio), Bl;* [*Enter*] SPERANTUS
[*and*] HALFPENIE [*on one side*], PRISIUS [*and* LUCIO *one the other*]. /
*Tydeman.*  144. is a token] *Q1;* is token *Q2, Bl.*  149. SD.] *This
ed.*  152. SD.] *This ed.*  face] *Q2, Bl;* fate *Q1.*

---

   139. *if*] that would have been the case if.

   140. *cozened of*] tricked into accepting.

   141–2. *dash...devices*] bring your schemes to ruin.

   143.] Rather than that, I will consent to your manumission. The agreement contributes to the play's conflation of historical periods, as at 5.1.16–17
above.

   SD.] As Andreadis notes (p. 212), though no scene break is introduced
at this point in *Q1, 2, Bl,* the fact that both speakers leave the stage before
a fresh set of characters is introduced suggests that Lyly may have intended
the group entrance at lines 143.1–2 below to signal the start of a new scene.

   144. *this smoke...fire*] a variation on the proverb, 'No smoke without
some fire' (Tilley, S569).

   144–5. *I like not...it*] this has an unlucky aspect. Though Dilke's emendation of *luck* to 'look' (see Appendix) is attractive as first sight, it is without
textual warrant, and has not been adopted by later editors, as the text makes
adequate sense as it stands.

   147. *rustle*] creep.

   149. *will to*] will go to.

   *quiet*] at peace in my mind.

   152–3. *bid...neighbourhood*] say farewell to any friendly association.

*Sperantus.* This is your old trick, to pick one's purse and then
        to pick quarrels! I tell thee, I had rather thou shouldest    155
        rob my chest than embezzle my son!
*Prisius.* Thy son! My daughter is seduced! For I hear say she
        is married, and our boys can tell. [*To Lucio*] How sayest
        thou? Tell the truth, or I'll grind thee to powder in my
        mill. Be they married?                                        160
*Lucio.* True it is they were both in a church.
*Prisius.* That's no fault; the place is holy.
*Halfpenny.* And there was with them a priest.
*Sperantus.* Why, what place fitter for a priest than a church?
*Lucio.* And they took one another by the hand.                       165
*Prisius.* Tush, that's but common courtesy.
*Halfpenny.* And the priest spake many kind words.
*Sperantus.* That showed he was no dumb minister. But what
        said they? Didst thou hear any words between them?
*Lucio.* 'Faith, there was a bargain during life. And the clock       170
        cried, 'God give them joy'.
*Prisius.* Villain! They be married!
*Halfpenny.* Nay, I think not so.

---

158. SD.] *Bond.*   171, 174. 'God...joy'] *Quotation marks / Andreadis.*

156. *chest*] money chest.
*embezzle*] cheat. The term is more heavily ironic than modern spelling of
*Q1, 2* 'imbesell' (see Appendix) suggests, in that Sperantus himself might
be said to have attempted to 'imbesell' his son in seeking to marry him to a
fool (i.e. an imbecile).
    159-60. *grind...mill*] The threat is adduced by Bond as further evidence
that Prisius is a fuller (see 2.5.–70n. above). The allusion is thus to a fulling
mill, rather than one used for the grinding of grain.
    168. *dumb minister*] obscure. Probably a reference to one of the 'silenced
clergy', i.e. those forbidden to preach because of their heterodox (usually
Puritan views), but possibly a term for an absentee priest as Tydeman suggests (p. 425).
    170. *clock*] Dilke's emendation to 'clerk' (see Appendix), accepted by
Tydeman (p. 425) on the grounds that *cried* in the next line is an unlikely
term for the pealing of a bell, is superficially attractive but, like the suggested
change at line 144 above, without textual authority. No emendation, is
necessary, moreover, if the reference to the clock is taken, as Bond suggests
(iii, p. 553), as confirmation that the wedding was conducted within legal
hours (i.e. before the clock struck twelve).

*Sperantus.* Yes, yes! 'God give you joy' is a binder. I'll quickly
  be resolved. [*He calls.*] Candius, come forth!                    175

          *Enter* CANDIUS [*from Sperantus' house*].

*Prisius.* And I'll be put out of doubt. [*He calls.*] Livia, come
  forth!

          [*Enter*] LIVIA [*from Prisius' house*].

*Sperantus.* The micher hangs down his head!
*Prisius.* The baggage begins to blush!
*Halfpenny.* [*Aside to Lucio*] Now begins the game.                    180
*Lucio.* [*Aside to Halfpenny.*] I believe it will be no game
  for us.
*Sperantus.* Are you married, young master?
*Candius.* I cannot deny it, it was done so lately.
*Sperantus.* But thou shalt repent it was done so soon.                    185
*Prisius.* Then 'tis bootless to ask you, Livia.
*Livia.* Ay, and needless to be angry.
*Prisius.* It shall pass anger; thou shalt find it rage.
*Livia.* You gave your consent.

---

175. SD.] *This ed.* 175.1.] *Bracketed material this ed.;* <Re-> *Enter*
CANDIUS. / *Bond.* 176. SD.] *This ed.* 177.1.] *Substantive bracketed material this ed.* 180. SD.] *Tydeman (subst.).* 181. SD.] *This ed.* 185. repent
it] *Punctuation as Dilke;* repent, it *Q1, 2, Bl.* 187. Ay] *Andreadis;* I *Q1, 2,
Bl.*

    174. *a binder*] the formulation sealing the contract.
    175. *resolved*] satisfied.
    175.1, 177.1.] The fact that the marriage between Candius and Livia is as
yet unacknowledged (and unconsummated, as lines 434–5 below suggest)
implies that the lovers are still living with their fathers, and hence emerge
from different houses, as indicated here.
    178. *micher*] truant.
    179. *baggage*] opprobrious term for a woman.
    180. *game*] sport.
    181. *game*] fun, source of amusement.
    184. *lately*] recently.
    185. *soon*] a grim rejoinder to Candius' *lately* in the previous line.
    186. *bootless*] pointless.
    188. *pass*] surpass.

*Prisius.* Impudent giglot! Was it not enough to abuse me, but     190
  also to belie me?

*Candius.* You, sir, agreed to this match.

*Sperantus.* Thou brazen-face boy! Thinkest thou by learning
  to persuade me to that which thou speakest? Where did
  I consent? When? What witness?                                    195

*Candius.* In this place. Yesterday. Before Dromio and Risio.

*Prisius.* I remember we heard a contract between Memphio's
  son and Stellio's daughter; and that our good wills being
  asked, which needed not, we gave them, which booted
  not.                                                              200

*Candius.* 'Twas but the apparel of Accius and Silena. We
  were the persons.

*Prisius.* Oh, villainy not to be borne! [*To Lucio*] Wast thou
  privy to this practice?

*Lucio.* In a manner.                                               205

*Prisius.* I'll pay thee after a manner!

*Sperantus.* [*To Halfpenny*] And you oatmeal groat, you were
  acquainted with this plot?

*Halfpenny.* Accessory, as it were.

*Sperantus.* Thou shalt be punished as principal. Here comes      210
  Memphio and Stellio. They belike were privy, and all
  their heads were laid together to grieve our hearts.

---

203. SD.] *Bond.* 206. pay] *Q1;* pray *Q2, Bl.* 207. SD.] *Tydeman.*

190. *Impudent giglot*] Impertinent hussy. Compare Erisichthon's angry
address to Ceres' nymphs in *Love's Metamorphosis*: 'Impudent giglots that
you are to disturb my game, or dare do honour to any but Erisichthon'
(1.2.71–3).
191. *belie*] misrepresent.
193. *brazen-face*] impudent.
199–200. *booted not*] was of no significance.
203–4. *Wast thou…practice?*] Were you a party to this device?
205.] After a fashion.
206. *pay…manner*] repay you (with connotations of striking or punishment) after a fashion (i.e. by beating, with a play on *manner* in the previous
line).
207. *oatmeal groat*] a further reflection on Halfpenny's diminutive stature.
As Dilke notes (p. 278n.), when topped, tailed, and stripped of their husks,
oats were known as groats or grits. The boy is thus being compared to a
single cropped grain.
210–11. *Here comes Memphio and Stellio*] The apparent lack of grammatical
agreement constitutes a further instance of a plural subject being conceived

*Enter* MEMPHIO, STELLIO [, DROMIO, *and* RISIO].

*Memphio.* Come, Stellio, the assurance may be made tomor-
    row, and our children assured today.
*Stellio.* Let the conveyance run as we agreed.                    215
*Prisius.* [*To Memphio and Stellio*] You convey cleanly, indeed,
    if cozenage be clean dealing; for in the apparel of your
    children you have conveyed a match between ours, which
    grieves us not a little.
*Memphio.* Nay, in the apparel of your children you have dis-    220
    covered the folly of ours, which shames us overmuch.
*Stellio.* But 'tis no matter. Though they be fools, they are no
    beggars!
*Sperantus.* And though ours be disobedient, they be no fools!
*Dromio.* [*Aside to Risio*] So, now they tune their pipes.    225
*Risio.* [*Aside to Dromio*] You shall hear sweet music between
    a hoarse raven and a screech owl.
*Memphio.* Neighbours, let us not vary. Our boys have played
    their cheating parts. I suspected no less at the tavern,
    where our four knaves met together.                    230
*Risio.* If it were knavery for four to meet in a tavern, your
    worships wot well there were other four.

---

212.1.] *Bracketed material* / *Dilke.*    216. SD.] *This ed.*    225, 226. SD.]
*Andreadis (subst.).*    227. screech owl] *Dilke;* schritch owle    *Q1, 2,*
*Bl.*    229. cheating] *Q1;* chearing *Q2, Bl.*    230. our four] *Bl (*foure*);* foure
foure *Q1;* fourc foure *Q2.*    232. worships] *Dilke;* wor. *Q1, 2, Bl.*

---

as a single entity as at 4.1.89–90 above. The comment suggests that Memphio
and Stellio are already visible to those on stage, although the printing of their
entry at line 212.1 follows the convention, observed elsewhere in *Q1* and followed in this edition, of marking an entrance immediately prior to the first
speech of the character heralded by the implied direction.
    211. *belike were privy*] were acquainted in all likelihood with this.
    213. *assurance*] financial settlement.
    214. *assured*] betrothed.
    215. *conveyance*] transfer of property by legal agreement.
    216. *convey*] (*a*) transfer property (as at line 215 above); (*b*) steal, delude.
*cleanly*] cleverly, adroitly.
    217. *clean*] plain (with a pun on *cleanly* in the previous line).
    218. *conveyed*] brought about (with a play on *convey* in line 216).
    220–1. *discovered*] revealed.
    225. *tune their pipes*] limber up for a heated exchange. The term *sweet
music* in the following line is ironic.
    228. *vary*] fall out, quarrel.
    232. *wot*] know.
    *other four*] i.e. the four old fathers.

*Stellio.* This villain calls us knaves, by craft!

*Lucio.* Nay, truly, I dare swear he used no craft, but means
plainly.                                                        235

*Sperantus.* This is worse! Come, Halfpenny, tell truth and
'scape the rod.

*Halfpenny.* As good confess here, being trussed, as at home
with my hose about my heels.

*Dromio.* [*To Sperantus*] Nay, I'll tell thee. [*To Halfpenny*] For   240
'twill never become thee to utter it.

*Memphio.* Well, out with it!

*Dromio.* Memphio had a fool to his son, which Stellio knew
not; Stellio a fool to his daughter, unknown to Memphio.
To cozen each other, they dealt with their boys for a          245
match. We met with Lucio and Halfpenny, who told the
love between their masters' children, the youth deeply in
love, the fathers unwilling to consent.

*Risio.* I'll take the tale by the end. Then we four met, which
argued we were no mountains, and in a tavern we met,           250
which argued we were mortal; and everyone in his wine

---

238. trussed] *Bond n.;* trust *Q1, 2, Bl.*    240. SDs.] *This ed.*    247. masters']
*Fairholt;* masters *Q1, 2, Bl.*    248. unwilling] *Dilke;* unwitting *Q1, 2, Bl.*

237. *'scape the rod*] escape a beating.

238-9. *being trussed...heels*] with the strings of my hose fastened (i.e. with
my breeches up) as at home with my breeches down (i.e. having the truth
beaten from me).

245. *cozen*] deceive.

245-6. *dealt...match*] plotted with their servants to bring about a marriage.

248. *unwilling*] Dilke's emendation of *Q1, 2, Bl* 'unwitting' (see collation
note) is adopted here (in common with all twentieth-century editions), as
the two words are readily confused in manuscript, and 'unwitting' does not
appear to make sense.

249. *tale*] pun: (*a*) story; (*b*) tail.

249-50. *Then...mountains*] an allusion to the proverb, 'Friends may
meet but mountains never greet' (Tilley, F738).

250-1. *in a tavern...mortal*] Bond (iii, p. 553) detects an allusion to the
concept of human life as an inn, citing lines from the poetic address by the
dying Loricus in the entertainment at Quarrendon, which he attributes to
Lyly (Bond, i, p. 468, 1–4). The parallel is an inexact, one, however, in that
the passage in question equates the body with an inn and the soul with a
guest, whereas the allusion in *Mother Bombie* turns on the fallibility of mortals
in their addiction to the pleasures of the flesh. Given the play's heavy reliance
on proverbs, it may be that the allusion is to a familiar saying.

told his day's work, which was a sign we forgot not our business. And seeing all our masters troubled with devices, we determined a little to trouble the water before they drank, so that in the attire of your children our  255
masters' wise children bewrayed their good natures, and in the garments of our masters' children yours made a marriage. This all stood upon us poor children and your young children, to show that old folks may be overtaken by children.  260

*Prisius.* Here's a children indeed! I'll never forget it.

*Memphio.* I will. [*He calls.*] Accius, come forth!

*Stellio.* I forgive all. [*He calls.*] Silena, come forth!

*Sperantus.* [*To Prisius*] Neighbour, these things cannot be recalled. Therefore as good consent, seeing in all our  265
purposes also we missed the mark; for they two will match their children.

*Prisius.* [*To Sperantus*] Well, of that more anon. [*He lowers his voice.*] Not so suddenly, lest our ungracious youths think

---

252. day's] *Andreadis;* dayes *Q1, 2 (*daies*), Bl.*    255. drank] *Dilke;* dronke *Q1;* drunk *Q2, Bl (*drunke*).*    256. masters'] *Fairholt;* masters *Q1, 2 (*maisters*), Bl. Also at line 257.*    261. a] *Q1, 2; not in Bl.*    262, 263, 264, 268-9. SD.] *This ed.*

253-4. *troubled with devices*] busied about plots.

254-5. *to trouble...drank*] proverbial expression (Tilley, C29) deriving from the behaviour of camels as recorded by Pliny (*Hist. nat.*, viii, 26). Compare *England*: 'The camel first troubleth the water before he drink' (p. 282), and *Pappe*, 'It is said that camels neuer drinke, til they haue troubled the water with their feete' (Bond, iii, p. 396). The behaviour was said to arise from the camel's reluctance to view the ugliness of its own shape, but the phrase is used here to denote a desire to cause mischief.

255. *your children*] i.e. the offspring of Prisius and Sperantus.

255-6. *our...children*] i.e. the offspring of Memphio and Stellio.

256. *bewrayed...natures*] revealed themselves to be fools. The good-natured character of fools was proverbial (cf. Tilley, F462, 'A fool is ever laughing', and F491, 'I am a fool, I love everything that's good').

258. *stood upon*] depended on.

259. *overtaken*] deceived.

261. *a children*] glossed by Tydeman as 'a breed of children' (p. 365), but it is possible that 'a clutch of children' was intended, looking back to the deliberately confusing repetition of the word *children* in Risio's preceding speech.

we dare do no other. But, in truth, their loves stirs up    270
nature in me.

[*Enter* ACCIUS *from Memphio's house, and* SILENA
*from Stellio's.*]

*Memphio.* Come, Accius, thou must be married to Silena.
How art thou minded?
*Accius.* What, for ever and ever?
*Memphio.* Ay, Accius, what else?                            275
*Accius.* I shall never be able to abide it. It will be so tedious!
*Stellio.* Silena, thou must be betrothed to Accius, and love
him for thy husband.
*Silena.* I had as lief have one of clouts!
*Stellio.* Why, Silena?                                      280
*Silena.* Why, look how he looks!
*Accius.* If you will not, another will!
*Silena.* I thank you for mine old cap!
*Accius.* And if you be so lusty, lend me two shillings!
*Prisius.* [*Aside to Sperantus*] We are happy we missed the  285
foolish match.
*Memphio.* [*To Accius*] Come, you shall presently be
contracted.
*Dromio.* Contract their wits no more; they be shrunk close
already.                                                     290
*Accius.* Well, father, here's my hand; strike the bargain!

---

271.1–2.] *This ed.; Enter* ACCIUS *and* SILENA. / *Bond (following line 263 this
ed.).* 275. Ay] *Dilke* (Aye); I *Q1, 2, Bl.* 285. SD.] *Bond (subst.).*
287. SD.] *Tydeman.*

270. *their loves stirs*] a further example of a plural subject being treated
grammatically as a single entity. Compare *Here comes Memphio and Stellio* at
lines 210–11 above.
271. *nature*] innate human bonds and sympathies.
273. *How...minded?*] What do you think about this?
279.] I would as gladly have a husband made of rags.
282.] Tydeman (p. 426) notes that the response is proverbial, often
concluded with 'so are all maidens married', but cites no authority or
comparable example.
283.] Thanks for nothing. The phrase has a proverbial ring, but no
parallel has been traced.
284. *lusty*] full of life.
288. *contracted*] betrothed.
289. *Contract*] Shrink (with a play on *contracted* in the previous line).

*Silena.* Must he lie with me?

*Stellio.* No, Silena, lie by thee.

*Accius.* I shall give her the humble bee's kiss.

*Enter* VICINIA [*with* MAESTIUS *and* SERENA].

*Vicinia.* I forbid the banns!                                     295

*Risio.* What, dost thou think them rats, and fearest they shall
     be poisoned?

*Memphio.* You, Vicinia? Wherefore?

*Vicinia.* Hearken. About eighteen years ago, I nursed thee a
     son, Memphio, and thee a daughter, Stellio.                   300

*Stellio.* True.

*Memphio.* True.

*Vicinia.* I had, at that time, two children of mine own, and,
     being poor, thought it better to change them than kill
     them. I imagined if, by device, I could thrust my children    305
     into your houses, they should be well brought up in their
     youth, and wisely provided for in their age. Nature
     wrought with me, and when they were weaned I sent
     home mine instead of yours, which hetherto you have
     kept tenderly, as yours. Growing in years, I found the        310
     children I kept at home to love dearly, at first like brother
     and sister, which I rejoiced at, but at length too forward
     in affection, which, although inwardly I could not mislike,

---

294.1.] *Bracketed material* / *Dilke (subst.).*     295. banns] *Daniel;* banes *Q1,*
*2, Bl.*     306. should] *Q1;* would *Q2, Bl.*

     292. *lie with*] share a room (or bed) with.
     293. *lie by*] have sexual intercourse with.
     294. *give her...kiss*] copulate with her. As Bond notes, '"sting" is
frequent in the dramatists of sexual action' (iii, p. 553).
     295. *banns*] capable of two meanings, obscured in modern English by
changes in spelling and pronunciation: (*a*) a public announcement of an
intention to marry (Vicinia's meaning); (*b*) rat poison (Risio's deliberate
misconstruction in the following lines, enabled by the sixteenth-century
spelling ('banes') of modern English 'banns').
     299–300. *nursed...son*] took in a son of yours for breast-feeding.
     300. *thee a daughter*] a daughter of yours.
     304–5. *kill them*] cause their death through my poverty.
     305. *device*] a trick.
     307–8. *Nature...me*] My maternal instincts worked upon me.
     312. *forward*] ardent.

yet openly I seemed to disallow. They increased in their
loving humours; I ceased not to chastise them for their          315
loose demeanours. At last, it came to my ears that my
son that was out with Memphio was a fool, that my
daughter with Stellio was also unwise, and yet, being
brother and sister, there was a match in hammering
betwixt them.                                                    320
*Memphio.* What monstrous tale is this?
*Stellio.* And, I am sure, incredible!
*Sperantus.* Let her end her discourse.
*Accius.* I'll never believe it.
*Memphio.* Hold thy peace!                                       325
*Vicinia.* My very bowels earned within me that I should be
author of such vild incest, an hindrance to lawful love. I
went to the good old woman, Mother Bombie, to know
the event of this practice, who told me this day I might
prevent the danger, and upon submission escape the        330
punishment. Hether I am come to claim my children,
though both fools, and to deliver yours, both loving.
*Memphio.* Is this possible? How shall we believe it?
*Stellio.* It cannot sink into my head.
*Vicinia.* This trial cannot fail. Your son, Memphio, had a mole   335
under his ear. I framed one under my child's ear by art.

327. vild] *Q1* (vilde), *2;* vile *Bl.*   328. good old] *Q1* (olde), *2;* gold
*Bl.*   332. yours] *Q2, Bl;* your *Q1.*   loving] *Q1;* living *Q2, Bl.*

314. *disallow*] disapprove.
315. *humours*] bent, fancies.
315–16. *ceased not...demeanours*] continued to reprove them for their
lascivious conduct.
319. *in hammering*] being devised.
326. *earned*] grieved. Compare *The Woman in the Moon:* 'Their sad depart
would make my heart to earn, / Were not the joys that I conceive in thee'
(3.1.63–4).
327. *vild*] vile.
329. *event*] outcome.
335–44.] The use of moles as a mark of recognition, a common device in
Roman New Comedy, was frequently deployed on the Renaissance stage.
Compare the confirmation that Polydore is the King's lost son in *Cymbeline*
by the 'sanguine star' on his neck (5.5.365), and the shared recollection in
the reunion of Viola and Sebastian in *Twelfth Night* that their father had 'a
mole upon his brow' (5.1.238).
335–6, 341–2. *a mole under his ear...on her wrist a mole*] Hazlitt (citing *The
Greenwich Fortune-Teller*) notes that 'A mole on the ear signifies riches and

You shall see it taken away with the juice of mandrake.
[*She rubs away the mole behind Accius' ear.*] Behold now
for your son's. [*She applies the herb, without success to the
mole behind Maestius' ear.*] No herb can undo that nature    340
hath done. Your daughter, Stellio, hath on her wrist a
mole, which I counterfeited on my daughter's arm, and
that shall you see taken away as the other. [*She rubs away
the mole on Silena's wrist.*] Thus you see I do not dissemble, hoping you will pardon me, as I have pitied them.    345
*Memphio.* [*Turning to Maestius*] This is my son! O, fortunate
Memphio!
*Stellio.* [*Turning to Serena*] This is my daughter! More than
thrice happy Stellio!
*Maestius.* How happy is Maestius, thou blessed, Serena, that    350
being neither children to poor parents, nor brother and

---

337-40. mandrake...No] *Punctuation this ed.;* mandrage, beholde nowe for
your sonnes, no *Q1, 2* (behold now...sons), *Bl.*    337. mandrake] *Daniel;*
mandrage *Q1, 2, Bl.*    338, 339-40. SD.] *This ed. Tydeman supplies / Shows*
MAESTIUS' *mole. / following* done (*line 341 this ed.*).    343-4. SD.] *This ed.
Tydeman supplies / Shows* SERENA'S *mole. /.*    346, 348. SD.] *This ed.*

---

respect. A mole on the neck promises riches', while 'A mole on the
wrist...shows an ingenious mind' (Hazlitt, W. C., p. 415). The discovery of
the moles of one set of children, and the removal of those of the other, thus
constitutes an emblematic representation of the reversal of their positions.
    336. *framed*] made.
    337. *mandrake*] mandragora, a plant with a range of mythical properties
and medical uses, reputed to scream when pulled up by the root.
    338, 339-40, 343-4. SD.] No indication is given in *Q1, 2, Bl* of how the
discovery scene was initially staged, and only Tydeman among modern
editors supplies any directions in the course of Vicinia's speech (see
Appendix). His brief interpolations, '*Shows* MAESTIUS' *mole*', following *done*
(line 341, this ed.), and '*Shows* SERENA'S *mole*', following *other* (line 343 this
ed.), imply that the removal itself takes place after the close of the play, and
that no evidence is afforded to the assembled company that some moles are
natural and others forged. The onstage acceptance of Maestius and Serena
indicates, however, that convincing proof of their identity is offered at this
point, justifying the stage directions supplied here.
    340. *that*] that which.
    345. *as I...them*] taken by Bond to mean that she did not kill the children
of Memphio and Stellio, 'as she had intended to do with her own offspring'
(iii, p. 553). It is doubtful, however, that Vicinia intended to murder her
children (see lines 304-5n. above), and more likely that she is alluding here
to the self-sacrificing revelation of her misconduct, which has allowed for
the transformation in the prospects of Maestius and Serena, and the fulfilment of their love. (*them* = Maestius and Serena.)

sister by nature, may enjoy their love by consent of
parents and nature.
*Accius.* Soft! I'll not swap my father for all this!
*Silena.* What! Do you think I'll be cozened of my father?      355
Methinks I should not! Mother Bombie told me, 'My
father knew me not, my mother bore me not; falsely bred,
truly begot.' A bots on Mother Bombie!
*Dromio.* Mother Bombie told us we should be found cozen-
ers, and in the end be cozened by cozeners. Well fare      360
Mother Bombie!
*Risio.* [*To Dromio*] I heard Mother Bombie say that thou shalt
die a beggar. Beware of Mother Bombie!
*Prisius.* Why, have you all been with Mother Bombie?
*Lucio.* All. And as far as I can see, foretold all.      365
*Memphio.* Indeed, she is cunning and wise, never doing harm,
but still practising good. Seeing these things fall out thus,
are you content, Stellio, the match go forward?
*Stellio.* Ay, with double joy, having found for a fool a wise
maid, and finding between them both exceeding love.      370
*Prisius.* Then to end all jars, our children's matches shall
stand with our good liking. Livia, enjoy Candius!

---

354. I'll not] *Q1 (Ile), 2;* I let *Bl.*      356–8. 'My father...begot'] *Quotation
marks / Fairholt.*      360. Well fare] *Daniel;* welfare *Q1, 2, Bl.*      362. SD.]
*Tydeman.*      369. Ay] *Dilke (Aye);* I *Q1, 2, Bl.*

---

352. *enjoy*] have full possession of. Compare Protea's request regarding
her lover in *Love's Metamorphosis*, having consented to be sold to satisfy her
father's hunger: 'And now, father, give me leave to enjoy my Petulius, that
on this unfortunate shore still seeks me, sorrowing' (4.2.19–21). The word
recurs, with the same force, at lines 372 and 373 below.
354. *Soft*] Just a moment.
*swap*] exchange.
355. *cozened of*] cheated out of.
358. *bots*] plague.
359–60. *found cozeners...cozeners*] discovered to be tricksters and ultimately deceived by impostors.
360. *Well fare*] an expression of good will (cf. Modern English 'Good
luck'), used here ironically.
366–7. *she is...good*] See Introduction, pp. 30ff., for a discussion of the
favourable representation of the figure of the wise-woman in this play.
366. *cunning*] knowledgeable.
368. *the match go forward*] that we proceed with the marriage.
370. *exceeding*] the utmost.
371. *jars*] quarrels, discord.

*Sperantus.* Candius, enjoy Livia!

*Candius.* How shall we recompense fortune, that to our loves
    hath added our parents' good wills!                    375

*Maestius.* How shall we requite fortune, that to our loves hath
    added lawfulness, and to our poor estate competent
    living!

*Memphio.* Vicinia, thy fact is pardoned, though the law would
    see it punished. We be content to keep Silena in the    380
    house with the new-married couple.

*Stellio.* And I do maintain Accius in our house.

*Vicinia.* Come, my children, though fortune hath not pro-
    vided you lands, yet you see you are not destitute of
    friends. I shall be eased of a charge both in purse and    385
    conscience; in conscience having revealed my lewd
    practice, in purse having you kept of alms.

*Accius.* [*To Silena*] Come, if you be my sister, it's the better
    for you.

*Silena.* [*To Accius*] Come, brother, methinks it's better than    390
    it was. I should have been but a bald bride. I'll eat as
    much pie as if I had been married.

*Memphio.* Let's also forgive the knavery of our boys, since all
    turns to our good haps.

*Stellio.* Agreed; all are pleased now the boys are    395
    unpunished.

    *Enter* HACKNEYMAN, SERGEANT, [*and*] SCRIVENER.

*Hackneyman.* Nay, soft, take us with you, and seek redress
    for our wrongs, or we'll complain to the Mayor.

*Prisius.* What's the matter?

---

386. having] *Dilke;* have *Q1, 2, Bl.*    388, 390. SD.] *This ed.*

377–8. *poor…living*] indigent condition a comfortable income.
379. *fact*] crime.
385. *charge*] (*a*) cost; (*b*) burden.
386–7. *lewd practice*] vile deception.
387. *kept of alms*] provided for by charity.
391. *but a bald*] a sorry, an unsatisfactory.
391–2. *eat…pie*] have as much to eat at the wedding feast (an index of
Silena's childishness). Pies of a variety of kinds were a staple sixteenth-
century dish.
394. *our good haps*] good fortune for us.
397. *soft…you*] stop, don't forget us.

*Hackneyman.* I arrested Memphio's boy for an horse. After    400
much mocking, at the request of his fellow wags, I was
content to take a bond, jointly of them all. They had me
into a tavern. There they made me, the Scrivener, and
the Sergeant drunk, pawned his mace for the wine, and
sealed me an obligation nothing to the purpose. I pray    405
you, read it!

*Memphio.* What wags be these! [*He looks over the bond.*] Why,
by this bond you can demand nothing; and things done in
drink may be repented in soberness, but not remedied.

*Dromio.* Sir, I have his acquittance; let him sue his bond!    410

*Hackneyman.* I'll cry quittance with thee!

*Sergeant.* And I, or it shall cost me the laying on freely of my
mace!

*Scrivener.* And I'll give thee such a dash with a pen as shall
cost thee many a pound, with such a *Noverint* as Cheapside    415
can show none such!

*Halfpenny.* Do your worst! Our knaveries will revenge it upon
your children's children!

*Memphio.* Thou boy! [*To the Hackneyman*] We will pay the
hire of the horse. Be not angry. The boys have been in a    420

---

400–1. horse…I ] *Punctuation as Bond;* horse after much mocking, at the
request of his fellowe wagges, I *Q1, 2, Bl* (fellow). 404. drunk] *Q2*
(drunke), *Bl;* dronke *Q1.* the wine] *Q1, 2;* his wine *Bl.* 407. SD.] *This
ed.* 415. Cheapside] *Dilke;* cheap side *Q1, 2, Bl.* 419–20. Thou boy…The
boys] *Punctuation this ed.;* Thou boy, we wil paie the hire of the horse, be
not angrie, the boyes *Q1, 2, Bl* (wee…boies). 419. SD.] *Bond (subst.).*

---

400. *for an*] over a.
404. *his*] the Sergeant's.
405. *nothing…purpose*] that availed me nothing.
407. *What…these*] What imps these boys are.
410. *acquittance*] written release from the debt.
411. *cry quittance*] get even (proverbial formulation: Tilley, Q18), with a
pun on *acquittance* in the previous line.
414. *give…pen*] draw up such a document against you.
415. Noverint] *Noverint universi* ('Let all men know'), the formal opening
of a writ.
*Cheapside*] the commercial heart of sixteenth-century London, stretching
from the north-east corner of St Paul's churchyard to the Poultry. Tydeman
notes that it 'was the home of the Court of Arches in the Church of St
Mary-le-Bow, from which legal summonses were sent out' (p. 426).
419. *Thou boy*] You little imp.

merry cozening vein, for they have served their masters
of the same sort. But all must be forgotten. [*To the
company at large*] Now all are content but the poor
fiddlers. They shall be sent for to the marriage, and have
double fees.                                                    425
*Dromio.* You need no more send for a fiddler to a feast than
a beggar to a fair.
*Stellio.* This day we will feast at my house.
*Memphio.* Tomorrow at mine.
*Prisius.* The next day at mine.                                430
*Sperantus.* Then at mine the last day, and even so spend this
week in good cheer.
*Dromio.* Then we were best be going whilst everyone is
pleased; and yet these couples are not fully pleased till
the priest have done his worst.                                435
*Risio.* Come, Sergeant, we'll toss it this week, and make thy
mace arrest a boiled capon!
*Sergeant.* No more words at the wedding. If the Mayor should
know it, I were in danger of mine office.
*Risio.* Then take heed how on such as we are you show a cast   440
of your office.
*Halfpenny.* If you mace us, we'll pepper you.

---

422–3. SD.]  *This ed.; To all.  / Andreadis.*    431. day]  *Q1; not in Q2, Bl.*

421. *cozening vein*] guileful mood.
421–2. *served...same sort*] behaved in the same way to their masters.
426–7.] proverbial (Tilley, F206: 'Fiddlers, dogs, and flies (flatterers)
come to feasts uncalled').
434–5. *are not...worst*] will not be fully satisfied (with sexual connotations) until the priest has performed all the marriage rites.
436. *toss it...week*] empty our drinking vessels for a week.
437. *capon*] castrated cock, fattened for the table.
438. *No more...wedding*] Say no more about it (with the implication that
those are some occasions on which it is best not to tell what one knows).
439. *were in danger of*] could lose.
440–1. *take heed...office*] be careful how you attempt to give a taste of
your authority over people like us.
440. *cast*] stroke or taste (*OED*, sb. 9. fig.). Compare Greene, *Menaphon*
(1589): 'Shew vs a cast of your cunning' (Grosart, vi, p. 82).
442.] a further play on the term used for the Sergeant's staff of office. (*a*)
If you threaten us with your authority, we will rain injuries in you; (*b*) If you
besprinkle us with spice (see 3.4.139n.), we will scatter a condiment on you.

*Accius.* [*To Silena*] Come sister, the best is we shall have good
        cheer these four days.
*Lucio.* And be fools for ever.                                        445
*Silena.* That's none of our upseekings!                    [*Exeunt.*]

                            FINIS


443. SD.] *This ed.*   446. SD.] *Bond.*

---

446. *upseekings*] a rare usage derived from a now obsolete verb denoting
to seek or sound out. *OED* cites Boys, *Workes* (1630), 462: 'We should not
expect untill other upseekes us, but that we should seeke and serue them'.
Though the word makes sense in the context, and its grandiose nature is
appropriate to Silena, given the archaic nature of the expression, it may be
that the play closes on yet another garbled proverb.

# APPENDIX
## Historical Collation

Characters...Appearance] *Not in Q1, 2, Bl. No two modern editions agree on the information supplied and/or the form or ordering of the characters' names. The first printed list was attempted by Dilke.*

SCENE] *Not in Q1, 2, Bl; Rochester, Kent. / first supplied by Fairholt and amplified by Bond, who (omitting Kent) adds / an open square or street. /. No scene is indicated by Dilke, Andreadis, or Tydeman.* Daniel locates the action *in* Wealthy estates in the English countryside around Rochester.

HT. A Pleasant...*Mother Bombie] Q1, 2, Bl; not in Dilke, Andreadis; assimilated to the title, and transferred to the title-page by Daniel.*

### ACTUS PRIMUS, SCENA PRIMA

0. primus] *Q2, Bl.; primus Q1 (turned letter).* 0.1.] *Stage directions derive from Q1, unless otherwise indicated. The following collation notes record substantive changes only, as when new stage directions or portions of stage directions have been added. The collation notes do not record routine amplifications, such as the supplying of an [Enter] where the entry is clearly implied in the Quarto by the listing of the characters' names, or an [and] in a series of names. Minor departures from directions supplied by previous editors, such as the ordering of names at the head of a scene, are not recorded.* 2. curst] *Q1, 2, Bl;* curs'd *Andreadis.* 5. maladies] *Q2, Bl;* mala-ladies *Q1.* 6. holly] *Q2, Bl;* holy *Q1.* 7. young²] *Q1 (yong), 2, Bl (young); not in Andreadis.* 10. Ay] *Andreadis;* I *Q1, 2, Bl;* Ah *Dilke (also at line 47).* 15. chickens] *Q1, Bl;* chichens *Q2.* 17. grown] *Q2, Bl (growne);* growen *Q1.* 20. coxcombs] *Andreadis;* cockescombes *Q1;* cockescomes *Q2, Bl;* cocks-combs *Dilke;* cock's-combs *Daniel.* 34. brought] *Q1, 2, Bl;* brough *Daniel.* 45. till thou¹] *Bond;* thou shalt *Q1, Bl;* thou shalr *Q2.* 53. arrant] *Dilke;* arrand *Q1, 2, Bl.* 57. skull] *Bl;* scull *Q1, 2.* 59. tongue] *Q1 (tong);* tougue *Q2.* 64. them] *Dilke;* him *Q1, 2, Bl.* 67. Well?] *Andreadis;* Well. *Q1, 2, Bl;* Well! *Fairholt.* 72. So, sir?] *Andreadis;* So sir *Q1, 2, Bl;* So, sir *Dilke.* 76. for ever] *Q1, 2, Bl;* forever *Andreadis.* 87. by] *Q2, Bl;* py *Q1 (turned letter).* 91. care] *Q2, Bl;* eare *Q1.* 95. hundreth] *Q1, 2, Bl;* hundred *Dilke;* hundredth *Fairholt.* 97. What else!] *This ed.;* What else? *Q1, 2, Bl.* 100. SD.] *Bond; Daniel encloses* I lack...son *(lines 100-2 this ed.) in brackets, denoting an aside.* 101. counsel] *Q1 (counsell), 2, Bl;* council *Dilke.* 102. SD.] *This ed.* 110. no] *Q1;* no no *Q2, Bl.* 110.1. SD.] *Bracketed material this ed.*

### ACT[US] I, SCE[NA] 2

0. Act[us] 1] *Fairholt (ACTUS PRIMUS); Act. 2 Q1, 2; Actus secundus Bl.* Sce. 2] *Q1, 2; Scaena secunda Bl.* 0.1. RISIO] *Dilke; Riscio / Q1, 2, Bl.* 1. Risio] *Q1 (in italics); Riscio / Q2, Bl.* 15.] *Tydeman supplies /*

*aside* / *following speech prefix.*    22. Risio] *Dilke; Riscio* / *Q1, 2, Bl.*
23. herself] *Q2* (*her selfe*), *Bl;* herselfe selfe *Q1.*      subtle; in this] *Dilke;*
subtile in this *Q1, 2, Bl.*    24. courtly; in this] *Dilke;* courtly, in this *Q1;*
courtlie: in this *Q2, Bl* (*courtly*).    26. SP.] *Q1; Riscio Q2, Bl.*    33. Risio]
*Q1; Risco* / *Q2; Riscio* / *Bl.*    35. compasses. And] *Punctuation as Andreadis;*
compasses, and *Q1, 2, Bl;* compasses: and *Tydeman;* compasses; and
*Daniel.*    36. they'll] *Andreadis;* the'il *Q1, 2, Bl.*    41. be a match] *Q1, 2,*
*Bl;* be made a match *Dilke.*    42. not I thirst] *Q1, 2, Bl;* not that I thirst
*Dilke.*    43. farm] *Q1* (*farme*), *2;* fame *Bl.*    44. SD.] *This ed.*    A very
good nature] *Signalled by Bond as an aside.*    50. Dromio] *Q1* (*in italics*);
*Romio* / *Q2, Bl.*    SD.] *Bond.*

## ACT[US] I, SCE[NA] 3

0.] *Q1* (*subst.*), *2;* Actus primus, Scaena tertia *Bl.*    5. sempster] *Q1, 2,*
*Bl;* sempstress *Dilke.*    to take to] *Q1;* to take too *Q2, Bl.*    8. winch] *Q1,*
*2, Bl;* wince *Dilke.*    9. your girl] *Q2* (*girle*), *Bl;* my girle *Q1.*    13. another
gate] *Q1;* another gates *Q2, Bl;* another gate's *Fairholt;* another-gate
*Andreadis.*    18. your] *Q1;* you *Q2, Bl.*    21. her] *Q1;* your *Q2,*
*Bl.*    22. nor my] *Q1, 2, Bl;* nor with my *Fairholt.*    23. If thou] *Q1;* for
if thou *Q2, Bl.*    SD.] *Bond* (*subst.*).    26. shake so, that] *Q1, 2;* shake,
so that *Bl.*    29. SD.] *This ed.*    35. princox] *Andreadis;* princockes *Q1,*
*2;* princocks *Bl.*    40–1] good, though I say it. He] *Punctuation as Daniel;*
good though I saie it, he *Q1, 2* (*thogh*), *Bl* (*say it, hee*); good, though I say
it, he *Dilke;* good. Though I say it, he *Andreadis;* good, though I saie it; he
*Tydeman.*    49. be] *Q1, 2;* he *Bl;* hie *Fairholt.*    58. hundreth] *Q1, 2, Bl;*
hundred *Dilke;* hundredth *Fairholt.*    61. to devise to] *Punctuation as Q1,*
*2, Bl;* to devise, to *Dilke.*    62. him] *Q1; not in Q2, Bl.*    67.] *Tydeman*
*supplies SD.* / *Looking offstage* / *following* heart ache.    69.1.] *This ed.;*
*They stand aside.* / *Dilke.*    69.2.] *Bracketed material* / *Tydeman*
(*subst.*).    70. SD.] *This ed.; aside* / *Bond.*    72. SD.] *This ed.; aside* /
*Tydeman.*    73. warrant, I, my] *Punctuation as Bond;* warrant I my *Q1;*
warrant I, my *Q2, Bl;* warrant I, my *Dilke;* warrant, ay, my
*Andreadis.*    80. hang] *Q1, 2, Bl; not in Andreadis.*    83. SD.] *Bond.*
Ay] *Andreadis;* I *Q1, 2, Bl;* Ah *Dilke.*    84. SP.] *Q1* (*Spe.*), *Bl; Lpe.* /
*Q2.*    SD.] *This ed.; aside* / *Tydeman.*    89. an] *Q1, 2, Bl;* a *Dilke.*
94. SD.] *Bond.*    picked] *Q1* (*pickt*), *2, Bl;* pricked *Dilke.*    95. work
out of] *Punctuation this ed.;* worke, out of *Q1, 2, Bl;* work? out of *Dilke;*
work? Out of *Andreadis.*    96. SD.] *This ed.; aside* / *Tydeman.*    103. join-
ture] *Dilke;* Ioynter *Q1, 2, Bl;* jointer *Daniel.*    108. SD.] *Bond.*    110.
whenas] *Q1* (*when as*); when *Q2, Bl.*    118. twenty] *Q1* (*twentie*), *Bl;*
20. *Q2.*    together] *Q1, 2, Bl;* not in *Dilke.*    119. make us] *Q1; not in*
*Q2, Bl.*    121. mine] *Q2, Bl;* min *Q1.*    124. deadly, if] *Punctuation as*
*Q1, 2, Bl;* deadly. If *Andreadis.*    126. SD.] *Bond.*    128. woo] *Q1, 2;*
woe *Bl.*    129–30. SD.] *Tydeman* (*subst.*).    132. cowslops] *Q1, 2, Bl;*
cowslips *Dilke.*    136–7. Venus. Among trees, the] *Punctuation as Bond;*
Venus among trees, the *Q1; Venus* among trees: the *Q2, Bl;* Venus; among
trees, the *Dilke.*    138. abeston] *Bond;* Abestor *Q1, 2, Bl;* asbestos *Dilke.*
139. thyme] *Andreadis;* Time *Q1, 2, Bl.*    142. SD.] *This ed.; aside* / *Bond.*
143. lerripoop] *Q1* (*lerripoope*), *2, Bl;* liripoop *Andreadis.*    144. SD.] *This*

*ed.; aside / Bond.*   Listen] *Q1, 2;* Listeu *Bl (turned letter).*   150. three] *Q2, Bl;* 3. *Q1.*   153. *placidam*] *Q1, 2, Bl; placitam / Dilke.*   exorare] *Dilke; euorare / Q1, 2, Bl.*   154. *duret*] *Dilke; ducet / Q1, 2, Bl.*   155. Candius] *Q2 (in italics), Bl; Cand. / Q1.*   conster] *Q1, 2, Bl;* construe *Dilke.*   156. parse] *Dilke;* pace *Q1, 2, Bl.*   159. that²] *Q1, 2, Bl;* not in *Dilke.*   162. SP.] *Q1 (Liu.), Bl; Lin. / Q2.*   165. *effectu*] *Dilke; effertu / Q1, 2, Bl.*   167. are] *Q1;* is *Q2, Bl.*   171. SD.] *Bond (subst.).*   173. SD.] *Tydeman (subst.).*   176. counsel] *Q1, 2, Bl;* council *Dilke.*   176. SD.] *This ed.*   177. hath] *Q1;* have *Q2, Bl.*   179. You have] *Q1;* and haue *Q2, Bl.*   186. fools, churls] *Q1 (*fooles, churles*), 2, Bl;* fools, and churls *Dilke.*   189–90. pains …pangs] *Text and punctuation as Q1;* paines, and with deadly pangs *Q2, Bl;* pains and, bringing it forth with deadly pangs *Andreadis;* pains and bringing it forth with deadly pangs *Daniel.*   191. it up with] *Q1, 2, Bl;* it with *Dilke.*   193. collop] *Q1;* collops *Q2, Bl.*   194. soul. With] *Punctuation as Andreadis;* soul, with *Q1, 2, Bl;* soul; with *Dilke.*   195. cheeks] *Q2, Bl;* checkes *Q1.*   196. heart, thou] *Punctuation as Q1, 2, Bl;* heart. Thou *Daniel.*   200. sewing] *Dilke;* sowing *Q1, 2, Bl.*   201. come] *Q1;* comes *Q2, Bl.*   212. idleness] *Q1 (*idlenesse*), Bl (*idlenes*);* idldnesse *Q2.*   216.] *Tydeman supplies SD. /* CANDIUS *hesitates. / following* alone.   220.1–2.] *Bracketed material this ed.*   228. 1.] *Bracketed material this ed.*

## ACT [US] 2, SCE [NA] I

0.] *Q1 (subst.), 2;* Actus secundus, Scaena prima *Bl.*   0.1–2.] *and initially…another / this ed.; Dromio. Risio. / Q1, 2, Bl (subst.); ⟨Enter at opposite sides⟩* DROMIO, RISIO. */ Bond; Enter from different directions* DROMIO *and* RISIO. */ Tydeman; Enter* DROMIO *and* RISCIO, *meeting. / Daniel.*   3. obviam] *Q1, 2, Bl;* obvium / *Dilke.*   4. on whom] *Q1 (*whome*), 2, Bl;* of whom *Dilke.*   5. should] *Q1, 2, Bl; not in Daniel.*   12. SD.] *Tydeman.   Hem quam opportune*] *Q1, 2, Bl;* Hem! *Quam opportune / Andreadis.*   14. SD.] *Tydeman.*   15. kiss my hand] *Q1 (*kisse*); not in Q2, Bl, Dilke, Fairholt.*   20. contract] *Bl;* controct *Q1, 2.*   28. this] *Q1, 2, Bl;* that *Dilke.*   30. are we] *Q1, 2, Bl;* we are *Dilke.*   wits' ends] *Andreadis;* wits endes *Q1;* wittes endes *Q2, Bl;* wits-ends *Dilke;* wit's ends *Daniel.*   37. will] *Q1, 2, Bl;* we'll *Fairholt.*   43. old] *Q1 (*olde*), Bl (*old*);* olke *Q2.*   44. as] *Q1;* is *Q2, Bl.*   45. if] *Q2, Bl;* is *Q1.*   46. too²] *Q1, 2, Bl;* to *Dilke.*   48.] *Tydeman supplies SD. / looking offstage / following SP.*   51.1.] *Positioning as Q1, 2, Bl. Transposed by Tydeman to line 50 this ed., following* cozenage.   54. an] *Q1;* a *Q2, Bl.*   56. you] *Q2, Bl;* you you *Q1.*   60. SD.] *This ed.; Tydeman supplies /* RISIO *grabs* HALFPENNY. */ following* steady *(line 59 this ed.).*   63. SD.] *This ed.*   70. Well?] *Punctuation as Andreadis;* Well. *Q1, 2, Bl;* Well! *Fairholt.*   71. SP.] *Q1 (Half.), Bl;* Aalf / *Q2.*   82. goose] *Q1, 2, Bl;* goose's *Dilke.*   84. Laudo] *Q1, Bl;* Lando / *Q2.*   85. Memphio] *Q1;* Memphios *Q2, Bl;* Memphio's *Dilke.*   89. SD.] *This ed.*   90. meantst] *Q1, 2;* meanest *Bl;* mean'st *Dilke;* meantest *Daniel (with it supplied erroneously before the following word).*   93. SD.] *Tydeman.*   94. thou] *Q1, 2, Bl;* thon *Fairholt.*   106.1.] *This ed.*   107. Go to] *Q1;* Go too *Q2, Bl.*   109. SD.] *This ed.*   110. SD.] *This ed.*   112. thee] *Q1;*

*not in Q2, Bl.*    117. *juventus*] *Bond n.; iuuentus / Q1, 2; inuentus / Bl; inventio / Dilke; inventus / Fairholt.*    121, 130. SP.] *Dilke (Luc.); Liu. / Q1, 2, Bl.*    123. SD.] *This ed.*    127–8. SD.] *This ed.*    130. irketh] *Q1;* liketh *Q2, Bl.*    130–1. behoveth. My] *Punctuation as Andreadis;* behoueth, my *Q1, 2, Bl;* behoueth; my *Bond.*    131. wits work] *Q1 (worke);* wits to worke *Q2, Bl.*    142. up] *Bl;* us *Q1, 2.*    143. disgest] *Q1, 2, Bl;* digest *Dilke.*    145. foot] *Q1, 2, Bl;* feet *Dilke.*    147. lanthorn] *Q1, 2, Bl;* lantern *Dilke.*    153. to] *Q1, 2, Bl;* to ⟨to⟩ *Bond.*    154. *philosophandum*] *Bl; philosophundum / Q1, 2.*    155. SD.] *This ed.*    158. SD.] *This ed.*    Why…Thou] *Punctuation as Bond;* Why, sayest thou that thou *Q1, 2 (*saiest*), Bl.*    160. singe] *Dilke;* sing *Q1, 2, Bl.*    an hot] *Q1, 2, Bl;* a hot *Dilke.*    162. SD.] *This ed.*    163.1–183] *Bl; not in Q1, 2; transferred to an Appendix by Andreadis. Daniel omits* SONG *(line 163.1. this ed.) and supplies / They sing. / following* throat *(line 163 this ed.).*    164, 182. Omnes] *Bl;* ALL *Daniel.*    165. callst] *Bl (call'st);* callest *Daniel.*    170. noll] *Andreadis; Nowle / Bl;* nole *Daniel.*    171. mak'st] *Bl;* makest *Daniel.*    men's] *Dilke;* mens *Bl.*    172. canst] *Bl; can* Dilke.    183.1.] *Bracketed material / Bond (subst.).*

## ACT [US] 2, SCE [NA] 2

0.] *Q1 (subst.), 2;* Actus secundus, Scaena secunda *Bl.*    0.1.] *Q1, 2, Bl; Enter* MEMPHIO. */ Dilke.*    5. SD.] *Exit / Q1; Exeunt / Q2, Bl. Bracketed material / Bond.*    5.1.] *Q1, 2, Bl; Enter* STELLIO. */ Dilke.*    8. loved] *Q1, 2, Bl;* loveth *Tydeman.*    11. ferret] *Dilke;* firrit *Q1, 2, Bl.*    13. SD.] *Bracketed material / Bond.*    13.1.] *Q1, 2, Bl; Enter* PRISIUS. *Dilke.*    15. errand] *Dilke;* arrande *Q1;* arrand *Q2, Bl.*    19. to] *Q1;* too *Q2, Bl, Daniel.*    20. suddenly] *Q1;* so suddainely *Q2, Bl (*suddenly*).*    22. SD.] *Bracketed material / Bond.*    22.1.] *Q1, 2, Bl; Enter* SPERANTUS. */ Dilke.*    26. too] *Q2, Bl;* to *Q1.*    his[2]] *Q1; not in Q2, Bl, Dilke.*    29. *sans*] *Dilke;* sance *Q1, 2, Bl.*    29–30. cats'…dogs'] *Fairholt (dogges');* cats…dogs *Q1;* cattes…dogges *Q2;* Cats…Dogges *Bl;* cat's…dog's *Dilke.*    33. th'other] *Q2 (*thother*);* thether *Q1;* the other *Bl.*    33.1.] *Bracketed material / Bond.*

## ACT [US] 2, SCE [NA] 3

0.] *Q1 (subst.), 2;* Actus secundus. Scaena tertia *Bl.*    0.1.] *Dilke; Candius. Silena. / Q1, 2, Bl (subst.);* CANDIUS, SILENA. ⟨*Enter* CANDIUS.⟩ *Bond.*    4. shall[2]] *Q1; not in Q2, Bl.*    8.1.] *Bracketed material this ed.; direction transposed by Tydeman to line 6 this ed., following* love.    8–9. her attire. By her face] *Punctuation as Q2, Bl;* attire, by her face *Q1.*    12. ay] *Andreadis;* I *Q1, 2, Bl;* ah! *Dilke.*    15. a way] *Dilke;* away *Q1, 2, Bl.*    16. if I her cunning] *Q1, 2, Bl;* if cunning *Dilke;* if I ⟨finde⟩ her coming *Bond;* If I find her cunning *Andreadis.*    18. SD.] *This ed.*    19. know] *Q1, 2, Bl;* knows *Dilke.*    21. Mother] *Q1; not in Q2, Bl.*    24. SD.] *Bond.*    27. passions] *Q1, 2, Bl;* passion's *Tydeman.*    31. SD.] *Bond.*    32. eyes] *Q1, 2, Bl;* eye *Dilke.*    37. SD. *Aside*] *Andreadis. To* Silena] *This ed., Aloud. / Andreadis.*    38. hether] *Q1;* hither *Q2, Bl.*    45. The] *Q1;* Thy *Q2, Bl.*    46. therefore should be] *Q1, 2, Bl;* therefore ⟨love⟩ should

be *Bond.* 52. Aha] *Andreadis;* A ha *Q1, 2, Bl;* Ha, ha *Dilke.*
53. SD.] *Dilke (following* try her, *line 54 this ed.).* 54. SD.] *This
ed; Aloud. / Andreadis.* 57. SD.] *Dilke (following* artificial, *line 58
this ed.).* 58. SD.] *This ed.; Aloud. / Andreadis.* 59. and am cunning]
*Q1, 2, Bl;* and cunning *Dilke.* 61. o'clock] *Daniel;* a clocke *Q1, 2,
Bl.* 62. SD.] *This ed.* 63–4. to your] *Q1, 2, Bl;* for your *Dilke.*
64. husband] *Q1, Bl;* busband *Q2.* 65. cranes'] *Q2 (*cranes*), Bl
(*Cranes*);* carnes *Q1;* crane's *Dilke.* 69. SD.] *Dilke (following* dissemble,
*line 71 this ed.).* wench] *Q1;* wretch *Q2, Bl.* 72. SD.] *This ed.; Aloud.
/ Bond.* 74. too] *Q2, Bl;* to *Q1.* 77. baked] *Dilke;* backt *Q1, 2, Bl;* bakt
*Bond;* bak'd *(hyphenated with* hard *in the previous line) Andreadis;* backed
*Daniel.* 78. SD.] *This ed.* hath] *Q1, 2, Bl;* hast *Dilke.* raked] *Dilke;*
rakt *Q1;* rackt *Q2, Bl;* rak'd *Andreadis;* racked *Daniel.* 81. jibing] *This ed;*
gybing *Q1, 2, Bl;* gibing *Andreadis.* 82. by-word] *Bl;* buy worde *Q1, 2
(*word*).* 87. SD.] *Bracketed material this ed.* 88. SP.] *Dilke (Sil.); Liu
/ Q1, 2, Bl.* 92.1.] *This ed.; Knocks at* MOTHER BOMBIE'S *door. / Bond;
Knocks at door. / Andreadis (following* God be here, *line 93 this ed.).* 93.1–
2.] *This ed.; Enter Mother Bombie. / Q1, 2, Bl.* 96. shouldst] *Q1 (*shuldst*);*
should *Q2, Bl.* 101.1–2.] *This ed.;* SILENA *holds it above her head. /
Tydeman.* 103–7] *Lineation as Bond; continuous prose in Q1, 2, Bl. Dilke
divides line 105 this ed. (*Falsely bred, / Truly begot*). Daniel divides line 106
(*Choice of two husbands, / But never tied in bands*).* 103. SD.] *This
ed.* 105. Falsely] *Q1;* falselie *Q2;* falsly *Bl;* fasly *Fairholt.* 108–15.]
*Lineation this ed.; continuous prose in Q1, 2, Bl.* 108. SD.]
*This ed.* 115. naught] *Q1, 2, Bl;* nought *Dilke.* 119.1.] *Bracketed mate-
rial this ed.*

## ACT [US] 2, SCE [NA] 4

0.] *Q1 (subst.), 2; Actus secundus. Scaena quarta / Bl.* 0.1–2.] *Ordering of
names as Daniel; Dromio. Risio. Lucio. Halfepenie. / Q1. 2, Bl (subst.); Fairholt
and Daniel print* RISCIO *for Risio; bracketed material / Tydeman.* 1. were] *Q1;*
are *Q2, Bl.* 4. cozenage] *Q2 (*cosonage*);* coosnage *Q1;* coozenage
*Bl.* 6. plod] *Q1, 2, Bl;* plot *Daniel.* 10. knavery] *Q1, 2 (*knauerie*);*
knauerie's *Bl.* 13. travail] *Daniel;* trauell *Q1, 2, Bl;* travel *Dilke.*
14. 'scaped] *Daniel (*scaped*);* scapt *Q1, 2, Bl;* escaped *Dilke;* 'scapt *Fairholt;*
'scap'd *Andreadis.* 21. SP.] *Dilke (Drom.); not in Q1, 2, Bl.* I prae...
and] *Bond (*bowle*); I presequar,* a bowle, and *Q1;* Ipresequam, a bowle,
and *Q2, Bl; I, prae sequar,* a bowl, and *Dilke; I prae-sequar,* a bowle, and
*Fairholt; I prae, sequar.* A bowl, and *Andreadis; I prae, sequar:* a bowle and
*Tydeman.* 22. cue] *Dilke;* que *Q1, 2, Bl.* 23. Ay] *Dilke (*Aye*);* I *Q1,
2, Bl.* 28. our] *Q1, Bl;* ou *Q2.* 30. us] *Q1, 2, Bl; not in Dilke.*

## ACT [US] 2, SCE [NA] 5

0.] *Q1 (subst.), 2;* Actus secundus, Scaena quinta *Bl.* 0.1. *from the
tavern] Tydeman.* STELLIO] *Q1 (*Stellio*), Bl;* Stellia / *Q2;* 0.2. tipsy]
*This ed.* 1. luckily] *Q1;* quickly *Q2, Bl.* 5. great-grandfather] *Q1 (*great
grandfather*), 2, Bl;* great great grandfather *Dilke.* 9. authentical]
*Bl (*authenticall*);* autentical *Q1;* autenticall *Q2.* 13. Ay] *Andreadis;*

I *Q1, 2, Bl;* Ah *Dilke.*     15. sayeth that]  *Q1* (saith); saith, that *Q2;* say, that *Bl;* say that *Dilke;* faith, that *Daniel.*     16–18. Old men…years.]  *Enclosed by Daniel in quotation marks.*     17. children]  *Q1;* yong men  *Q2, Bl.* cozened]  *Q1* (cosned); counted  *Q2, Bl.*     20. now]  *Q1;* wine  *Q2, Bl.* 21–2. We have…shillings]  *Q1; not in Q2, Bl.*     26. hogs']  *Andreadis;* hogges *Q1;* hogs *Q2, Bl;* hog's *Daniel.*     34. judge]  *Q1* (iudge), *Bl;* indge *Q2.*     38. struck]  *Andreadis;* stroke *Q1;* strooke *Q2, Bl.*     41–9.]  *Quotation marks / Fairholt.*     41. sovereignest]  *Dilke;* soueraigntest  *Q1, 2, Bl;* sovereigntest   *Andreadis.*     42. weathers…thunder,   though]  *Punctuation   as Andreadis;* weathers, if it thunder, though *Q1, 2* (thogh), *Bl;* weathers: if it thunder, though *Dilke;* weathers; if it thunder, though *Fairholt;* weathers if it thunder. Though *Daniel.*     50. hop-on-my-thumb]  *Andreadis;* hoppe on my thumbe *Q1, 2, Bl;* hop-o'-my thumb *Dilke.*     52. lear]  *This ed.;* leere *Q1, 2, Bl;* leer *Dilke.*     54. at]  *Q1;* of *Q2, Bl.*     56–7. 'Sine…Venus']  *Quotation marks / Andreadis.*     56. Cerere]  *Dilke;* Cere / *Q1, 2, Bl.*     59–60. But I must…business]  *Signalled by Dilke as an aside.*     be gone]  *Q1, 2, Bl;* begone *Dilke.*     62, 66, 70. SD.]  *Dilke (positioned following* done, about it, day's work, *lines 64, 68, 71, this ed.); Daniel encloses corresponding passages in brackets.*     63. been]  *Q2* (beene), *Bl;* bin *Q1.*     wit's]  *Dilke;* wittes *Q1, 2;* wits *Bl;* wits' *Andreadis;* wittes' *Tydeman.*     72. Halfpenny]  *Q1* (Halfepenie), *Bl* (Halfpenie); Palfpenie / *Q2.*

## ACT [US] 3, SCE [NA] 1

0.]  *Q1 (subst.), 2;* Actus tertius, Scaena prima *Bl.*     4. into]  *Q1, 2, Bl;* in *Dilke.*     6. without]  *Q1, 2, Bl;* with *Dilke.*     7–8. can then]  *Q1, 2, Bl;* then can *Dilke.*     9. father's]  *Daniel;* fathers *Q1, 2, Bl;* fathers' *Dilke.* 10. combat]  *Q2, Bl* (combate); comhat *Q.*     14–17. Yet this…stretch so.]  *Incorrectly assigned to Serena by Dilke and Fairholt (though the correct reading is given in Fairholt's notes), consequent upon the omission of lines 18–20 this ed., in Q2, Bl (see below) resulting in consecutive speeches being assigned to Maestius.*     18. SP.]  *Q1; not in Q2, Bl.*     18–20.]  *Q1; not in Q2, Bl.*     32.1.]  *Andreadis (subst.);*  MAESTIUS *knocks at* MOTHER BOMBIE'S *door. / Tydeman.*     33. SD.]  *This ed.*     33.1–2.]  *Bracketed material this ed.; Enter Mother Bombie. / Q1, 2, Bl.*     35. SD.]  *Tydeman.*     39. your]  *Q1, 2, Bl;* you *Dilke.*     40. SD.]  *This ed.*     41–6.]  *Lineation as Dilke; continuous prose in Q1, 2, Bl.*     41–2. hand, By]  *Q1* (by), *2;* hand, and by *Bl.* 42. God, Nature]  *Q2, Bl;* good nature *Q1;* good Nature *Tydeman.*     46. true, call]  *Q1* (without comma); true, then call *Q2, Bl.*     old fool]  *Q1* (olde foole), *2, Bl;* an old fool *Dilke.*     47–50.]  *Lineation this ed.; continuous prose in Q1, 2, Bl.*     47. SD.]  *This ed.*     51.]  *Tydeman supplies SD. / to* MAESTIUS */ following SP.*     54.]  *Tydeman supplies SD. / to* BOMBIE */ following* brains.     57.1.]  *This ed.*     59–60. enjoy our love]  *Q1;* enioy them *Q2, Bl.*

## ACT [US] 3, SCE [NA] 2

0.]  *Q1 (subst.);* Act. 3. Sce. 3: *Q2;* Actus tertius. Scaena tertia. *Bl.*     0.1.  DROMIO [*and*] RISIO]  *Dilke;* Dromio. Risio. Halfepenie. Luceo. / *Q1;* Dromio. Risio. Halfepenie. Lucio. / *Q2, Bl (the latter dividing names by commas);* DROMIO. RISIO. HALFEPENIE. LUCEO. ⟨*Enter* DROMIO *and*

RISCIO.) *Bond; Enter* DROMIO *and* RISCIO. / *Daniel. from different directions*] *Tydeman.* 1. SD.] *This ed. pretiosius*] *Bl; pretiotius* / *Q1, 2; pretiosus*] *Dilke.* 2. wherein] *Q1, 2, Bl;* where *Daniel.* 4. SD.] *This ed. barbarie est*] *Q1, 2, Bl; barbaria est* / *Dilke; barbaries* / *Bond; barbaries est* / *Andreadis.* 7. wrung all] *This ed;* rong all *Q1;* roong al *Q2;* rung all *Bl;* rong all [out] *Tydeman.* 9. I] *Q1, 2, Bl;* Ay *Andreadis;* Aye *Daniel.* 14. *io*] *Andreadis;* to *Q1, 2, Bl; O* / *Dilke.* 19. I$^2$] *Q1;* we *Q2, Bl.* 20. and could] *Q1, 2, Bl;* could *Dilke.* 26. told that] *Q1, 2, Bl;* told him that *Fairholt.* 28. marking] *Q1;* thanking *Q2, Bl.* 34. mo] *Q1;* my *Q2, Bl;* any *Dilke;* many *Fairholt;* mo' *Andreadis.* 42. fodges] *Q1, 2;* fadges *Bl.* Lucio] *Q2, Bl;* Luceo *Q1.* 43. excellent] *Q2, Bl;* exccellent *Q1.* 44. my] *Q1, 2, Bl;* by *Daniel.* 44.1. LUCIO] *Q2, Bl; Luceo* / *Q1.* SD. *transposed by Tydeman to line 44 this ed., following* come. 56–7. quadripartite] *Andreadis;* quadrapertit *Q1, 2;* quadrapertite *Bl;* quadrupartite *Dilke.* 58. your] *Q1, 2, Bl;* our *Dilke.* 59. their] *Q1;* your *Q2, Bl.* parents'] *Fairholt;* parents *Q1, 2, Bl;* parent's *Dilke.* 65.1. LUCIO] *Q2, Bl; Luceo* / *Q1.* 65.2–3.] *Bracketed material this ed.; Enter Accius and Silena* / *Q1, 2, Bl; Tydeman supplies* / *separately.* 67. master] *Q1;* Maister *Q2;* Masters *Bl;* master's *Fairholt.* 69. out] *Q1;* our *Q2, Bl.* 70. the] *Q1, 2, Bl;* their *Dilke.* cue] *Dilke;* que *Q1, 2;* Q *Bl.* 71. SP.] *Q1, (Dro.), Bl; Dra.* / *Q2.* 72. woo] *Bl;* woe *Q1, 2.* one another] *Q1, 2, Bl;* one to another *Dilke.* 74.1. *severally...houses*] *This ed.* 74.2.] *Daniel (positioned following* Act[us] 3, Sce[na] 3 *this ed.).*

## ACT[US] 3, SCE[NA] 3

0.] *Q1 (subst., following 3.3.01. this ed.), 2 (subst.);* Actus tertius, Scaena tertia *Bl (following 3.3.14 this ed.). Positioning here as Bond.* 0.1.] *Andreadis (following 3.2.74.1 this ed.); Memphio and Stellio singing.* / *Q1 (following* / *Exeunt.* / *3.2.74.1 this ed.), 2, Bl;* ACCIUS *and* SILENA *singing.* / *Bond (positioning as this ed.);* ACCIUS *Sings.* / *Daniel (positioning as this ed.).* 0.2– 14.] *Bl (following SD. at 3.2.74.1 this ed.); not in Q1, 2, Andreadis (text). Positioning here as Bond. Daniel omits* SONG. 1. SP.] *Daniel;* Memp. *Bl (Memphio); Sil.* / *Bond (Silena).* 5. held] *Dilke;* hel'd *Bl.* 6.] *Daniel supplies SD.* / *Silena sings* / *following* kill. 7. SP.] *Daniel;* Stel. *Bl (Stellio); Acc.* / *Bond (Accius).* 8. wise man] *Fairholt;* wiseman / *Bl.* 13. SP.] *Tydeman; lines assigned to previous singer in other eds.* 14.1–2.] *Bracketed material this ed.* / *Enter* MEMPHIO *and* STELLIO, *separately.* / *Daniel.* 18. your] *Q1;* a *Q2, Bl.* 18.1–2.] *Bracketed material this ed.; Exeunt* / *Q2, Bl; Exunt* / *Q1,* 19, 21. SD.] *Bond.* 24. SD.] *This ed.* 27. SD.] *Bond.* 29. SD.] *Bond (subst.).* 30. make] *Q1, 2, Bl;* makes *Dilke.* 33. lies] *Q1, Bl;* likes *Q2 (Boston and Huntington copies only).* 38. courtesy] *Daniel;* cursie *Q1, 2, Bl;* cursy *Dilke;* cur'sie *Fairholt;* cur'sy *Andreadis.* business I] *Punctuation as Q1, 2, Bl;* business, I *Dilke;* business; I *Daniel.* 40. SD.] *Dilke. Daniel encloses the corresponding passage in brackets.* 40–1. Perhaps move] *Q1, 2, Bl;* Perhaps I may move *Fairholt.* 41. be long] *Q2, Bl;* belong *Q1.* 42. SD.] *Dilke; Daniel encloses corresponding passage in brackets.* Good silly Stellio! We] *Punctuation this ed.;* Good silly *Stel.* we *Q1;* Good sillie *Stellio,* we *Q2, Bl (silly);* Good, silly Stellio, we *Dilke.* shortly.] *Q2 (shortlie.), Bl;* shortly, *Q1.*

## ACT [US] 3, SCE [NA] 4

0.] *Q1 (subst.), 2;* Actus tertius, Scaena quarta *Bl.*    0.1–2.] *Bond (subst.);*
*Halfepenie. Luceo. Rixula. Dromio. Risio.* / *Q1,* 2 *(Lucio), Bl;* HALFPENNY,
LUCIO, *and* RIXULA. *Dilke;* HALFEPENIE, LUCIO, RIXULA, DROMIO,
RISCIO. *Fairholt.*    1 the whole] *Q1;* our whole *Q2, Bl.*    5. *Omnem*]
*Q1, 2, Bl; omne* / *Dilke.*    10. cannot] *Q1, Bl;* cannon *Q2.*    12. away.] *Q2,*
*Bl;* away, *Q1.*    21. SD.] *This ed.*    22. masters] *Q1,* 2 *(*Maisters*), Bl;*
master *Daniel.*    27. SD.] *This ed.*    28. speeches] *Q1;* words *Q2,*
*Bl.*    31. beatest] *Q 1, 2;* beatedst *Bl;* beated'st *Fairholt.*    41. song] *Q1,*
*2;* soug *Bl (turned letter).*    41.1.] *Q1, 2, Bl. Not in Dilke, Daniel. Not*
*distinguished as SD. from previous speech in Q1, 2 (*song, Cantant.*).*    41.2–
61.] *Bl. Not in Q1, 2, Andreadis (text). Daniel omits* SONG *(line 41.2. this ed.)*
*and supplies* / *Enter* DROMIO *and* RISCIO *during the song.* RIXULA *sings.* /
*following* song. *line 41 this ed.).*    52, 55, 60. SP.] *This ed.;* 4. Pag. *Bl*
*(4.* Pa. *at line 60); The men* / *Dilke;* 2 Pag. *Fairholt; The Pages* / *Bond;* FOUR
PAGES *Daniel.*    56–9.] *Quotation marks* / *Tydeman.*    61.1–2.] *from Mem-*
*phio's house...from Stellio's house* / *this ed.; other bracketed material* / *Tydeman*
*(subst.); Enter Dromio, Risio.* / *Q1; Enter Dromio, Rosio.* / *Q2, Bl; Enter*
DROMIO, RISIO *⟨carrying the clothes of* ACCIUS *and* SILENA *respectively⟩.* /
*Bond. Daniel transposes the direction to the end of line 41 this ed. (see 41.2–61n.*
*above).*    62. stands] *Q1, 2, Bl;* stand *Dilke.*    68. SP.] *Q1 (Rix.), 2;*
*Ri.* / *Bl; Ris.* / *Fairholt.*    of] *Q1, 2, Bl;* on *Dilke.*    73. utrumque]
*Dilke; untranque* / *Q1; utramque* / *Q2, Bl.*    74. or to run] *Q1, 2, Bl;* or run
*Dilke.*    83.] *Andreadis supplies* SD. / *They walk towards* Mother Bombie's
*house.* / *following quickly.*    84.1–3.] *This ed.; no entry marked in Q1, 2,*
*Bl; They knock at Bombie's door.* / *Dilke. Bond supplies* / *Enter* MOTHER
BOMBIE. / *following Dilke's direction.*    88. SD.] *Tydeman.*    89. SP.] *Q1*
*(Dro.); not in Q2, Bl. Dilke prints the ensuing speech as a continuation of Half-*
*penny's preceding exclamation.*    SD.] *Tydeman.*    95. an] *Q2, Bl;* a *Q1.*
105. upon] *Q1, 2, Bl;* on *Dilke.*    brewish] *Q1, 2, Bl;* brewis *Andreadis.*
106. powdered] *Dilke;* poudred *Q1;* powdred *Q2, Bl;* powder'd *Andreadis.*
107. troubled] *Bl;* trobled *Q1;* troubed *Q2.*    108. sack] *Q1;* wine *Q2,*
*Bl.*    111. cushion] *Q1, 2;* cushing *Bl.*    113. hand awaked] *Q1 (*awakt*);*
hand I awakt *Q2, Bl.*    119–20. in, unless...leg?] *Punctuation as Q2 (ten*
*extant copies, see Introduction, n. 20), Bl;* in, vnlesse it had bin a leg, *Q1;* in?
vnlesse it had bin a leg, *Q2 (Boston and Huntington copies only).*    128–
30.] *Lineation as Dilke; continuous prose in Q1, 2, Bl.*    128. morning
sleep] *Q1, 2, Bl;* morning's sleep *Dilke;* morning-sleep *Andreadis.*
135. judges] *Q2 (*Iudges*), Bl;* indges *Q1 (turned letter).*    137. of a riot] *Q1,*
*2;* of riot *Bl.*    clunged] *Q1, 2, Bl;* clung *Dilke.*    138. raisins] *Andreadis;*
raisons *Q1, 2, Bl.*    139. whole] *Q1, 2, Bl;* old *Fairholt.*    145. SP.] *Q1*
*(Dro.), 2, Bl; Bom.* / *Dilke.*    152. unsensible] *Q1;* vincible *Q2, Bl.*
155–7.] *Lineation as Dilke; continuous prose in Q1, 2, Bl. (Also at lines 161–3*
*below.)*    159. gammer] *Q1, 2;* Grammer *Bl.*    165. SD.] *This ed.*
166. SD.] *This ed.*    167. it will] *Q1;* will *Q2, Bl.*    168. Ay] *Andreadis;*
I *Q1, 2, Bl;* Ah *Dilke.*    perchance] *Q1, Bl;* perehance *Q2;* perhaps
*Dilke.*    170.] *Tydeman supplies* / *Exit* RIXULA. / *following* me.    171. missed]
*Daniel; mist Q1, 2, Bl; miss'd Andreadis.*    173. SD.] *This ed.*    174–6] *Lin-*
*eation as Dilke; continuous prose in Q1, 2, Bl.*    174. dye] *Dilke;* die *Q1, 2,*

*Bl.*  177. SP.] *Dilke (Ris.); Ri.* / *Q1, 2, Bl; Rixula.* / *Andreadis;* RISCIO.
*Daniel.*  I would] *Q1;* I I would *Q2;* I, I would *Bl;* Ah! I would
*Dilke.*  179. dyer] *Dilke;* diar *Q1, 2; Dyar* / *Bl.*  and ] *Dilke;* but *Q1, 2,*
*Bl.*  180. believe, Mother] *punctuation as Bond;* beleeue *Mother* / *Q1, 2*
(mother*), Bl.*  186. SD.] *Tydeman.*  Ay] *Andreadis;* I *Q1, 2, Bl;* Ah
*Dilke.*  188. fodge] *Q1, 2;* fadge *Bl.*  189–91.] *Lineation as Dilke; con-*
*tinuous prose in Q1, 2, Bl.*  192. Gramercy…We] *punctuation as Tydeman;*
Gramercie mother *Bombie,* we *Q1, 2 (Mother), Bl;* Gramercy, Mother
Bombie, we *Dilke;* Gramercie! *Mother Bombie,* we *Fairholt;* Gramercy,
Mother Bombie; we *Andreadis;* Gramercy, Mother Bombie. We *Daniel.*
193.] *Bond supplies SD.* / *Offering money.* / *following* pains.  195.1.] *This ed.;*
*Exit Bom.* / *Q1, 2, Bl. Tydeman inexplicably differentiates* BOM[bie] *(sic) from*
*SD. and prints as text following* Farewell.  196. but to go] *Q1, 2, Bl;* but
go *Dilke.*  197. SD.] *This ed.*  199. Lucio] *Q2, Bl;* Linceo *Q1.*

ACT[US] 4, SCE[NA] 1

0.] *Q1 (subst.), 2;* Actus quartus, Scaena prima *Bl.*  0.1.] *This ed.;Candius,*
*Liuia, Dromio, Risio, Sperantus, Prisius.* / *Q1, 2 (subst.), Bl; Enter* CANDIUS
*and* LIVIA. / *Dilke; Enter* CANDIUS *and* LIVIA, *in the clothes of* ACCIUS *and*
SILENA, *respectively.* / *Bond (following listing of characters' names as in early eds);*
*Enter* CANDIUS *dressed in* ACCIUS' *clothes and* LIVIA *dressed in* SILENA'S
*clothes.* / *Tydeman (following listing of characters' names as in early eds); Enter*
CANDIUS *and* LIVIA, *disguised.* / *Daniel; Fairholt as Q1, 2, Bl but with* RISCIO
*for* / *Risio.*  5. fool, and he wise. What] *Punctuation as Daniel;* foole, and
hee wist what *Q1, 2 (he), Bl;* fool; and he wise, what *Dilke;* foole, and hee
wise; what *Bond;* fool and he wist what *Andreadis.*  wise] *Dilke;* wist *Q1, 2,*
*Bl.*  6. conclusion, I marvel.] *Punctuation as Q1, 2, Bl;* conclusion
I marvel? *Dilke;* conclusion, I mervaile! *Tydeman;* conclusion. I marvel.
*Andreadis.*  10. SP.] *Q1 (Liu.), 2; Lu.* / *Bl.*  13. 'Livia…word'] *Quota-*
*tion marks supplied by Daniel.*  33. heart[1]] *Q2, Bl;* hart *Q1.*  34. Molle]
*Q1; Male* / *Q2, Bl.*  enim inviolabile] *Q1, 2, Bl;* est violabile / *Dilke .*  36,
37. hart] *This ed.;* heart *Q1, 2, Bl.*  40. I] *Q1, 2, Bl;* Ah *Dilke.*
41. coming] *Q1, 2, Bl;* coughing *Dilke.*  46. key] *Q1; not in Q2, Bl.*
47. was never] *Q1, 2, Bl;* never was *Dilke.*  49–50. SD.] *Andreadis*
*(subst.).*  51, 53, 56, 57. SD.] *This ed.*  52. my solace] *Q1, 2, Bl;* the
solace *Daniel.*  58. brings] *Q1;* bringeth *Q2, Bl.*  hundred] *Q1, Bl;* hundreth *Q2.*  dangers in the church] *Q1, 2, Bl;* dangers: in the church *Dilke*
*(omitting the comma following* church *in all early eds).*  59. too] *Q2, Bl;* to
*Q1.*  61. SD.] *This ed.; aside* / *Tydeman.*  62. be] *Q1, 2, Bl;* is
*Daniel.*  63, 65, 66, 69, 71, 73, SD.] *This ed.*  65. Agreed] *Q1, 2, Bl;*
Agree *Daniel.*  81. remedy, that I] *Q1,2,Bl;* remedy, I *Dilke.*  83. SP.] *Q1*
*(Ri.); Riu.* / *Q2, Bl.*  84. use…as though] *Q1, 2, Bl;* use them as though
*Dilke.*  86. Not I] *Q2, Bl;* Not, I *Q1.*  88. SD.] *This ed.; to* CANDIUS /
*Tydeman.*  here's] *Q1 (heres);* heere *Q2;* here *Bl.*  89. loves] *Q1, 2, Bl;*
love *Fairholt.*  91. is] *Q1, 2, Bl;* are *Dilke.*  92. bad] *Q1;* hard *Q2,*
*Bl.*  SD.] *Bond. Daniel signals an aside by enclosing* This cottons…ear *(lines*
*92–3 this ed.) in brackets.*  94. SD.] *This ed.*  95. other] *Q1; not in Q2,*
*Bl.*  98. because] *Q1, Bl;* bccause *Q2.*  101. Ay] *Dilke (Aye);* I *Q1, 2,*
*Bl.*  will, let] *Bond;* will let *Q1, 2, Bl.*

ACT[US] 4, SCE[NA] 2

0.] *Q1 (subst.), 2;* Actus quartus, Scaena secunda *Bl.*    0.1.] *Dilke (subst.);
Accius, Silena, Linceo, Halfepenie.* / *Q1, 2 (Halfpenie), Bl (Lincio, Halfpenie);*
ACCIUS, SILENA, LINCEO, HALFEPENIE. ⟨*Enter* LUCIO *and* HALFPENNY.⟩
*Bond; Accius. Silena. Lucio. Halfepenie.* [*Enter* LUCIO *and* HALFPENNY.] /
*Tydeman.*    1. SP.] *Dilke (Luc.); Lin.* / *Q1, 2, Bl.*    time] *Q2, Bl;* tiwe
*Q1.*    3. Silena.] *Q2 (Silena.), Bl;* Silena *Q1.*    4. was] *Q1, 2, Bl;* would
be *Dilke.*    6.1.] *from Memphio's house* / *this ed.; other bracketed material* /
*Bond; Tydeman supplies* / *dressed as* CANDIUS.    7.1.] *This ed.*    7.2.] *from
Stellio's house* / *this ed.; other bracketed material* / *Bond;* / *Tydeman supplies* /
*dressed as* LIVIA.    8. SD.] *This ed.*    9. another boy's] *Dilke;* anothers
boyes *Q1;* an other boies *Q2, Bl.*    11. SD.] *This ed.; aside* /
*Tydeman.*    13. SD.] *This ed.*    mine] *Q1;* my *Q2, Bl.*    15. SP.] *Fairholt;
Lin.* / *Q1; Liu.* / *Q2, Bl; Liv.* / *Dilke.*    15, 17. SD.] *This ed; aside* /
*Tydeman.*    18. SD.] *This ed.*    20. SD.] *This ed.; aside* / *Tydeman.*
22. SP.] *Dilke (Luc.); Lin. Q1; Siu. Q2, Bl.*    22, 24. SD.] *This ed.;
aside* / *Tydeman.*    25. SD.] *This ed.*    26. SD.] *Tydeman.*    30. SD.]
*This ed.; aside* / *Tydeman.*    Ay,] *Andreadis;* I *Q1, 2, Bl;* Ah!
*Dilke.*    32. joint] *Bl (*ioynt*);* ioynd *Q1, 2;* join'd *Andreadis;* joined
*Daniel.*    33. SP.] *Dilke; Linceo* / *Q1; Liu.* / *Q2, Bl.*    SD.] *This ed.;
aside* / *Tydeman.*    38. SD.] *This ed.; aside* / *Tydeman.*    Whether] *Q1, Bl;*
Whither *Q2.*    39. cobblers'] *Tydeman (*coblers'*);* coblers *Q1, 2, Bl;*
cobler's *Dilke;* cobbler's *Andreadis.*    45. gaskins] *Andreadis;* gascoins
*Q1, 2;* gascoines *Bl;* gascoyns *Dilke.*    hose] *Q1, 2;* house *Bl.*
46. father's] *Fairholt;* fathers *Q1, 2, Bl.*    are] *Q1, 2, Bl;* were *Dilke.*
47. crimson] *Q2, Bl;* Crimosin *Q1.*    48. That's] *Q2, Bl (*thats*);* That
*Q1.*    49. SD.] *This ed.; aside* / *Tydeman.*    two] *Dilke;* three *Q1, 2, Bl.*
51. SP.] *Dilke (Luc.); Lin.* / *Q1; Liu.* / *Q2, Bl.*    51, 52. SD.] *This ed.;
aside* / *Tydeman.*    55. SD.] *This ed.*    56. preface] *Q1;* pretie face *Q2,
Bl (*prettie*).*    hair] *Q1 (*haire*), 2, Bl;* heir *Dilke.*    57. Wisely you]
*Punctuation as Q1, 2, Bl;* Wisely! you *Bond.*    63. lief] *Q1 (*liefe*), 2;* leuue
*Bl;* leaue *Dilke.*    64, 66. SD.] *This ed.; aside* / *Tydeman.*    67.1.]
*This ed.*    68. SD.] *This ed.; aside* / *Tydeman.*    issues] *Q1;* issue *Q2, Bl.*
69. SD.] *Bond.*    72. SD.] *Tydeman (subst.).*    a] *Q1;* not in *Q2,
Bl.*    gleek] *Andreadis;* glieke *Q1;* glicke *Q2, Bl;* glick *Dilke.*    73. SD.]
*Bond.*    74. 'tis] *Q1 (*tis*);* it is *Q2, Bl.*    a clock] *Q1, 2, Bl;*
o'clock *Dilke.*    76.] *Tydeman supplies SD.* / *aside* / *following SP. and* / *To*
SILENA / *following* nest.    struck] *Dilke;* stroke *Q1;* strooke *Q2, Bl.*
80. passes] *Bl;* passe *Q1, 2.*    recognizance] *Dilke;* recognoscence *Q1, 2,
Bl.*    80.1–2.] *This ed.; Enter Memphio, Stellio.* / *Q1, 2, Bl; Enter* MEMPHIO,
STELLIO ⟨*severally behind*⟩. / *Bond; Enter* MEMPHIO [*and*] STELLIO [*separately, unseen by the other, at the rear of the stage*]. / *Tydeman.*    86. SD.] *Tydeman
(subst.).*    88. stitched] *Q1 (*stitcht*), Bl;* stirch *Q2.*    90. SP.] *Bond (correcting this and the five subsequent speech prefixes of all early eds);* Mem. / *Q1,
2; Memp.* / *Bl.*    SD.] *This ed.; aside to* LUC. / *Bond.*    91. SP.] *Bond;
Half.* / *Q1, 2, Bl.*    SD.] *This ed.; aside* / *Tydeman.*    92. SP.] *Bond;
Mem.* / *Q1, 2; Memp.* / *Bl.*    SD.] *This ed.; aside* / *Tydeman.*    fodges] *Q1,
2;* fadges *Bl.*    93. SP.] *Bond; Stel.* / *Q1, Bl; Ste.* / *Q2.*    SD.] *This ed.;
aside to* HALF. / *Bond.*    95. SP.] *Bond; Lin.* / *Q1, 2; Liu.* / *Bl; Luc.* /

*Dilke.*  SD.] *This ed.; aside / Tydeman.*  96. SP.] *Bond; Stel. / Q1, 2,*
*Bl.*  SD.] *This ed.; aside / Tydeman.*  97. SD.] *The ed.*  98. SD.] *Bond*
*(subst.); aside / Tydeman.*  101. SD.] *Bond (subst.); aside / Tydeman.*
103. SD.] *Bond (subst.).*   off] *Q2, Bl; of Q1.*   105. SD.] *This ed.*   I'll
look] *Bond*  (looke*);*  I   looke   *Q1,   2,   Bl.*   107. SD.] *This*
*ed.*   108. Memphio] *Q1, Bl; Mem. / Q2.*   109. SD.] *This ed.; to* MEMP.
*/ Bond.*   112. SD.] *This ed.*   My...ashamed!] *Punctuation as Bond;* My
sonne and I ashamd, / *Q1, 2* (ashamde*), Bl* (asham'd*);* My son, and I
ashamed *Dilke;* My sonne and I asham'd! *Fairholt.*   113. SD.] *This*
*ed.*   115. SD.] *This ed.*   116. SP.] *Dilke (Luc.); Lin. / Q1, 2; Liu. /*
*Bl.*   SD.] *Tydeman (subst.).*   117. SD.] *This ed.*   117, 118. hether] *Q1;*
*hither Q2, Bl. Also at line 124.*   120.] *Punctuation as Q1, 2, Bl;* How chance?
Dromio bid me. *Dilke.*   121. SD.] *This ed.*   Thy] *Q1, 2, Bl;* my
*Dilke.*   123,   124. SD.] *This ed.*   126. am[2]] *Q1;*   came   *Q2, Bl.*
128. Ay] *Andreadis;* I *Q1, 2, Bl;* Ah *Dilke.*   an hard] *Q1, 2, Bl;* a hard
*Dilke.*   130. SD.] *Bond.*   that] *Q1, 2, Bl; not in Tydeman.*   132–3.
*Stellio...*Memphio's son] *Q1; not in Q2, Bl (see line 133n. below).*   132.
SD.] *Bond.*   133. and plead...daughter] *Q1; assigned to Memphio as a*
*continuation of the preceding speech in Q2, Bl.*   134. SP.] *Q1, 2, Bl; not in*
*Dilke, Fairholt (avoiding repetition of SP. / Memphio / consequent upon omission*
*of / Stellio...*Memphio's son *(lines 132–3 this ed.) / in Q2, Bl).*   SD.]
*Bond.*   that] *Q1, 2, Bl; not in Dilke.*   136. SD.] *Bond.*   138. SP.]
*Dilke (Luc.); Lin. / Q1; Liu. / Q2, Bl.*   SD.] *Tydeman.*   138–9. mules
weep] *Q1;* mules to weepe *Q2, Bl.*   140. SD.] *This ed.*   141. preg-
nant] *Q1;* repugnant *Q2 Bl.*   142,   143,   145. SD.] *This ed.*
146. SP.] *Dilke (Luc.); Lin. / Q1; Liu. / Q2, Bl.*   SD.] *This ed.; to* STELLIO
*/ Bond.*   149. SD.] *Bond.*   150. Sperantus'] *Bond; Prisius Q1, 2 Bl*
*(Prisius).*   153. SP.] *Dilke (Luc.); Lin. / Q1; Liu. / Q2, Bl.*   SD.]
*Bond.*   And so...Education] *Punctuation as Andreadis;* And so sir for your
daughter, education *Q1, 2, Bl;* And so, sir, for your daughter education
*Dilke;* And so, sir, for your daughter, education *Fairholt.*   159. Ay]
*Dilke* (Aye*);* I *Q1, 2, Bl.*   too] *Q2, Bl;* to *Q1.*   166.1–2.] *Bracketed*
*material this ed.*   167. Ass] *Q1* (Asse*), 2, Bl;* as *Andreadis.*   168. world?
Now we] *Punctuation this ed.;* worlde, now we *Q1, 2* (world, now wee*), Bl;*
world now we *Dilke;* worlde now? We *Bond.*   171. SP.] *Dilke (Luc.); Lin.*
*/ Q1; Liu. / Q2, Bl.*   175. if underhand this] *Q1;* if I understand this *Q2,*
*Bl;* if I understand, if this *Dilke.*   178. Halfpenny] *Q2* (Halfepenie*), Bl*
*(Halfpeny);* Halfepnle *Q1.*   178.1.] *Q1 (subst.), 2, Bl. Tydeman supplies /*
*unseen by the others / .*   181. q.] *Dilke;* que *Q1, 2, Bl;* farthing *Fairholt;* cue
*Andreadis.*   183. SP.] *Dilke (Luc.); Lin. / Q1; Liu. / Q2, Bl.*   in in] *Q1;*
*in Q2, Bl, and all later eds.*   184. SD.] *Bond (subst.); stepping forward and*
*placing his hand on* DROMIO'S *shoulder / Tydeman.*   189. an horse] *Q1, 2,*
*Bl;* a horse *Dilke.*   but[1]] *Q1; not in Q2, Bl.*   191. ale-acy] *Tydeman n.*
*(subst.);* alecie *Q1, 2, Bl;* alecy *Dilke;* ale-cy *Daniel.*   195.] *Tydeman supplies*
*SD. / to* DROMIO */ following SP.* ridst] *Q1, 2, Bl;* ridest *Bl[2].*   197. SP.] *Dilke*
*(Luc.). / Lin. / Q1; Liu. / Q2, Bl.*   200. forty] *Q1, 2, Bl;* twenty
*Dilke.*   204. SP.] *Fairholt; Ri. / Q1, 2, Bl; Ris. / Dilke; Risio / Andreadis;*
*Riscio / Daniel.*   for] *Q1; not in Q2, Bl.*   205. an horse] *Q1, 2, Bl;* a horse
*Dilke.*   211. is he] *Q1;* hee is *Q2, Bl.*   was, I'll warrant. He'll] *Punctua-*
*tion as Andreadis;* was, Ile warrant, heele *Q1;* was Ile warrant heele *Q2, Bl;*

was; I'll warrant he'll *Dilke;* was. Ile warrant heele *Bond;* was, I'le warrant!
Hee'le, *Tydeman;* was. I'll warrant he'll *Daniel.*   215. 'wyhie'] *Spelling
as Q1, 2, Bl;* whyie *Andreadis;* wyyheee *Daniel.   Quotation marks supplied
by Tydeman.*   216. thorough] *Q1;* through *Q2, Bl.*   217. SP.] *Dilke
(Luc.);Lin./Q1;Liu./Q2,Bl.*   225. thy] *Q1;*thine *Q2,Bl.*   226. stay] *Q1;
not in Q2, Bl.*   229. to his] *Q1;* of his *Q2, Bl.*   231. adzes] *Daniel;*
addeces *Q1, 2;* addices *Bl.*   240. rheum] *Bl* (rheume*); rume *Q1,
2.*   240–1. an handkercher] *Q1, 2, Bl;* a handkerchief *Dilke.*   244. SP.]
*Q1 (Ri.); Li. (i.e. Lucio)* / *Q2, Bl; Luc. (i.e. Lucio)* / *Dilke.*   fellow] *Q1;
not in Q2, Bl.*   245. knowest] *Q1, 2, Bl²; not in Bl.*   250. poor] *Q2*
(poore*), Bl;* poort *Q1.*   252. a] *Q1, 2, Bl; not in Dilke.*   254. SD.] *This
ed.*   258. SP.] *Dilke (Luc.); Lin.* / *Q1; Liu. Q2, Bl.*   259. Well] *Q1, 2,
Bl;* We'll *Andreadis.*   260. SP.] *Q1 (Ser.); Seg:* / *Q2; Serg.* / *Bl.*
260.1.] *Dilke (subst.); Exit* / *Andreadis.*   261. to a Sergeant's] *Q2, Bl;* to
Sergeants *Q1.*   262. frieze] *Daniel;* freese *Q1;* freeze *Q2, Bl.*
262.1.] *Andreadis; not in Q1, 2, Bl. Bond supplies / within / following SP. line
263 this ed.;Tydeman supplies / entering / at the same point.*   267. SD.] *Bracketed material / Tydeman (subst.); Exeunt.* / *Q1, 2, Bl; Exeunt all but Risio.* /
*Dilke; Exeunt ⟨all but* RISCIO⟩. / *Bond; Exeunt.* [*Manet* Risio.] /
*Andreadis.*   268. our¹] *Q1, 2, Bl;* your *Daniel.*   269. They] *Q1, 2, Bl;*
we *Dilke.*   271. SD.] *Bracketed material / Tydeman; not in Daniel.*

## ACT[US] 5, SCE[NA] 1

0.] *Q1 (subst.);* Act. 5. Sce. 8 *Q2;* Actus quintus. Scaena prima
*Bl.*   0.1–2.] *Tydeman (subst.); Dro, Risio, Linceo, Halfpenie.* / *Q1, 2; Dromio,
Risio, Linceo, Halfepenie.* / *Bl;* DROMIO, RISIO, LUCIO *and* HALFPENNY
*Dilke; Enter* DROMIO, LUCIO *and* HALFPENNY *to* RISCIO, *who remains.* /
*Daniel.*   4. SP.] *Dilke (Luc.); Lin.* / *Q1; Liu.* / *Q2, Bl.*   8. 'Jost…
Richard'] *Quotation marks* / *Dilke.*   Jost] *Fairholt;* Iost *Q1, 2 (iost),
Bl.*   up, bay] *Punctuation as Q2, Bl;* up bay *Q1.*   10. acquittance] *Q1;*
acquaintance *Q2,Bl.*   such a bond] *Q1;*such bonds *Q2,Bl.*   13. SD.] *This
ed.*   14. appease] *Q1;* appeale *Q2, Bl.*   SD.] *This ed.*   15. the
late] *Q1;* your late *Q2, Bl.*   18. let's] *Dilke;* lettes *Q1;* lets *Q2,
Bl.*   19. fire] *Q2, Bl; not in Q1.*

## ACT[US] 5, SCE[NA] 2

0.] *Q1 (subst.), 2;* Actus quintus. Scaena secunda *Bl.*   0.1.] *Bond (follow-
ing Q1* VICINIA. BOMBIE.*); Vicina. Bombie.* / *Q2, Bl; Enter* VICINIA *and*
MOTHER BOMBIE, *separately.* / *Daniel.*   1–2. misgives me, since] *Punc-
tuation as Q1, 2, Bl;* misgives me. Since *Daniel.*   2. such] *Q1;* some *Q2,
Bl.*   2–3. Rochester. My] *Punctuation as Bond;* Rochester, my *Q1, 2, Bl;*
Rochester; my *Dilke;* Rochester, my *Daniel.*   3. hath] *Q1;* have *Q2,
Bl.*   4. with congealed] *Q1* (conieaied*); with this conieaied *Q2, Bl*
(congealed*); with this concealed *Dilke;* with conjealed *Tydeman.*
9–10. SD.] *Bond (subst.). Bond, Andreadis and Tydeman all indicate that
Mother Bombie enters at this point.*   10.1.] *This ed. No entry indicated in Q1,
2, Bl.*   12. SP.] *Bl (Vic.);Vin.* / *Q1, 2.*   15–16. tell what] *Q1, 2;* tell me
what *Bl.*   17–22.] *Lineation as Dilke; printed as continuous prose in Q1, 2,*

*Bl.* 19. a] *Q1; not in Q2, Bl.* natural] *Q1* (naturall)*, Bl;* uaturall
*Q2.* 23. hast] *Q1, 2, Bl;* has *Daniel.* 27. SD.] *This ed.; Exit Bom.* / *Q1,
2 (subst.); Exit. Bomb.* / *Bl; Exit* [Mother] Bombie. / *Andreadis.*

### ACT[US] 5, SCE[NA] 3

0.] *Q1 (subst.), 2;* Actus quintus. Scaena tertia *Bl.* 0.1–2.] *Q1 (Bedu-
nens), 2 (Bedunenus), Bl;* SYNIS, NASUTUS, BEDUNENUS, *three Fiddlers.* /
*Dilke; Three Fidlers. Synis. Nasutus. Beduneus.* [*Enter the* FIDDLERS.] /
*Tydeman; Enter the three fiddlers,* SYNIS, NASUTUS, *and* BEDUNENS. /
*Daniel.* 6. SD.] *This ed.* 8–9. SD.] *This ed.* 10. loses] *Dilke;* looses
*Q1, 2, Bl.* rosin] *Dilke;* rosen *Q1;* roson *Q2;* Rozen *Bl;* resin
*Andreadis.* 'cush, cush'] *Quotation marks* / *Tydeman;* cush-cush *Daniel.*
13. SD.] *This ed.* 14. SD.] *This ed.* 16. I'll throw] *Q1* (Ile); I throw
*Q2;* ile throw *Bl.* hobbler] *Andreadis;* hobler *Q1, 2, Bl.* 17. SD.] *This
ed.* There's a time] *Q1* (theres); there is time *Q2, Bl.* 18. that should
not] *Q1, 2, Bl;* that should not say it *Dilke.* 23. SD.] *This ed.* 25. 'The
Love Knot'] *Quotation marks* / *Andreadis.* 25.1.] *First differentiated from
text as SD. by Bond (following a note by Fairholt). Printed as part of Synis'
speech at lines 25–6 this ed. in Q1* (bridall. Sing. God)*, 2, Bl* (Bridall. Sing.
Good); *They sing.* / *Daniel.* 26–7.] *Assigned to Synis in Q1, 2, Bl but transferred to Nasutus without authority by Dilke. Daniel supplies SP.* ALL THREE.
*and prints as verse* (Good morrow, fair bride, / And send you joy of
your bridal.)*.* 26. Good] *Bl;* God *Q1, 2.* 27.1.] *Q1, 2, Bl. Tydeman
adds* / *of an upstairs window.* /. 28. make] *Q1, 2, Bl;* makes *Dilke.* twan-
glers] *Q1;* twangers *Q2, Bl.* 32–3. bridegroom God] *Punctuation as Q2,
Bl;* bridegroome, God *Q1;* bridegroom; God *Dilke.* 34. Here's] *Bl;* hers
*Q1;* heres *Q2.* 35–6. married…Yet] *Punctuation this ed.;* maryed, though
you seeme strange, yet *Q1, 2, Bl* (with spelling variants); married; though you
seem strange, yet *Dilke;* maryed: though you seeme strange, yet *Bond;*
married. Though you seem strange, yet *Andreadis.* 38. My son,
villain!] *Punctuation as Dilke;* My sonne villaine, *Q1, 2* (son); My sonne
villaine! *Bl;* My son? Villain! *Andreadis.* 40.1.] *This ed.* 41. SD.] *This
ed.* 42. SD.] *This ed.* 45. SD.] *Andreadis; not in Q1, 2, Bl; Bond
supplies* / *Exit* CANDIUS. / *following* married (line 47 this ed.)*.* 48. SP.] *Q1,
Bl; not in Q2.* Oho!] *Dilke;* O ho *Q1, 2, Bl;* O, ho, *Andreadis.* thether] *Q1;*
thither *Q2, Bl.* 49. SD.] *This ed.; Exit.* / *Andreadis; Exit* SPERANTUS. /
*Tydeman.* 53. Mayor's] *Dilke;* Maiors *Q1, 2, Bl;* major's *Daniel.*
56. Ay] *Andreadis;* I *Q1, 2, Bl;* Ah *Dilke.* 56–7.] *Quotation marks* /
*Andreadis. Daniel prints as a single quotation, including* and. 57. and] *Not
in Bl, Tydeman.* 58. one's] *Q1* (ones); my *Q2, Bl.* 59. SD.] *This
ed.* 61. SD.] *This ed.; They cross the stage.* / *Tydeman.* 63. SP.]
*Q1* (Syn.); Lyn. / *Q2, Bl.* 64.1.] *Q1; as text, following* catch, *line 64 this
ed.* / *Q2, Bl.* 64.2–84] *Bl; not in Q1, 2.* 65. All 3] *Bl; All three* /
*Dilke;* ALL *Daniel (also at lines 71 and 78).* 68. SP.] *Bl* (Fid.). *Daniel
substitutes* FIRST *for numeral.* 69, 70, 72, 73, 74, 75, 76, 77. SP.] *Bracketed
material* / *Dilke. Daniel substitutes* FIRST, SECOND, THIRD *respectively for
numerals.* 85. God] *Q1, 2;* Good *Bl.* 85.1.] *This ed.; not in Q1, 2, Bl;
Memphio looks out.* / *Dilke; Enter* MEMPHIO *and* DROMIO *above.* / *Tydeman;*

*Bond supplies* / *above* / *following SP. line 86 this ed.*    86. crowding] *Dilke;* crouding *Q1, 2, Bl.*    94. mock his] *Q1;* mock with his *Q2, Bl. Tydeman supplies SD.* / *To* FIDDLERS / *following* with him.    97. SD.] *This ed.*    fair] *Q1 (faire), Bl;* faires *Q2.*    98. feet] *Q1, Bl;* feeet *Q2.*    knave] *Q1, 2, Bl;* knaves *Dilke.*    99.] *Andreadis supplies SD.* / *Enter* Dromio. / *following* wise, sir.    101. rogues] *Q1;* tongues *Q2, Bl.*    103. Mayor] *Dilke;* maior *Q1, 2, Bl;* major *Daniel.*    104.] *Bond supplies SD.* / *above* / *following SP.* been] *Q1, 2;* bin *Bl.*    105.1.] *Tydeman (subst.).*    106. SD.] *This ed.*    108. SD.] *This ed.*    112. SD–112.1.] *Substantive bracketed material this ed. (otherwise as Q1, 2, Bl; Exeunt.* [*Manent*] Memphio, Dromio. / *Andreadis; Exeunt.* MEMPHIO [*and*] DROMIO [*reappear in the street.*] / *Tydeman; Exeunt* FIDDLERS. *Enter* MEMPHIO *and* DROMIO. / *Daniel.*    116. advised] *Q1;* advise *Q2, Bl.*    122. Ay] *Andreadis;* I *Q1, 2, Bl;* Ah *Dilke.*    132. hang] *Q1, 2, Bl;* hung *Dilke.*    133. off, do] *Punctuation as Dilke;* off. Do *Q1, 2, Bl (*Doe*).*    139. Ay] *Dilke (*Aye*);* I *Q1, 2, Bl.*    143.1–2.] *Bracketed material this ed.; Sperantus, Halfepenie, Prisius, Linceo.* / *Q1, 2 (Lincio), Bl; Enter* SPERANTUS, HALFPENNY, PRISIUS, *and* LUCIO. / *Dilke;* [*Enter*] Sperantus, Halfpenny, Lucio. / *Andreadis;* [*Enter*] SPERANTUS [*and*] HALFPENIE [*on one side*], PRISIUS [*and* LUCIO *on the other*]. / *Tydeman.*    144. is a token] *Q1;* is token *Q2, Bl.*    145. luck] *Q1 (*lucke*), 2, Bl;* look *Dilke.*    148.] *Andreadis supplies* / *Enter* Prisius / *following* such words.    149. SP.] *Q1, (*Spe.*), Bl;* Lpe. / *Q2.*    SD.] *This ed.*    150. God] *Q1, 2, Bl;* Good *Dilke. Daniel supplies SD.* / *Enter* PRISIUS. / *following the greeting.*    152. SD.] *This ed.*    face] *Q2, Bl;* fate *Q1.*    155. shouldest] *Q1;* shoudst *Q2, Bl.*    156. embezzle] *Dilke;* imbesell *Q1, 2;* imbeasell *Bl;* embezzel *Andreadis.*    158. SD.] *Bond.*    159. powder] *Bl;* pouder *Q1;* powdeded *Q2.*    161, 165, 170. SP.] *Dilke (Luc.);* Lin. / *Q1; Liu.* / *Q2, Bl.*    170. clock] *Q1, 2 (*clocke*), Bl;* clerk *Dilke.*    171, 174. 'God…joy'] *Quotation marks* / *Andreadis.*    175. SD.] *This ed.*    175.1.] *Bracketed material this ed.;* ⟨*Re-*⟩ *Enter* CANDIUS. / *Bond.*    176. SD.] *This ed.*    177.1.] *Subtantive bracketed material this ed.*    180. SD.] *Tydeman (subst.).*    181. SP.] *Dilke (Luc.);* Lin. / *Q1, 2; Liu.* / *Bl.*    SD.] *This ed.*    185. repent it] *Punctuation as Dilke;* repent, it *Q1, 2, Bl;* repent. It *Andreadis.*    187. Ay] *Andreadis;* I *Q1, 2, Bl;* Ah *Dilke.*    189. consent] *Q1, Bl;* consenr *Q2.*    190. giglot] *Q1, 2, Bl;* giglet *Daniel.*    203. SD.] *Bond.*    205. SP.] *Dilke (Luc.);* Lin. / *Q1, 2; Liu.* / *Bl.*    206. pay] *Q1;* pray *Q2, Bl.*    207. SD.] *Tydeman.* And you…groat] *Punctuation as Q1, 2, Bl;* And you, oatmeal groat *Dilke.*    212.1.] *Bracketed material* / *Dilke.*    216. SD.] *This ed.*    221. overmuch.] *Q2, Bl;* overmuch *Q1.*    225, 226. SD.] *Andreadis (subst.).*    227. screech owl] *Dilke;* schrith owle *Q1, 2, Bl;* schrith-owle *Fairholt;* scritch-owl *Andreadis.*    228. Neighbours] *Q2, Bl;* Neigbbours *Q1.*    229. cheating] *Q1;* chearing *Q2, Bl;* cheering *Dilke.*    230. our four] *Bl (*foure*);* foure foure *Q1;* fourc foure *Q2.*    231. to] *Q1, 2;* to to *Bl.*    232. worships] *Dilke;* wor. *Q1, 2, Bl;* worship *Andreadis.*    234. SP.] *Dilke (Luc.);* Lin / *Q1, 2, Bl.*    236. Halfpenny] *Bl (Halfepenie);* Half. / *Q1, 2.*    238. confess] *Q2 (*confesse*), Bl;* honfesse *Q1.*    trussed] *Bond n.;* trust *Q1, 2, Bl.*    240. SDs.] *This ed.*    thee] *Q1, 2, Bl; not in Dilke.*    244. unknown] *Q2 (*vnknowne*), Bl;* vnknowen *Q1.*    246. Lucio] *Dilke;* Lincio *Q1, 2, Bl.*    247. masters'] *Fairholt;* masters *Q1, 2,*

*Bl;* master's *Dilke.* 248. unwilling] *Dilke;* unwitting *QI,* 2,
*Bl.* 252. day's] *Andreadis;* dayes *QI,* 2 *(daies), Bl;* days *Dilke.*
255. drank] *Dilke;* dronke *QI;* drunke *Q2, Bl (drunke).* 256.
masters'] *Fairholt;* masters *QI,* 2 *(maisters), Bl.* 257. masters'] *Fairholt;*
masters *QI, Bl;* maisters *Q2;* master's *Dilke.* 261. a] *QI,* 2; *not in*
*Bl.* 262, 263, 264, 268, 268–9 SD.] *This ed.* 270. loves stirs] *QI*
*(stirres),* 2 *(stirs), Bl;* loves stir *Dilke;* loue stirres *Bond.* 271.1–2.] *This*
*ed.; Enter* ACCIUS and SILENA. / *Bond (following line 263 this ed.). Daniel*
*supplies* / *Enter* ACCIUS. / *following line 262 this ed.* and / *Enter* SILENA. /
*following line 263.* 272. Silena] *Q2, Bl;* Silenena *QI.* 274. for ever] *QI*
*(euer),* 2, *Bl;* forever *Andreadis.* 275. Ay] *Dilke (Aye);* I *QI,* 2,
*Bl.* 279. lief] *QI (liefe),* 2, *Bl;* leave *Dilke.* 285. SD.] *Bond (subst.).*
287. SD.] *Tydeman.* 294.] *Tydeman supplies SD.* / *He kisses* SILENA. /
*following kiss.* 294.1.] VICINIA] *QI,* 2; *Vicina* / *Bl. Bracketed material* /
*Dilke (subst.).* 295. banns] *Daniel;* banes *QI,* 2, *Bl.* 296. shall] *QI,* 2,
*Bl;* should *Dilke.* 298. Vicinia] *QI;* Vicina *Q2, Bl.* 302. True] *QI, Bl;*
*True* / *Q2.* 306. should] *QI;* would *Q2, Bl.* 309. hetherto] *QI;* hith-
erto *Q2, Bl.* 326. earned] *QI,* 2, *Bl;* yearned *Dilke.* 327. vild] *QI*
*(vilde),* 2; vile *Bl.* an] *QI,* 2, *Bl;* and *Dilke.* 328. good old] *QI (olde),*
2; gold *Bl.* 331. Hether] *QI;* hither *Q2, Bl.* 332. yours] *Q2, Bl;* your
*QI.* loving] *QI;* living *Q2, Bl.* 337. with] *QI,* 2, *Bl;* by *Dilke.* man-
drake] *Daniel;* mandrage *QI,* 2, *Bl.* 337–40. mandrake…No] *Punctua-*
*tion this ed.;* mandrage, beholde nowe for your sonnes, no *QI,* 2 (behold
now…sons), *Bl;* mandrage; behold. Now for your son's; no *Dilke;* mandrage; beholde nowe for your sonnes, no *Bond;* mandrage; behold now for
your sonne's, no *Fairholt;* mandrage. Behold now for your son's: no
*Andreadis;* mandrage; beholde nowe for your sonnes: no *Tydeman;* mandrake. Behold now, for your son's, no *Daniel.* 338, 339–40. SD.] *This ed.*
*Tydeman supplies* / *Shows* MAESTIUS' *mole.* / *following done (line 341 this*
*ed.).* 343–4. SD.] *This ed. Tydeman supplies* / *Shows* SERENA'S *mole.* / .
346, 348. SD.] *This ed.* 350. thou] *QI,* 2, *Bl;* how *Bond.* 352. their]
*QI,* 2, *Bl;* our *Dilke.* 354. I'll not] *QI (Ile),* 2; I let *Bl.* 356–8. 'My
father…begot'] *Quotation marks* / *Fairholt.* 360. Well fare] *Daniel;*
welfare *QI,* 2, *Bl;* farewell *Dilke;* wel fare *Fairholt.* 361. Bombie] *QI*
*(Bomby); Bom.* / *Q2, Bl.* 362. SD.] *Tydeman.* 365. SP.] *Dilke (Luc.);*
*Lin.* / *QI,* 2, *Bl.* see, foretold] *Q2;* see foretolde *QI, Bl (foretold);* see she
foretold *Dilke.* 369. Ay] *Dilke (Aye);* I *QI,* 2, *Bl.* 379. Vicinia] *QI;*
Vicina *Q2, Bl.* 382. do] *QI (doo),* 2 *(do), Bl;* to *Daniel.* 386. having]
*Dilke;* have *QI,* 2, *Bl.* 387. practice] *QI (practise),* 2, *Bl;* practises
*Dilke.* of] *QI,* 2, *Bl;* off *Daniel.* 388. SD.] *This ed.* it's] *QI (its);*
tis *Q2, Bl ('tis).* 390. SD.] *This ed.* it's] *QI,* 2; 'tis *Bl;* it is *Dilke.*
398. Mayor] *Dilke;* Maior *QI,* 2, *Bl;* major *Daniel. Also at line 438.*
400. an] *QI,* 2, *Bl;* a *Dilke.* 400–1. horse…I] *Punctuation as Bond;*
horse after much mocking, at the request of his fellowe wagges, I *QI,* 2, *Bl*
*(fellow);* horse; after much mocking, at the request of his fellow wags, I
*Dilke;* horse after much mocking at the request of his fellow wags. I *Andreadis;*
horse after much mocking. At the request of his fellow wags, I
*Daniel.* 404. drunk] *Q2 (drunke), Bl;* dronke *QI.* pawned] *Dilke;*
paunde *QI;* pawnde *Q2, Bl.* the wine] *QI,* 2; his wine *Bl.* 406.] *Tydeman*
*supplies SD.* / *Hands* MEMPHIO *the bond.* / *following read it.* 407. SD.]

*This ed.* 410. acquittance] *Q2;* acquittaunce *Q1;* acquaittance *Bl.* 415.
Cheapside] *Dilke;* cheap side *Q1, 2, Bl.* 417. revenge] *Q2* (reuenge*), Bl;*
renenge *Q1 (turned letter).* 419–20. Thou boy…The boys] *Punctuation
this ed.;* Thou boy, we wil paie the hire of the horse, be not angrie, the boyes
*Q1, 2, Bl* (wee…boies*);* Then, boy, we will pay the hire of the horse; be
not angry. The boys *Dilke;* Thou boy! 〈*To* HACKNEYMAN.〉 We wil paie the
hire of the horse: be not angrie; the boys *Bond;* Thou boy, we will pay the
hire of the horse. [*To* Hackneyman, Sergeant, *and* Scrivener.] Be not angry.
The boys *Andreadis;* Thou boy! [*To* HACKNEYMAN] We wil paie the hire of
the horse; be not angrie: the boyes *Tydeman;* Thou boy, we will pay the hire
of the horse; be not angry. The boys *Daniel.* 421. cozening] *Dilke;*
cosning *Q1;* cousoning *Q2;* cousening *Bl.* 422–3. SD.] *This ed.; To all. /
Andreadis.* 431. day] *Q1; not in Q2, Bl.* 438.] *Tydeman supplies / Aside
/ following* wedding. 443. SD.] *This ed.* 445. SP.] *Dilke (Luc.); Lin. /
Q1;Liu. / Q2,Bl.* for ever] *Q1* (euer*),2,Bl;*forever *Andreadis.* 446. SD.]
*Bond.* 446.1.] *Q1, 2, Bl; not in Fairholt, Daniel.*

# Index

Page numbers refer to the Introduction; 'Characters' to Characters in Order of Appearance; act-scene-line numbers to the Commentary; 'n' after a page reference indicates the number of the note on that page. An asterisk (*) preceding an entry indicates that the commentary note in this edition adds materially to the information given in the *OED*. Individual words appearing in various inflected forms are usually grouped under one form; phrases are indexed in the form in which they appear in the text. When a gloss is repeated in the annotations, only the initial occurrence is indexed.

214 INDEX

Lightning Source UK Ltd.
Milton Keynes UK
UKOW04f1918240814

237443UK00007B/102/P